When Growth Is Not Enough

DIRECTIONS IN DEVELOPMENT
Poverty

When Growth Is Not Enough

Explaining the Rigidity of Poverty in the Dominican Republic

Francisco Galrão Carneiro and Sophie Sirtaine, Editors

 **WORLD BANK GROUP**

Contents

Figures

Foreword

The Dominican Republic has enjoyed one of the strongest growth rates in Latin America and the Caribbean over the past 25 years. Since 2014, growth has averaged 7 percent per year, raising the country's income per capita to 92 percent of the regional average, versus 57 percent in 1992. Yet, despite this remarkable economic performance, economic growth in the Dominican Republic has not been as inclusive as in the rest of the region, as one in three Dominicans remains below the poverty line.

The key challenge that the Dominican economy faces at this time is to understand the conundrum of rapid growth with limited poverty reduction and to address it through policies that sustain economic growth while making it more inclusive. This book tests a set of three hypotheses that could help explain the country's disconnect between growth and poverty reduction.

The first hypothesis tested is whether the observed pattern of fast economic growth with persistent poverty is partly driven by a poverty methodology that does not account for price variation that distinctly affects the consumption patterns of low-income and better-off households. An important result found by the authors is that there is no evidence of any problems with the methodology used to calculate poverty or economic growth.

The second hypothesis tests whether the pattern of specialization in the Dominican Republic might be such that it does not favor unskilled labor. Here, the evidence presented shows that the country's patterns of trade—which rely on a relatively low endowment of skilled workers—are not the most likely sources of inequality in the country. This finding is important because it confirms the need for government policy to promote greater equity and inclusion through more efficient, targeted public spending.

Finally, the third hypothesis investigates whether poverty in the country is affected not only by immigration but also by emigration. On this point, the results are less conclusive, owing to severe data limitations. Nonetheless, after making use of robust, state-of-the-art methodological approaches to investigate this question, the evidence presented by the authors suggests that the impact of immigration on the more skilled workers is minimal and relatively benign for the formal, low-skilled workers.

The Dominican Republic is well positioned to build on its successes and generate more inclusive growth. With this book, the authors hope to inform the national policy dialogue on how to advance on the most pressing challenge that the Dominican Republic faces at this time: namely, to sustain its exemplary growth while ensuring that this growth is inclusive and brings greater prosperity to its most vulnerable population.

Tahseen Sayed
Regional Director for the Caribbean
The World Bank Group

Acknowledgments

This book presents the results of research by leading experts from the World Bank and the Dominican Republic on some of the most important development issues faced by a nation that wants to share more widely the benefits of its strong growth performance.

The editors would like to acknowledge the financial support from the World Bank Group's Development Economics Department through their Research Support Budget program, which financed work associated with chapters 1, 2, and 5. The editors also thank the Poverty and Equity Global Practice of the World Bank, which funded work associated with chapters 3 and 4.

The support of the Macroeconomics and Fiscal Management Global Practice, the Development Economics Department, the Office of the Chief Economist of the Latin America and the Caribbean Region, and the Caribbean Country Management Unit is also greatly acknowledged. The authors are grateful to McDonald Benjamin, Oscar Calvo-Gonzalez, and Cecile Thioro Niang for their insightful and useful peer reviewer comments.

The logistical support provided by Carla Bordas Portela, Alejandra De La Paz, Maria J. Hermann, Elizabeth Mekonnen, Virginia Ricart Giro, and Mohammed Edreess Sahak, as well as the encouragement and support from Tahseen Sayed, World Bank Regional Director for the Caribbean, and Alessandro Legrottaglie, World Bank Country Manager for the Dominican Republic, was essential for the successful completion of this project.

About the Editors

Francisco Galrão Carneiro is the lead economist and program leader for the Caribbean at the World Bank. Since joining the World Bank in 2003, he has worked in multiple regions of the world. Before 2003, Carneiro was professor of economics at the University of Brasilia and at the Catholic University of Brasilia, and he served as economic adviser in the Ministry of External Relations in Brazil. He has authored and coauthored a number of academic papers and World Bank reports on a range of topics that include macroeconomics and growth, natural resource revenue management, trade, labor market institutions, poverty, and inequality. Born in Brazil, he received his PhD in economics from the University of Kent in the United Kingdom in 1996.

Sophie Sirtaine is director, Strategy and Operations, at the Independent Evaluation Group of the World Bank. Previously, she worked for more than 16 years in the World Bank, in various country, corporate, and sectoral positions. Her most recent post was as country director for Caribbean countries in the Latin America and the Caribbean Region, where she led the definition and implementation of the World Bank program in the Dominican Republic. Prior to joining the World Bank, Sirtaine worked in London in investment banking at JP Morgan and as an infrastructure economist for Halcrow Fox and Associates.

Abbreviations

ACS	American Community Survey
ADESS	administradora de subsidios sociales (administrator of social subsidies)
AFP	admininistradoras de fondos de pensiones (pension fund administrator)
BCRD	Banco Central de la República Dominicana (Central Bank of the Dominican Republic)
CCTs	conditional cash transfers
CI	confidence interval
CPI	consumer price index
CTP	Comité Técnico Interinstitucional de Medición de la Pobreza (Interinstitutional Technical Committee for Poverty Measurement)
DECDG	Development Data Group–Survey Unit (World Bank)
DIGEPRES	Dirección General de Presupuesto (National Budget Office)
DIOC	Database on Immigrants in OECD and Non-OECD Countries
ENCFT	Encuesta Nacional Continua de Fuerza de Trabajo (Monthly National Labor Force Survey)
ENFT	Encuesta Nacional de Fuerza de Trabajo (National Labor Force Survey)
ENI	Encuesta Nacional de Inmigrantes de la República Dominicana (National Survey of Immigrants from the Dominican Republic)
ENIGH	Encuesta Nacional de Ingresos y Gastos de los Hogares (National Survey of Income and Expenses of Households)
FIES	Fondo Para el Fomento de la Investigacion Economica y Social (Social and Economic Research Support Fund)
FII	financial intermediation and insurance
GDP	gross domestic product
GMI	gross mixed income
GNI	gross national income
HBR	hotels, bars, and restaurants

IL	inferior limit
INTEC	Instituto Tecnológico de Santo Domingo (Technological Institute of Santo Domingo)
ISIC	International Standard Industrial Classification
ISO	International Organization for Standardization
LAC	Latin America and the Caribbean
LFS	Labour Force Survey (International Labour Organization)
MEPyD	Ministerio de Economía, Planificación y Desarrollo (Ministry of Economy, Planning and Development)
OECD	Organisation for Economic Co-operation and Development
ONE	Oficina Nacional de Estadística (National Statistics Office)
PL	poverty line
PO	poverty incidence
PPP	purchasing power parity
RCA	revealed comparative advantage
SEZ	special economic zone
SL	superior limit
SNA	System of National Accounts (Dominican Republic)
TFP	total factor productivity
UNIDO	United Nations Industrial Development Organization
UNSTATS	UN National Accounts Statistics
WITS	World Integrated Trade Solution

Overview

Francisco Carneiro and Sophie Sirtaine

The Dominican Economy: Strong albeit Barely Inclusive Growth

The Dominican Republic has enjoyed one of the strongest growth rates in Latin America and the Caribbean (LAC) over the past 20 years. Between 1992 and the year 2000, the Dominican Republic's economy grew at an average rate of 6.7 percent per year, being the top performer in the region. During 2001–13, growth remained high, at an average rate of 5.1 percent, placing the Dominican economy's performance at fourth in the region (after Argentina, Panama, and Peru). This overall dynamic growth has enabled a convergence of the Dominican Republic's gross national income (GNI) per capita (US$4,959 in 2013) with that of the region, from 57 percent of the regional average in 1992 to 90 percent in 2013.[1] In fact, estimates show that if the pace of growth observed during 2008–13 remains the same, the gap would disappear by 2020 (Baez et al. 2014). Although the country weathered the global economic slowdown of 2008–09 well, declining domestic demand and weak performance in richer economies worldwide have contributed to decreased growth in the Dominican Republic since 2011—in fact, gross domestic product (GDP) growth dropped by almost half, falling from 7.8 percent in 2010 to 4.1 percent in 2013.

Despite this remarkable economic performance, growth has been widely believed as being not inclusive in the Dominican Republic. In 2000 the poverty incidence in this country was below the regional average; about 33 percent of Dominicans lived on less than US$4 a day, compared with 42 percent of those

The authors express their gratitude to McDonald Benjamin (adviser, Operational Services), Oscar Calvo-González (practice manager, Poverty and Equity Global Practice), and Cecile Thioro Niang (program leader, Caribbean Country Management Unit) for their useful comments and suggestions.

Francisco Carneiro is lead economist and program leader for the Caribbean in the Latin America and the Caribbean Region of the World Bank. He holds a doctorate in economics from the University of Kent in the United Kingdom. Please direct correspondence to fcarneiro@worldbank.org.

Sophie Sirtaine is director of strategy and operations in the Independent Evaluation Group of the World Bank. She holds a master of science in development economics from the London School of Economics in the United Kingdom. Please direct correspondence to ssirtaine@worldbank.org.

living in LAC. In fact, another important characteristic of the Dominican economy has been limited upward economic mobility. Over the past decade, just under 7 percent of the population in the Dominican Republic moved up in the income ranks (for example, from vulnerable to middle class), in contrast to 41 percent in the LAC region (Baez et al. 2014). This is a striking fact given the rapid increase in the country's GNI per capita.

Following the 2003–04 banking crisis, the country's GDP that had grown by 6 percent in 2002 contracted by 0.3 percent in 2003. Thus, a financial and economic crisis followed, with an estimated 1.7 million persons moving into poverty, and the poverty rate reaching 50 percent of the population in 2004—up from 33 percent in 2000.

When the economy recovered after the crisis, poverty rates began to fall but returned to the precrisis level only by 2015 (Baez et al. 2014.), albeit a level considered above the average for LAC (see figure O.1).[2] On the other hand, inequality improved between 2000 and 2015 (with the Gini index falling from 0.507 to 0.455). Evidence also exists that between 2004 and 2011 income growth for the lower quintiles of the population was faster than for the higher quintiles; yet, this growth has been insufficient to compensate for the effects of the 2003–04 banking crisis, which disproportionately affected the poor.

Figure O.1 Fast GNI Growth versus Slowly Declining Poverty and Inequality in the Dominican Republic, 2000–15

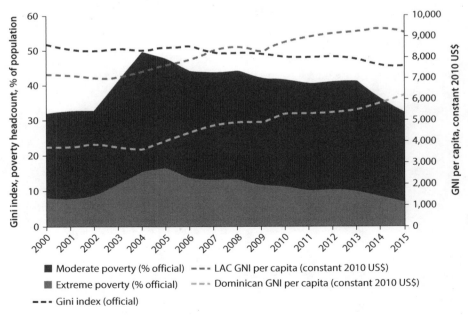

Sources: Based on data from the World Bank's World Development Indicators and from Comité Técnico Interinstitucional de Medición de la Pobreza (Interinstitutional Technical Committee for Poverty Measurement, CTP).
Note: Poverty line used for the calculation is the level of US$4 PPP per capita per day.

Recently, official estimates suggest that poverty has fallen substantially in the Dominican Republic. After remaining at above 40 percent since the crisis, poverty calculations for 2014 point to a sizable one-year reduction, and data from the first semester of 2015 suggest a continued reduction in poverty six months later. While the mechanisms of this reduction are being studied to gain a full understanding, the focus of this book is twofold: (a) on the slow gains in poverty reduction through 2013, and (b) on the possible explanations for why the country's high growth failed to translate into significant reductions in poverty during the period 2000–13. A better understanding of these mechanisms can also shed light on some of the possible reasons for the poverty reduction recently experienced in the Dominican Republic.

Why Has High Economic Growth Not Led to Better Equity Outcomes?

The combination of stubborn poverty rates despite high economic growth remains a puzzle, but this is not a phenomenon unique to the Dominican Republic. Some characteristics of this economy may help explain why poverty has not fallen faster despite rapid growth, including (a) a labor market that does not translate productivity gains into salary increases; (b) a domestic economy with weak intersectoral linkages; and (c) a public sector that does not commit enough resources or deploy them particularly well to reduce poverty. In addition, the country remains largely exposed to natural disasters and exogenous shocks (earthquakes and hurricanes, for example) that, if not mitigated properly, may affect the sustainability of growth over the medium and longer terms.

Rising Productivity and Stagnant Real Wages

Real earnings declined after the 2003–04 banking crisis and have not returned to their precrisis level, despite significant productivity gains. Real hourly earnings fell to RD$10.3 in 2004, and only recovered nine years later to reach RD$12 in 2013—compared with an average of RD$16 during 2001–02 (figure O.2). In fact, real earnings fell or remained stagnant in many sectors, including manufacturing as well as transport and communications, where productivity has grown since 2002. Likewise, in the public sector, real earnings rose over the same period while productivity stagnated (Abdullaev and Estevão 2013).[3]

Since 2004, some of the sectors that contributed the most to GDP growth (manufacturing, telecommunications, and financial services) have not produced as many jobs, and their shares in employment remain low (Abdullaev and Estevão 2013).[4] In fact, the share of manufacturing jobs in total employment has almost halved, declining from 19 percent in 1996 to 10 percent in 2013, which partly explains productivity increases in the sector (that has moved to relatively more capital-intensive activities). Moreover, the financial services and insurance sector employed only a small share of the workforce, that is, 2.6 percent. In 2013, the mining sector emerged as a potential driver of economic growth with a contribution of almost 1 percentage point. Yet, the sector hired less than 1 percent of all employed Dominicans (Abdullaev and Estevão 2013).

Figure O.2 Real Earnings and Productivity Indexes, 1991–2013

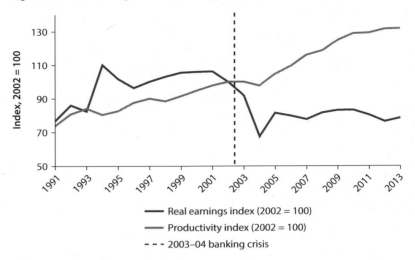

Sources: Based on Conference Board Total Economy Database™ and Central Bank of the Dominican Republic data.

On the other hand, faster-expanding sectors created mostly unskilled jobs (retail and wholesale trade; hotels, bars, and restaurants; and other services). For instance, since 2002 the retail and wholesale trade industries have employed, on average, one in five Dominicans. The percentage of jobs in the hotel, restaurant, and bar sector with respect to total employment increased from 5.2 percent in 2002 to 6 percent in 2013, but productivity increased only by 13 percent during the same period. Other services (such as housekeeping and certain low-value-added self-employment activities) have gained importance, employing one in every four Dominicans, in 2013 compared to one in five in 2002. This trend toward higher growth in unskilled worker employment is reflected in labor market outcomes, as unemployment rates remain lower among the least educated. As of April 2014, for example, the working age population with no education level recorded an open unemployment rate of 2.4 percent, whereas the population with primary, secondary, and tertiary education levels registered unemployment rates of 4.8, 8.7, and 8.4 percent, respectively.[5] As can be observed in figure O.3, real hourly wages have been stagnant (and much lower than a decade ago) despite rising output per worker.

The stagnation of real wages prevents the lower strata from moving out of poverty. One possible reason for this disconnect between productivity growth and real wage levels can be attributed to rising informality in the labor market, at least in the most low-skill and labor-intensive sectors. Informality levels have increased slightly, from 54 percent in 2004 to 56 percent in 2013, despite the effective establishment of the social security system—possibly because a large proportion of the new jobs have been created in low-value-added services (housekeeping, petty commerce), often as a result of self-employment.

Figure O.3 Rising Productivity versus Declining Real Hourly Earnings in the Manufacturing and the Hotel, Bar, and Restaurant Sectors, 1996–2013

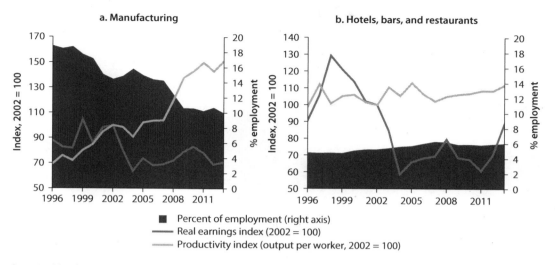

Source: World Bank estimations based on data provided by the Central Bank of the Dominican Republic.

Informal workers in the Dominican Republic are a very diverse group, and informality is widespread across sectors (Guzmán 2007). Some workers are forced to accept informal contracts. Moreover, some small business owners do not register their businesses because they find it burdensome and costly (in particular, those that do not plan future business expansion). This may negatively impact productivity, as business fragmentation due to informality may prevent the attainment of economies of scale.

In addition, high levels of informality push people outside of the social security safety nets, strip the state of potential tax resources, and limit their participation in organized worker unions. The historical weakness of labor unions in the Dominican Republic (Ondetti 2009) may partly explain the observed decrease in the real return to labor, despite the rising productivity, because unions do not enjoy a strong bargaining position vis-à-vis entrepreneurs when negotiating minimum wages. At the same time, in a context of rising real exchange rates in the aftermath of the 2003–04 banking crisis, keeping wages down may have been the only way to continue attracting foreign direct investment and preserving external competitiveness.

A Domestic Economy with Weak Intersectoral Linkages

The disconnection between high-value-added sectors (with limited job generation) and low-value-added sectors (with informality and high employment growth) is a symptom of a divided economy, evident also in the structure of exports. Firms operating under special economic zones (SEZ) produce and export higher-value-added products when compared to exporters that are subject to the national regime. Whereas the former group specializes in products such as clothing, medical devices, and jewelry, the latter group specializes mostly in resource-based products, such as minerals (gold, ferronickel) and agricultural products (figure O.4). On the surface, the Dominican export basket looks well diversified in terms of products, but only a handful of goods are meaningful in terms of export value. Manufactured products that require some level of industrial transformation typically come from SEZs; some examples include cigars, T-shirts, medical instruments, and electrical circuit breakers.

Exports and employment in SEZs fell dramatically during the past decade, in the context of expiring textile preferences. At the beginning of the 2000s, Dominican exports were dominated by textile exports (accounting for a third of total exports), when the clothing industry received benefits from the U.S. quotas defined by the global Multi-Fibre Arrangement, which had been in place for over three decades. The phasing out of this global arrangement, completed at the beginning of 2005, led to a decline in the textile industry in the Dominican Republic, which was unable to compete with cheaper clothing from Bangladesh; China; Hong Kong SAR, China; and Vietnam. Faced with this phaseout, the Dominican Republic was a latecomer to the Central America Free Trade Agreement, between the Central American region and the United States, joining it in 2007. Since then, SEZs have been able to diversify the export basket into emerging products such as medical devices, footwear, and pharmaceuticals. However, this transformation has not brought net employment creation, with jobs in SEZs falling from 140,000 in 2000 to just about 40,000 in 2012.

Another challenge of the SEZs is that they are relatively isolated from the rest of the economy, reducing the potential for positive externalities and spillovers. The literature on SEZs in the Dominican Republic (Burgaud and Farole

Figure O.4 Technological Composition of SEZ versus Non-SEZ Originating Exports, 2002–12

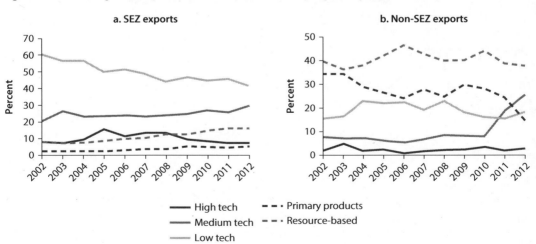

Source: World Bank 2014.
Note: This figure shows the evolution of the technological content of the Dominican Republic's exports using the classification suggested by Lall (2000).

2011; Sánchez-Ancochea 2012) discusses at length the lack of backward link-ages, although direct evidence is scant. Using enterprise surveys, the World Bank (2014b) finds that Dominican foreign direct investment firms (mostly located in SEZs) import almost 70 percent of their inputs, compared with 49 percent for the Caribbean, 58 percent for Central America, and 43 percent for Mexico and South America.[6] SEZs are not buying inputs from domestic suppliers, which limits the potential for knowledge transmission, learning-by-doing processes, and efficiency gains. Another tentative interpretation is that the lack of linkages with the rest of the economy may also indicate that most of the wealth generated in the export process remains in SEZ companies that are usually foreign-owned.

Public Spending Could Be More Equitable

The third possible explanation for slow improvements in inequality and poverty reduction in a context of high growth rates is the Dominican Republic's limited fiscal space for conducting equity-enhancing public policies. On the tax side, for example, the Dominican Republic is characterized by limited revenue-generation capacity, and in this regard, it underperforms in relation to other countries in the LAC region (figure O.5). Tax revenues have declined from an average of 15.1 percent of GDP in 2005–08 to an average of 13.3 percent of GDP in 2009–13. This decline is mostly explained by the dismantling of tariffs and duties in the context of the Central America Free Trade Agreement that the Dominican Republic joined. It is also worth noting that the executive branch of the government unsuccessfully tried to prevent the decline in fiscal revenues

Figure O.5 Share of Tax Revenue in Selected LAC Countries, 2012

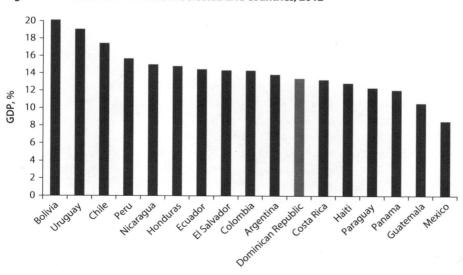

Source: Computed using CEPALSTAT Statistics and Indicators data.

by adopting a total of six tax reforms between 2004 and 2012. One of the most significant measures (in terms of revenue collection capacity) introduced was the increase in value-added tax rates from 12 percent to 16 percent (Law 288–04) and then 18 percent (Law 253–12), which was likely moderately regressive.[7]

On the expenditure side, a series of rigidities have limited the fiscal space to conduct redistributive policies. First, the 2003–04 banking crisis had a large fiscal cost, associated with the bailout of one of the country's main financial entities; hence, since 2007 the government of the Dominican Republic has been devoting about 1 percent of GDP to the recapitalization of the nation's Central Bank. Second, while the Dominican Republic's stock in nonfinancial public sector debt declined from about 29 percent of GDP in 2003 (following the crisis) to 18 percent in 2007, it has expanded again, reaching 38.3 percent of GDP in 2013. As such, the International Monetary Fund warned in 2014 that the Dominican Republic is facing large public gross financing needs, representing about two thirds of expected revenues.[8] Third, inefficiencies in the electricity sector (Rufín et al. 2014), which have entailed government transfers averaging 1.3 percent of GDP in 2009–12, have posed another rigidity as well as a severe burden for the competitiveness of Dominican companies (figure O.5).

With limited fiscal resources, the Dominican Republic has faced difficulties in implementing equity-enhancing public policies. During 1991–2010, the Dominican Republic spent just about 2 percent of GDP on public education, ranking at the bottom of Latin American countries.[9] Despite a notable expansion in school enrollment over the past two decades, the system has been characterized by high student-to-teacher ratios, double-shifting by teachers, inadequate formation, and high repetition and dropout rates (Sánchez and Senderowitsch 2012). To address these challenges, and following extensive citizen protests in December 2010, the government increased allocations for education to 4 percent of GDP for the first time in the 2013 budget. The health sector presents a similar situation, having registered notable improvements in terms of coverage, but facing some persistent challenges in terms of effective access, as private out-of-pocket expenditures still represent 66 percent of total spending, and purchasing medicines is a heavy burden for the poorer strata of the population.

In sum, a vicious cycle seems to limit the capacity of the Dominican government to redistribute wealth. Sánchez and Senderowitsch (2012) observe how individuals in the Dominican Republic, especially those in the middle class, opt out from public services in light of their limited quality, choosing instead private solutions (for example, private schools and health insurance). This seems to make them less likely to engage in collective action, demanding increasing accountability from the public sector, and less inclined to pay taxes, thus further limiting state resources to improve the quality of public service delivery. This low-level equilibrium is likely preventing the country from attaining a welfare state and hampering prospects for poverty reduction.

Why Is Growth Insufficient to Reduce Poverty in the Dominican Republic? An Empirical Analysis of Factors Contributing to Limited Shared Growth

The available evidence strongly supports the role of three distinguishing characteristics of the Dominican economy in explaining why prosperity has not been shared more broadly in a country that does not seem to have a growth problem. In the authors' view, these three characteristics are part of a more complex puzzle; additional pieces could help craft a clearer view of why growth has not been enough to contribute to faster poverty reduction. This book attempts to map out this puzzle and identify complementary explanations about why the Dominican Republic continues, to this date, to experience high growth with limited poverty reduction. The authors strongly believe that the assessment of Dominican labor market functioning—with a focus on equity—can contribute to inform the ongoing policy debate about the necessary reforms needed to enhance the linkages between economic growth, labor incomes, and poverty reduction. The contribution of the book, thus, lies in precisely offering a more careful exploration of specific issues regarding common explanations for the Dominican Republic's shortcomings in accelerating poverty reduction.

With this objective in mind, this book assembles a collection of empirical analyses that explore three complementary hypotheses that could help decipher the puzzle of growth with limited shared prosperity in the Dominican Republic.

Hypothesis 1: Poverty Methodology Might Not Account for Price Variation of Consumption between Income Levels

The first hypothesis tests whether the observed pattern of fast economic growth with persistent poverty and inequality in this country is partly driven by a poverty methodology that does not account for price variation that distinctly affects the consumption patterns of low-income and better-off households. If this hypothesis holds, the Dominican Republic may face a situation in which household income for households at the bottom of the distribution is underestimated.

Hypothesis 2: The Pattern of Specialization Might Not Favor Unskilled Labor

The second hypothesis tests whether the pattern of specialization in the Dominican Republic might be such that it does not favor unskilled labor. If this hypothesis holds, then returns to capital are probably much higher than returns to labor; this would be an indication that the Dominican Republic has had a comparative advantage in products that are capital-intensive instead of labor-intensive.

Hypothesis 3: Poverty and Wage Inequality Might Be Affected by Both Immigration and Emigration

The third hypothesis investigates whether poverty and wage inequality in this country are affected not only by immigration but also by emigration.

Haitian emigration might be supplying unskilled labor that attenuates the effect on wages of increases in labor demand usually associated with high GDP growth rates. However, many Dominicans have moved abroad over past decades, mainly to the United States, where they formed one of the largest migrant diasporas in the country. Thus, it is necessary to conduct an economic analysis of labor market impact, considering these two migration flows simultaneously.

The analysis of three complementary hypotheses tested in this book yields interesting findings that reveal the complexity of the phenomenon of growth with limited poverty reduction in the Dominican Republic. Regarding the first hypothesis, an important result is that there is no evidence of any methodological problems with the methodology applied to calculate poverty or economic growth in this country. As is discussed in chapter 1, the share of household income that is not factored into the calculation of the poverty incidence is not substantive enough to have a significant impact on the poverty rate.

Regarding the second hypothesis, the evidence presented in chapters 2 and 3 shows that the patterns of trade of the Dominican Republic—a relatively low endowment of skilled workers—are not the most likely sources of inequality in the country. This is important because it confirms the importance of government policy to promote greater equity and inclusion through more efficient, targeted public spending. On the other hand, the results presented in chapter 3 point to a negative association between sectoral changes in labor shares and growth in the country. This is suggestive of the importance of supply-side policies to improve both labor force skills and participation. With a better-educated labor force, it may indeed be easier for the country to move toward a more virtuous circle of higher productivity, higher growth, and faster employment creation.

Finally, the third hypothesis is concerned with the effects of migration on poverty and wage inequality. In this book, the findings are less conclusive owing to severe data limitations. Nonetheless, after making use of robust, state-of-the-art methodological approaches to investigate this question, the evidence presented in chapters 4 and 5 remains highly relevant. The analysis shows that the impact of immigration on more skilled workers is minimal and relatively positive for those with low skills in the formal sector. The effects of emigration are consistent with economic theory and suggest that high-skilled Dominicans who decide not to migrate tend to benefit from emigration because of the decline in supply, and that low-skilled workers tend to lose more relative to high-skilled ones, owing to their complementary role in production.

Overview

Chapter 1 addresses the adequacy of the methodology to measure price variation, focusing on whether the low responsiveness of the poverty rate to the strong, robust level of economic growth recorded by the Dominican Republic during the past decade may be partly explained by a price index that does not reflect differences in consumption patterns across income groups. An additional concern is that the definition of *household income* used in the micro-data may overlook components that represent an important source of income for poor households such as social transfers, which have increased in recent years as the country has introduced new social safety nets.

Adding to the concerns is the issue that the reliability of poverty figures in the Dominican Republic has been recently questioned.[10] After exhaustively assessing the concerns noted above, Aristy-Escuder finds that the quality of the household surveys in the country could indeed be improved to include more detailed information on the sources of income, mainly related to social programs and agricultural income. However, his main conclusion is that the share of income that is not taken into consideration to calculate the poverty incidence is not large enough to have a significant impact on the poverty rate. His results are robust vis-à-vis the use of different consumer price indexes to calculate the Dominican Republic's poverty rate, which did not change much for each different index used in this experiment.

Chapter 2 examines the role of factor endowments, technology, and capital mobility in job creation, and investigates the following question: why, in the face of outstanding growth performance, has the Dominican Republic not been able to generate enough formal jobs to absorb its abundant labor force (in light manufacturing, for example). This chapter ponders this question by exploring the relationship between factor endowment and comparative advantage in the Dominican Republic. In particular, the authors test the hypothesis that the factors of Dominican exports are not labor-intensive. In that context, they estimate Rybczynski coefficients for the global economy and for the Dominican Republic in particular, and then test whether the Dominican estimates differ from global estimates. With this, they then assess whether the Dominican Republic has had a comparative advantage in products that are capital-intensive instead of labor-intensive.

Chapter 3 considers whether labor market outcomes in the Dominican Republic suffer from capital-biased technical change, providing additional insights into the questions addressed in the previous chapter. In this chapter, the authors study the recent evolution of the labor income share in the Dominican Republic to test whether biased technical change can help explain why the country's observed strong economic growth has not translated into improved labor market outcomes. More specifically, they analyze whether wage stagnation in the context of favorable economic growth is driven by a decrease in labor income shares. If capital-biased technical change is indeed a factor, then sectors that experienced higher output growth also experienced a decrease in the labor income share, the authors conclude. Their results indicate that the labor share in the Dominican Republic fell significantly during the 2003–04 banking crisis, resulting in a significant wage correction. Although recent national accounts data suggest that the labor share has recovered to precrisis levels, it remains low by international comparison, though similar to other developing Latin American economies. Declines in labor share are notable in the sectors largely driving economic growth, possibly owing to "biased" technical change that increases productivity while lowering labor demand. Specifically, the authors find a negative relationship between sectoral changes in labor shares and growth, both before and after the crisis. A decomposition analysis finds that, in most years, it has been a decrease in labor share within sectors that is driving the decrease in labor shares, rather than a change in the composition of output.

Chapter 4 focuses on the wage effects of Haitian migration in the Dominican Republic, delving into the complex, sensitive debate on whether labor market outcomes in the Dominican Republic are affected by migrants from neighboring Haiti. In this chapter, the authors test the hypothesis that higher Haitian immigration results in lower wages for local workers. The extent to which immigration affects wages in local labor markets is, in large part, determined by whether immigrants' skills substitute for or complement those of local workers. If they are substitutes, this can result in increased competition for jobs, although complementary skills can lead to increased productivity for local workers.

To explore this question while exploiting the heterogeneity in the distribution of Haitian immigrants in the Dominican Republic, Sousa, Sanchez, and Baez test for a relationship between the size of the local Haitian immigrant population and wages of Dominican-born workers. Their analysis finds that Haitian workers in the Dominican Republic are highly clustered—in unskilled work categories, specific sectors, and geographic locations. In particular, given the relatively low levels of schooling among Haitian immigrants and the low levels of employment among Haitian immigrant women, it would be expected that competition for jobs with Haitian labor would be primarily felt by Dominican men with low levels of schooling. Their analysis finds no negative relationship between the proportion of the local labor force that is Haitian-born and the wages of local labor once individual characteristics are considered. The authors have also tested whether Haitian migration affects only some types of workers by looking at workers with certain levels of schooling and considering only the proportion of the Haitian local labor force that is of the same educational group and gender. This analysis also does not yield a negative effect or correlation. It does not find evidence supporting the hypothesis that Haitian labor in the Dominican Republic has led to stagnating wages for local workers. Instead, the findings suggest that because Haitian immigrant labor is largely limited to unskilled and informal employment in agriculture and construction, Haitian immigrants are more likely to be complements than substitutes to both capital as well as the relatively more skilled Dominican workers.

Chapter 5 considers the labor market implications of immigration and emigration in the Dominican Republic, going one step further in this debate. Kone and Ozden add a new and important dimension to the discussion by acknowledging that the Dominican Republic occupies a unique place in the migration landscape as both an immigration and emigration country. While it hosts many Haitians, who have migrated to escape poverty and the effects of the massive 2010 earthquake, the Dominican Republic also has a similarly large diaspora in the United States. The authors construct an elegant, sophisticated stylized nested production model that captures the extent of substitution between natives and migrants, high- and low-skilled workers, and the formal and informal sectors. The authors then simulate the effects of migration for a range of parameter values and immigration levels; this simulation is intended to circumvent the severe data constraints associated with the measurement of migration flows. Their results show that low-skilled workers in the informal sector are most negatively affected owing to their direct substitutability with immigrants. As the analysis in chapter 4 had anticipated, the impact of immigration is minimal for the formal high-skilled but relatively positive for the formal low-skilled. The effects of emigration, more on the high-skilled than natives, are as important. Kone and Ozden find that the nonmigrant high-skilled gain owing to a decline in supply and that the low-skilled lose due to their complementary role in production. An important caveat in their analysis is that the extent of the negative impact on the formal and informal low-skilled depend on the extent of formality among the emigrants.

Notes

1. Computation based on the *World Bank Atlas* Method, instead of simple exchange rates. as well as on the World Bank's World Development Indicators. For detailed information on the *Atlas* Method, visit https://datahelpdesk.worldbank.org/knowledgebase /articles/378832-the-world-bank-atlas-method-detailed-methodology.

2. See SEDLAC (CEDLAS and World Bank) data files on poverty, including regional poverty estimates. http://sedlac.econo.unlp.edu.ar/eng/statistics-detalle.php?idE=34.

3. It is highlighted that measuring productivity as output per worker (as in this chapter) or as output per hour (as computed by Abdullaev and Estevão 2013) leads to similar result.

4. The authors would like to note, however, that gains in productivity in manufacturing (figure O.3) may be also affected by the reduction of manufacturing employment in the SEZs in the 2000s, although Abdullaev and Estevão (2013) use output per hour as a proxy and obtain similar results.

5. Open unemployment rates consider only respondents who are actively looking for a job over the previous month. It is worth noticing that labor market participation rates among individuals with tertiary (77 percent) and secondary (64 percent) education are significantly higher than those with primary or no education (about 50 percent), according to the National Labor Force Survey (Encuesta Nacional de Fuerza de Trabajo 2014) conducted by the Central Bank of the Dominican Republic. For more information, see http://www.bancentral.gov.do/estadisticas_economicas /mercado_trabajo/.

6. The authors look at the Dominican *foreign direct investment firms* (defined as those with a percentage of foreign ownership above 10 percent of social capital), using World Bank–IFC Enterprise Surveys. The Dominican survey sample consists of only 57 observations; hence, the results should be interpreted with caution.

7. According to microsimulation exercises conducted by the Ministry of Economy, Planning, and Development of the Dominican Republic, with the support of the World Bank, in January 2013.

8. "Press Release: IMF Executive Board Concludes 2014 Article IV Consultation and Second Post-Program Monitoring Discussion with the Dominican Republic," Press Release No. 14/281, dated June 13, 2014, http://wwbw.imf.org/external/np/sec /pr/2014/pr14281.htm.

9. World Bank's World Development Indicators and SISDOM (Sistema de Indicadores Sociales de República Dominicana), Ministry of Economy, Planning, and Development of the Dominican Republic.

10. See Edwin Ruiz, "'Milagro dudoso': Más de 539 mil dejan pobreza en 6 meses," *Diario Libre*, August 11, 2014, http://www.diariolibre.com/economia/2014/08/11/i740371 _milagro-dudoso-539-mil-dejan-pobreza-meses.html.

References

Abdullaev U., and M. Estevão. 2013. "Growth and Employment in the Dominican Republic: Options for a Job-Rich Growth." IMF Working Paper WP/13/40, International Monetary Fund, Washington, DC.

Baez, J. E., L. F. Lopez-Calva, A. Castaneda, and A. Sharman. 2014. *When Prosperity Is Not Shared: The Weak Links between Growth and Equity in the Dominican Republic.* Washington, DC: World Bank Group.

Burgaud, J.-M., and T. Farole. 2011. "When Trade Preferences and Tax Breaks Are No Longer Enough: The Challenge of Adjustment in the Dominican Republic's Free Zones." In *Special Economic Zones: Progress, Emerging Challenges, and Future Directions,* edited by T. Farole and G. Akinci, 159–89. Washington, DC: World Bank.

Guzmán, R. M. 2007. *La informalidad en el mercado laboral urbano de la Republica Dominicana.* Santo Domingo: Banco Central de la República Dominicana.

Lall, Sanjaya. 2000. *The Technological Structure and Performance of Developing Country Manufactured Exports, 1985–1998.* Oxford (UK): Queen Elizabeth House, University of Oxford.

Ondetti, G. 2009. "Democratization and Redistributive Policymaking: Taxation, Social Spending and Labor Market Regulation in Brazil and the Dominican Republic." Paper presented at the American Political Science Association meeting, Toronto, September 3–6.

Rufín, C., D. Zucchini, R. Senderowitsch, and M. E. Sánchez-Martín. 2014. "The Dominican Republic: Moving from Exit to Voice—Shifting Incentives in the Power Sector." In *Problem-Driven Political Economy Analysis: The World Bank's Experience,* edited by B. Levy, V. Fritz and R. Ort. Washington, DC: World Bank.

Sánchez-Ancochea, D. 2012. "A Fast Herd and a Slow Tortoise? The Challenge of Upgrading in the Dominican Republic." *Studies in Comparative International Development* 47 (2): 208–30.

Sánchez, M. E., and R. Senderowitsch. 2012. "The Political Economy of the Middle Class in the Dominican Republic: Individualization of Public Goods, Lack of Institutional Trust and Weak Collective Action." Policy Research Working Paper 6049, World Bank, Washington, DC.

———. 2014. *How to Sustain Export Dynamism by Reducing Duality in the Dominican Republic: A World Bank Trade Competitiveness Diagnostic.* Washington, DC: World Bank. http://documents.worldbank.org/curated/en/863411468233087995/pdf/AUS6804 -REVISED-WP-P145785-PUBLIC-Box391428B.pdf.

CHAPTER 1

Income Definition, Price Indexes, and the Poverty Headcount in the Dominican Republic

Jaime Aristy-Escuder

Historically, the Dominican Republic's economy has had relatively high growth rates. From 1991 to 2015, the average real economic growth rate was 5 percent. Macroeconomic and political stability were factors driving this economic performance, along with the implementation of structural reforms that improved the resource allocation process and encouraged domestic and foreign direct investment.[1] This high growth rate has been explained by capital accumulation—followed by an increase in total factor productivity and, to a lesser extent, higher employment levels (Johnson 2013).

Since the early 1990s, the Dominican Republic has been one of the fastest growing economies in Latin America and the Caribbean. Between 1992 and 2000, the rate of growth of the annual gross domestic product (GDP) was 6.5 percent, making the Dominican Republic the region's top performer. But throughout 2001–14, the country's average growth rate decreased to 4.5 percent as a result of the Dominican banking crisis (2003–04), the increase of international oil prices (2008), and the Great Recession (2008–09). The banking crisis provoked an inflation rate of 42.7 percent and a GDP contraction of 1.3 percent in 2003. Thus, poverty incidence jumped from 33.4 percent (September 2002)

The author expresses his gratitude to collaborators for their help in data collection and in data analysis and interpretation—namely, Mabely Díaz (Oficina Nacional de Estadística, ONE), Ramón Gonzalez, Antonio Morillo (Ministerio de Economía, Planificación y Desarrollo, MEPyD), Jaime Pérez (Dirección General de Presupuesto, DIGEPRES), and Elina Rosario (Central Bank of the Dominican Republic). Also to McDonald Benjamin, Juan Carlos Parra, and Miguel Sánchez (all of the World Bank) for their important comments and suggestions.

Jaime Aristy-Escuder is professor of economics at the Instituto Tecnológico de Santo Domingo (INTEC), Dominican Republic. He holds a master of science degree in financial mathematics from the University of Chicago and a doctorate in economics from the University of Barcelona. Please direct correspondence to jaimearisty@gmail.com.

to 50 percent (September 2004)—or in other words, more than 1.7 million persons moved into poverty. The Great Recession also had a negative impact on the Dominican economy.

In sum, the reduction of international trade flows, rising oil prices, and the slowdown of global growth caused a significant decline in economic activity. The negative impact of these external shocks was noticeable. In one year, 218,479 persons became poor, increasing poverty incidence from 43.8 percent (September 2007) to 45.2 percent (September 2008).

This chapter examines the issue of poverty incidence and associated trends with a focus on income definition, price indexes, and the poverty headcount. It is worth noting that, despite the relatively rapid GDP growth recovery since the 2003–04 Dominican banking crisis, the reduction of poverty incidence has been sluggish. Until September 2013, poverty incidence was 41.8 percent, showing that the economy had not achieved precrisis poverty levels. However, an improvement in poverty indicators has been observed since 2014 in the context of the recent acceleration of economic growth during 2014–15 (with rates over 7 percent per year). The most recent official publications indicated poverty incidence at 31.5 percent (September 2015) and subsequently at 30 percent (ONE and MEPyD 2015b).

Against this backdrop, this chapter examines the following question: given the strong economic performance, why has growth not led to faster poverty reduction in the Dominican Republic? In doing so, two hypotheses will be evaluated. The first considers the possibility that the household surveys do not capture all the income sources, including cash and in-kind social transfers, needed to correctly determine poverty incidence. As such, household income is decomposed in this analysis to determine if income concepts that are not included in the definition of *wellness* have a significant impact on poverty measures.[2]

The second hypothesis establishes that the general consumer price index (CPI), used to periodically adjust the poverty lines, does not properly reflect the evolution of the cost of consumption basket of poor households.[3] Consumption patterns for poor and nonpoor households are compared with the consumption basket implicit in the general CPI to determine whether poverty line adjustments, using the CPI for the whole population, ignore heterogeneous price variations—and thus purchasing power—across different income groups. In this case, this would distort the measures of the poverty headcount.

Poverty in the Dominican Republic

The official methodology used to define *poverty* in the Dominican Republic corresponds to a monetary approach measured by household income (ONE and MEPyD 2012).[4] The official definition of *monetary poverty* considers a welfare indicator, defined from household disposable income: a basic food basket and a basic nonfood basket, the latter of which considers essential needs such as clothing, shelter, water, electricity, schooling, and reliable health care.[5] Both baskets are constructed based on the observation of the consumption pattern of a population of reference, and evaluated and adjusted accordingly to nutritional criteria. According to this approach, *monetary poverty* is defined as the state in which a deficit exists in the amount of resources (income) considered necessary for a household to purchase a minimum food and nonfood basket.

Based on these indicators, a person or a household monetary poverty condition is established with two thresholds: the extreme poverty line and the general poverty line. The first represents the money needed to purchase a food basket with the minimum daily calorie requirement for an equivalent adult. The second threshold used to define poverty represents the monetary resources needed to purchase basic goods and services, besides food, that have been identified as necessary to well-being.[6] In addition, urban-versus-rural poverty lines, depending on residence, are also considered to establish household monetary poverty.

Poverty lines are adjusted periodically using the CPI calculated by the Central Bank of the Dominican Republic. The jump in the inflation rate during the banking crisis (2003–04) significantly increased the value of poverty lines (figures 1.1 and 1.2). From September 2002 to September 2004, the national poverty line almost doubled, increasing from RD$1,372.40 to RD$2,702.20. This trend increased the number of persons living in poverty. In September 2015, the general poverty line was RD$4,582.10; the extreme poverty line, RD$2,109.50; the general urban poverty line, RD$4,748.70; and the general rural poverty line, RD$4,228.00.

Figure 1.1 General Poverty Lines: General, Urban, and Rural, 2000–15

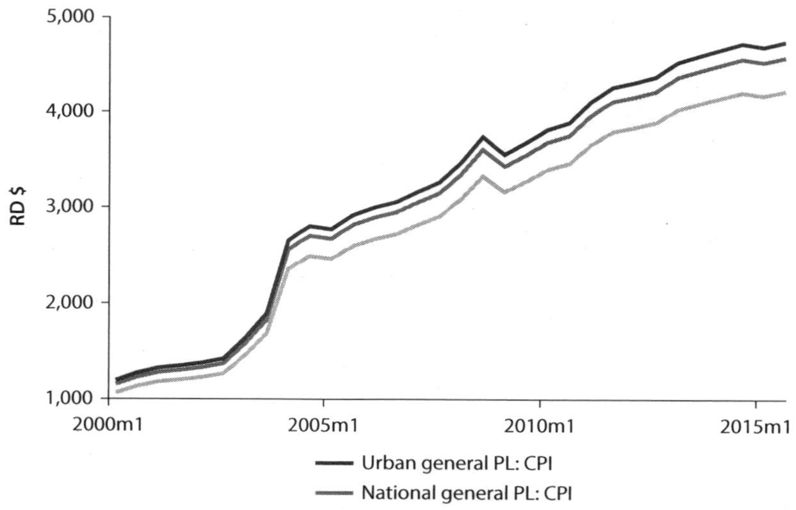

Source: Based on data from ONE and MEPyD (2015b).
Note: CPI = consumer price index; MEPyD = Ministerio de Economía, Planificación y Desarrollo (Ministry of the Economy, Planning and Development); ONE = Oficina Nacional de Estadística (National Bureau of Statistics); PL = poverty line.

Figure 1.2 Extreme Poverty Lines: General, Urban, and Rural, 2000–15

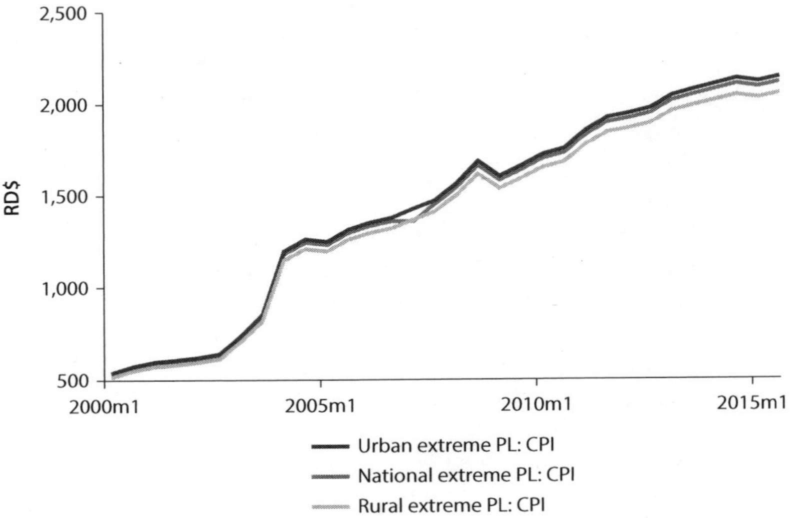

Source: Based on data from ONE and MEPyD (2015b).
Note: CPI = consumer price index; MEPyD = Ministerio de Economía, Planificación y Desarrollo (Ministry of the Economy, Planning and Development); ONE = Oficina Nacional de Estadística (National Bureau of Statistics); and PL = poverty line.

When examining poverty as a share of the population, the most recent official estimation (September 2015) reveals that the overall general poverty incidence rate was 31.5 percent. In general, a persistent decline is evident in the overall incidence of poverty since September 2013, with September 2015 levels at pre-crisis 2000–02 levels. It is worth noting that from September 2013 to September 2015, general poverty incidence was reduced by 10.3 percentage points (figure 1.3). By area of residence, in September 2015, the rate of general poverty was higher in rural areas (38.3 percent) than in urban areas (28.2 percent).

In comparison, extreme poverty affects 6.8 percent of the total population, with urban area incidence (4.9 percent) lower than in rural areas (10.6 percent) (figure 1.4). From September 2013 to September 2015, extreme poverty declined by 3.0 percentage points (ONE and MEPyD 2015b).

Sources of Income and the Poverty Headcount

ENIGH 2007: Overview of the 2007 National Survey of Income and Expenses of Households

The input used to define the basic food and non-food consumption baskets (discussed above) is the 2007 National Survey of Income and Expenses of Households (ENIGH 2007, Encuesta Nacional de Ingresos y Gastos de los Hogares). ENIGH 2007 aimed to obtain data on household income and expenditures as well as on the population's general welfare from a representative national sample, by region and area of residence.

Figure 1.3 General Poverty Incidence: National, Urban, and Rural, 2000–15

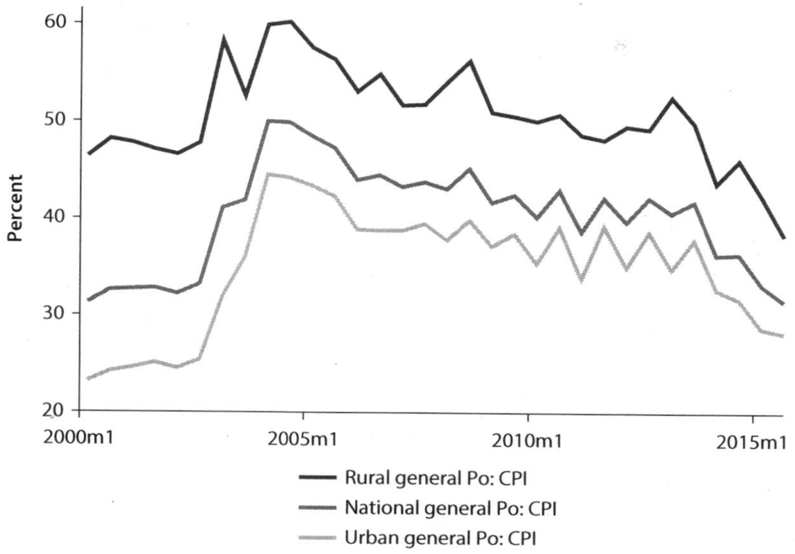

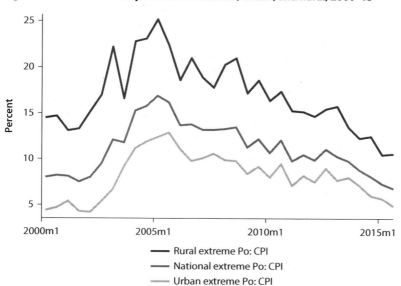

Source: Based on data from ONE and MEPyD (2015b).
Note: CPI = consumer price index; MEPyD = Ministerio de Economía, Planificación y Desarrollo
(Ministry of the Economy, Planning and Development); ONE = Oficina Nacional de Estadística
(National Bureau of Statistics); and Po = poverty incidence.

Figure 1.4 Extreme Poverty Incidence: National, Urban, and Rural, 2000–15

Source: Based on data from ONE and MEPyD (2015b).
Note: CPI = consumer price index; Po = poverty incidence; MEPyD = Ministerio de Economía, Planificación y
Desarrollo (Ministry of the Economy, Planning and Development); ONE = Oficina Nacional de Estadística
(National Bureau of Statistics).

Spatially, the ENIGH 2007 survey covered the national district and the country's 31 provinces. It is important to note that in most cases, the sample size in each province did not allow inferences with acceptable accuracy at that level. Also, the sample was divided in proportion to the population reported to the planning regions (Decree 710–2004), in the Dominican Republic's VIII National Population and Housing Census of 2002, and classified by area of residence: urban or rural. The temporary coverage for data captured was 12 months, that is, between January 8, 2007, and January 17, 2008.

The effective sample from the ENIGH 2007 resulted in 8,318 houses, 8,363 households, and 30,937 persons. Data were collected from the selected households through four questionnaires: the first regarded the characteristics of the dwelling and of the household and its members; the second, daily household expenses; the third, personal daily expenses of the household members with independence of some expenses; and the last, agricultural activity.

Based on the survey results and using the expansion factors, the total population in 2007 was 9,353,700; 49.7 percent men and 50.3 percent women. By area of residence, 67.2 percent of the population lived in urban areas and the remaining 32.8 percent in rural areas.

ENIGH 2007: Sources of Income

The ENIGH 2007 captures the following types of income: monetary labor income, in-kind labor income, national transfers, foreign transfers, and imputed rent of homeownership. However, labor income, both monetary and in kind, and national transfers income have traditionally been the main sources of income, with labor income being the most relevant and having more impact on poverty estimation.

For the general population, total labor income accounts for 71.4 percent of total household income. National transfers income follows, with 11.2 percent, and imputed rent of homeownership represents 8.5 percent. Dividing the population into five parts, using quintiles, they could be ordered from the poorest (included in the first quintile) to the wealthiest (members of the fifth quintile). For the first quintile, total labor income reduces to 53.4 percent and national transfers income jumps to 27.7 percent, while imputed rent of homeownership is 14.2 percent. In comparison, for the top quintile, labor income accounts for 74 percent of total household income, national transfers income represents 7.5 percent, and imputed rent homeownership is 7.8 percent.[7]

Some income sources are not included as income for poverty calculations, however, because they are considered as being occasional (for example, inheritance income, insurance payments, and occasional foreign transfers). Even though the welfare indicator does not include some occasional income, this source does not have a significant weight in the total household income.[8] The total income not included in the poverty calculation accounts only for 1.5 percent of total household income.

Official computations of poverty do not consider as income other types of income because they are not found in the National Labor Force Survey

(ENFT, Encuesta Nacional de Fuerza de Trabajo), which is used periodically to compute general and extreme poverty in the Dominican Republic. In the process of homologation of the income definition to be used to construct the welfare indicator that defines monetary poverty in the Dominican Republic, some sources of income were not considered because they were not included in the ENFT. These sources of income are (a) occasional income, (b) other national transfers for the past month and the past 12 months, and (c) other foreign occasional income. The income that is not considered in the wellness indicator only represents 0.4 percent of total household income.

For the first quintile, the amount of income not included in poverty calculations accounts for 3.7 percent of total household income.[9] The income not considered represents 0.2 percent of the total household income of that quintile. These results show that the poverty headcount should not be significantly different if these occasional incomes and other types of income (for example, other national transfers) are considered in poverty analysis.

ENFT: Overview of the National Labor Force Survey

The ENFT is conducted semiannually to periodically update the poverty measurements—with a series of surveys taken into consideration for poverty estimation beginning in the year 2000.[10] The survey is designed to provide information on the labor market. The ENFT provides information about average income generated by the employed. Comparing this information with the poverty line results in the determination of poverty incidence twice a year.

Comparison of ENFT with ENIGH 2007

Both surveys, ENIGH 2007 and ENFT, capture the main types of income of Dominican households, even though they do this with different specifications in terms of periodicity. For some questions, the ENFT captures the aggregate amount on a monthly and yearly basis, and the ENIGH captures the declared amount on a monthly basis.

The ENIGH 2007 contains some concepts that are not included in the ENFT 2007, such as income tax deductions and pension discounts through the pension fund administrator (Admininistradoras de Fondos de Pensiones, AFP) declared in the survey, the incentives and representation expenses considered as part of labor income, and some occasional income. As stated above, the differences between the total amount of the concepts of income included in ENIGH 2007 and ENFT to calculate poverty indicators are relatively small.

The main difference between the questionnaires of these two surveys is that the ENIGH 2007 has a richer, detailed set of questions for salaried workers, independent workers, and farmers than those in the ENFT. For salaried and independent workers, the same detailed questions are asked for the principal occupation as well as the secondary one. The main difference between both surveys is found in the sources of farmer income; in the ENIGH 2007, a specific questionnaire was included to determine household income devoted to farming, which examined the source of income (agricultural or livestock) and expenses incurred for the development of the activity to obtain household income.

Table 1A.4 (in the annex) presents the income concepts included in ENFT 2015 to calculate official poverty indicators. As in ENIGH 2007, labor income, imputed rent of homeownership, and national transfers income are the main sources of income for Dominican households. In September 2015, for the first quintile, the sources of income account for 67.6 percent, 11.0 percent, and 17.3 percent, respectively. The table also shows the income concepts not included in the wellness indicator. For the first quintile, these incomes represent 1.0 percent of total household income, a small amount that would not significantly change the poverty headcount.[11]

Social Programs

Public in-kind transfers (for example, education and health services) are not included as income to calculate poverty for these surveys. The in-kind transfers considered are those types made in exchange for labor (for example, payments made with food, a house, transport, fuel, a telephone, and other types of in-kind arrangements) and those received from family and friends.

The only types of social programs considered in the ENFTs are conditional cash transfers (CCTs). Because, throughout the survey, investigators ask the interviewee about the amount of money received and the program name, this generally affects the quantity reported by the program administrator. If the household receives government transfers from different programs (for example, Comer es Primero, Bono Luz, Bono Gas), these income transfers are shown as an aggregate amount in the questionnaire.

Even though the name of the social program is known to the ENFT, the published databases do not identify the program. It is well known that the informant's declarations are biased toward the most popular programs and those established at the beginning of CCT programs, such as the Dominican Republic's Solidaridad program. Because of this and the increasing need to visualize social programs separately, the new survey methodology, currently being implemented by the Central Bank, will contain detailed specifications for these programs.

The definition of *income* captures improvements in welfare brought about by the introduction and expansion of CCT schemes put in place after the 2003–04 crisis and during the economic slowdown of 2008–09. An increasing number of government social program beneficiaries are captured in the survey. Table 1.1 presents the number of government transfer beneficiaries that (a) were registered with the Dominican Republic's social subsidies administration (Administradora de Subsidios Sociales, ADESS) and (b) identified in the ENFT. In 2015, the difference in total beneficiaries was 18.2 percent (953,783 versus 806,663 persons). Moreover, there is a difference of 8 percent between per capita transfers received by beneficiaries, according to ENFT (RD\$1,172/month) and to ADESS (RD\$1,266/month).

Simulating an Increase in Household Income

Table 1.2 shows the impact of an increase in official income used to compute poverty indicators. It is worth noting that the percentage of income excluded from the definition of income (1.0 percent for the poorest 20 percent of households (CPI 1, or the first quintile) and the social conditional transfers are not included in the September 2015 ENFT as a percentage of total household income (0.3 percent). Thus, it could be assumed that the proportion of income to be adjusted would be less than 5 percent. Thus, the absolute change in general poverty would be about 1.8 percentage points.[12] This reveals that considering additional income sources (for example, occasional transfers) or adjusting the conditional transfer amount by the underreporting of CCT revenues has a relatively small impact on poverty measures.

Table 1.1 Government Beneficiary Transfers and Per Capita Transfers, 2005–15

Year	Government beneficiary transfer (no.)		Per capita transfers (RD$)	
	Labor force survey (ENFT)	Social subsidies manager (ADESS)	Labor force survey (ENFT)	Social subsidies manager (ADESS)
2005	36,803	196,226	547	269
2006	157,833	216,152	648	561
2007	169,435	313,327	640	491
2008	322,445	791,950	702	475
2009	561,193	818,340	776	792
2010	624,504	824,932	846	876
2011	618,757	860,711	868	870
2012	720,973	831,811	1,019	1,113
2013	720,650	906,504	1,174	1,202
2014	777,555	945,463	1,191	1,264
2015	806,663	953,783	1,172	1,266

Sources: Based on ADESS and ENFT data.
Note: ADESS = Administradora de Subsidios Sociales (Social Subsidy Administration); ENFT = Encuesta Nacional de Fuerza de Trabajo (National Labor Force Survey).

Table 1.2 Poverty Incidence and Income Growth, September 2015 Baseline

Poverty line type	Severity	Official income			
		Baseline (Sept. 2015)	5% increase	10% increase	15% increase
National	General	31.51	29.75	27.39	25.76
	Extreme	6.75	6.04	5.53	5.03
Urban	General	28.20	26.47	24.26	22.71
	Extreme	4.88	4.30	3.92	3.66
Rural	General	38.33	36.51	33.85	32.03
	Extreme	10.60	9.62	8.84	7.83

Source: Based on April 2015 ENFT data.
Note: ENFT = Encuesta Nacional de Fuerza de Trabajo (National Labor Force Survey)

When Growth Is Not Enough • http://dx.doi.org/10.1596/978-1-4648-1036-7

Recommendations on the Survey Data Collection

The information collected on the governmental transfers must be improved because it is impossible to identify the program from which the support is received in both surveys, ENIGH 2007 and ENFT. This could help determine the impact each specific social program has on poverty.[13]

The information collected on farmers and independent workers could also be improved. Part of this effort was made by including a specific questionnaire in ENIGH 2007, but that information could not be taken into consideration because there is no comparable concept within the ENFT. It was established in the conclusions of the report *Construction of the Aggregates of Income and Expenditure*, published by the Dominican Republic's National Office of Statistics in 2011, that the results of the evaluation of the questions for the farmers included in questionnaire 1 (used in the wellness indicator) and questionnaire 4 (a specific module with more detailed information) in ENIGH 2007 establishes that the latter is much better.

Price Indexes and Poverty Incidence

This section evaluates the impact on the poverty headcount of different price indexes used to adjust poverty lines. First, the consumption basket of the poor—that is, the first poorest quintile (20 percent) and first and second poorest quintiles (40 percent) of the population—is compared with the consumption basket of the "representative consumer" used to calculate the general CPI. Then, the evolution of these price indexes is studied to determine if there is a significant impact on the poverty line updated, using weights that reflect the consumption patterns of the poor. Finally, the poverty incidence for each price index, and poverty lines, are discussed.

Consumption Baskets

The Central Bank of the Dominican Republic reports a monthly general CPI and five other CPIs by income bracket, using 2010 as the base year.[14] The weights for the CPI are the shares of different types of consumption obtained from ENIGH 2007, which captures data from 2,640 goods and services consumed by household members. For the general CPI, the Central Bank selected a basket of 305 goods and services that represent 90 percent of total household consumption.

The Central Bank also computes consumption baskets by each quintile. The first quintile (Q1 CPI) by income bracket is based on the expenditure pattern of the bottom or poorest 20 percent of the population. The second quintile (Q2 CPI) is based on the expenditure pattern of the second 20 percent of the population, and so on.

As expected, there is a significant difference in consumption patterns between the richest 20 percent of households (that is, Q5 CPI, or the fifth quintile) and the poorest 20 percent of households (Q1 CPI, or the first quintile) (figure 1.5). Food and nonalcoholic beverages account for only 12.4 percent of the total

Figure 1.5 Consumption Basket of Richest (Q5 CPI) versus Poorest (Q1 CPI) Dominican Households, 2010

Percent

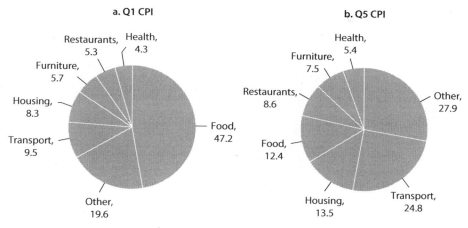

Source: Based on ONE and BCRD data.

Note: Q1 CPI = first-quintile consumption weights, or poorest 20 percent of households; Q5 CPI = fifth-quintile consumption weights, or richest 20 percent of households; ONE = Oficina Nacional de Estadística (National Bureau of Statistics); BCRD = Banco Central de la República Dominicana (Central Bank of the Dominican Republic).

consumption of the top quintile. On the other hand, these goods represent 47.2 percent of the total consumption of the bottom quintile population. Notice that the share of transport services consumption (24.8 percent) of the fifth (highest) quintile more than doubles the share of the first (lowest) quintile. This means that a reduction of fuel prices would benefit more the richest population. It can also be noted that droughts, which increase the prices of agricultural goods, affect the poorest more than the richest quintiles.

The general CPI can be interpreted as a weighted average of household indexes. The weight of each household is given by its total expenditures (Ley 2001, 3). In 2010, food and nonalcoholic beverages accounted for 25.1 percent of the consumption basket used to calculate the general CPI.[15] In terms of weights, transport is the second group of goods and services, with a share of 18 percent. Housing, restaurant, and furniture expenses follow (figure 1.6). Significant differences arise when comparing the consumption pattern of the poorest 40 percent of households (which includes both CPI Q1 and CPI Q2, or the first and second quintiles) or the poorest 20 percent of households (CPI Q1, or the first quintile), with the structure of consumption used to calculate the general CPI. The poorest 40 percent of households (CPI Q1 and Q2 quintiles, also referred to as the P-40% CPI) have a much higher share of food and nonalcoholic beverages, as well as a smaller share of transport services in total consumption. For this group of households, food and nonalcoholic beverages account for 42.1 percent of their total consumption, and transport services represents 11.1 percent. This means that the general CPI has a weight structure for a type of household with a level of income higher than the poorest 40 percent of households.

Figure 1.6 Consumption Basket for General CPI and P-40% CPI Households, 2010

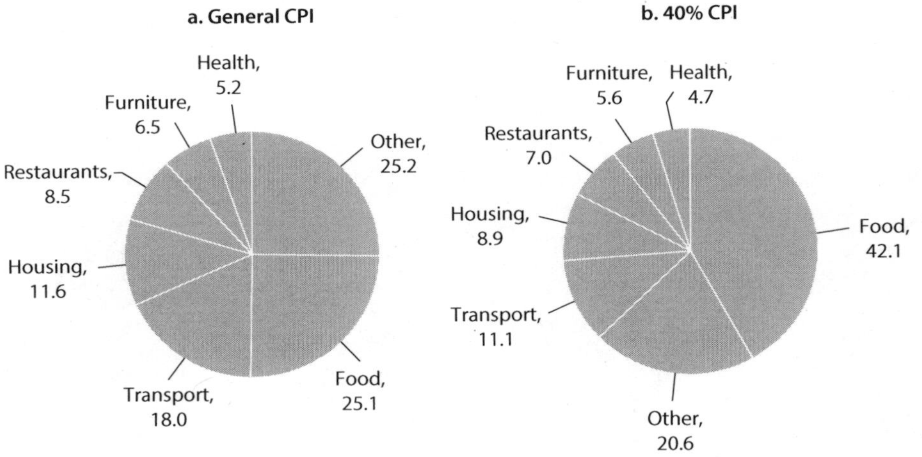

a. General CPI

Health, 5.2
Furniture, 6.5
Restaurants, 8.5
Housing, 11.6
Transport, 18.0
Food, 25.1
Other, 25.2

b. 40% CPI

Furniture, 5.6
Health, 4.7
Restaurants, 7.0
Housing, 8.9
Transport, 11.1
Food, 42.1
Other, 20.6

Source: Based on ONE and BCRD data.
Note: Consumption weights are used to calculate General CPI. 40% CPI = first- and second-quintile consumption weights, or poorest 40 percent of households; BCRD = Banco Central de la República Dominicana (Central Bank of the Dominican Republic); ONE = Oficina Nacional de Estadística (National Bureau of Statistics).

The formula of vector distance allows one to determine which of the different CPIs is closest to the general CPI.[16] Using the weights of goods and services for the CPI presented in table 1A.5 (in the annex), the distance is calculated and depicted in figure 1.7. The result shows that the specific CPI with the minimum distance to the general CPI is the one representing the consumption basket of fourth quintile's population (Q4 CPI). This means that the evolution of prices of different components of the consumption basket could have an impact on the poverty headcount.

Consumer Price Indexes

In general, the CPI for the richest 20 percent (Q5 CPI, or the fifth quintile) and the general CPI increases at a slightly higher (or similar) rate than the price index for the bottom 20 percent. The biggest positive difference between the general CPI and Q1 CPI rose from June 2005 to September 2007 (figure 1.8). This means that the price of the consumption basket of the poor increased at a lower rate in that period. Since August 2014 the price index of the poorest population has been increasing faster, owing to the impact of drought on food prices and to the reduction of fuel prices, which are included in transport services costs, thus having a higher weight in the consumption basket of the wealthiest population.[17]

Figure 1.8 shows the following price indexes: the general CPI, the Q1 CPI, and the Q5 CPI from 1999 to 2015.

Figure 1.9 shows that food prices had a moderate rate of growth from mid–2005 to September 2007. At the same time, transport services costs increased continuously, peaking in September 2008, when they started a temporary decline. Given the consumption pattern per quintile, these price movements

Figure 1.7 Distance between Various CPIs and the General CPI Consumption Basket

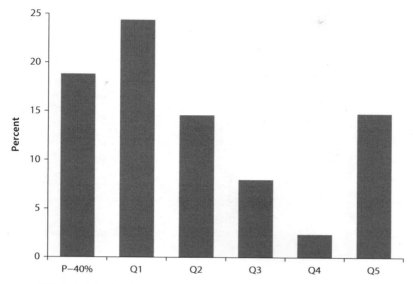

Source: Original calculations based on Central Bank of the Dominican Republican data.
Note: P-40% = poorest 40 percent of households, or first and second quintiles; Q1 = poorest 20 percent of households, or first quintile; Q2 CPI = second quintile; Q3 = third quintile; Q4 = fourth quintile; Q5 = richest 20 percent of households, or fifth quintile.

Figure 1.8 General CPI, Q1 CPI, and Q5 CPI, 1999–2015

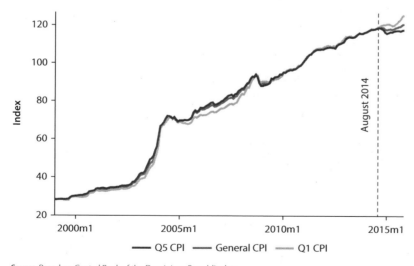

Source: Based on Central Bank of the Dominican Republic data.
Note: CPI = consumer price index; Q1 CPI = first quintile, or poorest 20 percent of households; Q5 CPI = fifth quintile, or richest 20 percent of households.

Figure 1.9 Food and Transport Services Prices, 2000–15

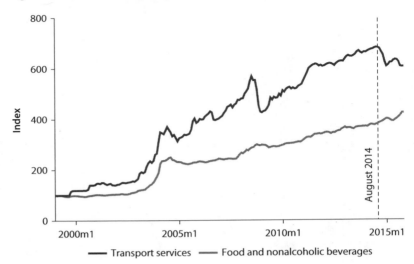

Source: Based on Central Bank of the Dominican Republic data.

provoked a rise in the general CPI at a higher rate than the CPI specific to the poorest 20 percent of the population. This suggests that, in this period, using general CPI to calculate welfare tends to overestimate the poverty incidence because poverty lines were slightly higher than they would be if adjusted by the CPI specific to poor households. Since August 2014, transport services prices decreased, owing to the significant reduction of international fuel prices, and food prices increased, owing to weather conditions. These price movements benefited the wealthiest population more.

Using these CPIs, inflation rate differentials between income groups are computed.[18] This allows one to determine if price adjustments, using a general CPI for the whole population of the Dominican Republic, (a) ignore heterogeneous price variation—and thus purchasing power—across different income groups and thus (b) distort the measures of the poverty headcount.

The Dominican Central Bank also computed a price index for the poorest 40 percent of the population (40% CPI) from December 2010 to October 2015. This index, along with the general CPI and the Q1 and Q5 CPIs, are shown in figure 1.10. The CPI computed with the consumption basket corresponding to the bottom 40 percent follows a similar path as the first-quintile CPI, even after August 2014, when fuel prices started their decline. When compared with the evolution of different price indexes, it can be shown that the general CPI is closer to the price index weighted with the consumption pattern of the fourth quintile. Since August 2014, the reduction in fuel prices and the increase in food and beverage goods prices explains the difference between the general CPI and the 40% CPI—that is, the poorest 40 percent (or in other words, CPI Q1 plus Q2).

Figure 1.10 Consumer Price Indexes: CPI, 40% CPI, Q1 CPI, and Q5 CPI, 2010–15

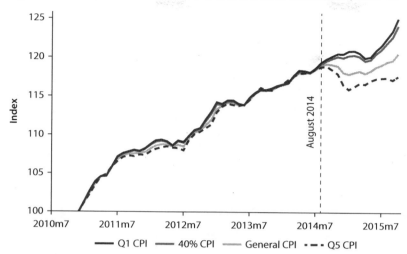

Source: Based on Central Bank of the Dominican Republic data.
Note: Q1 CPI = poorest 20 percent of households, or first quintile; 40% CPI = poorest 40 percent of households, or first and second quintiles; Q5 CPI = richest 20 percent of households, or fifth quintile.

The "plutocratic bias" (B) is defined as the difference between the general CPI (CPI_G) and a weighted CPI (CPI_S) that takes into consideration the consumption pattern of a selected group. A positive bias means that the goods consumed by the average representative population experience higher-than-average inflation and that those consumed by the selected population (for example, the poorest 40 percent of the population) experience lower-than-average inflation. A negative bias means that the prices of goods consumed by the selected group increased faster than the goods consumed by the average representative agent (Ley 2001, 8).

$$B = (CPI_G - CPI_S)$$

The "plutocratic bias" for the first quantile is −3.6 from December 2010 to October 2015. The median for the whole period was −0.33 (figure 1.11). It means that in this period, the goods consumed by the poorest 20 percent exhibit slightly higher inflation than the goods consumed by the general population. It is worth noting that up to July 2014, the plutocratic bias was close to zero. Thus, the CPI differential was created from August 2014 to October 2015. Price movements reduced the level of welfare of the poor.

For the poorest 40 percent of the population (40% CPI), the plutocratic bias from December 2010 to October 2015 was −4.5 points. The median for the whole period was −0.23 (figure 1.12). It is worth noting that up to June 2014, the bias was negligible (figure 1.13). This means that the negative bias originated when the general CPI had a negative movement from August 2014 to October 2015. As said before, the reduction of the general CPI inflation rate was explained mainly by the contraction of fuel and transport services prices.

Figure 1.11 Plutocratic Bias: Q1 CPI, December 2010–October 2015

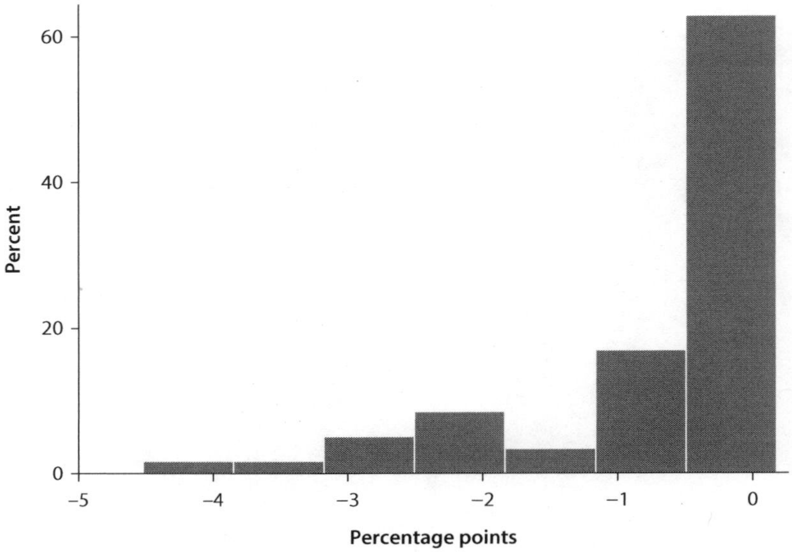

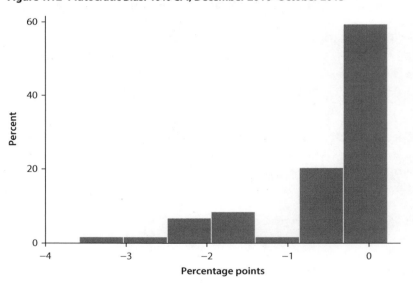

Source: Based on Central Bank of the Dominican Republic data.
Note: Q1 CPI = first quintile.

Figure 1.12 Plutocratic Bias: 40% CPI, December 2010–October 2015

Source: Based on Central Bank of the Dominican Republic data.
Note: 40% CPI = poorest 40 percent of households.

Figure 1.13 Plutocratic Bias: Q1 CPI and 40% CPI, 2010–15

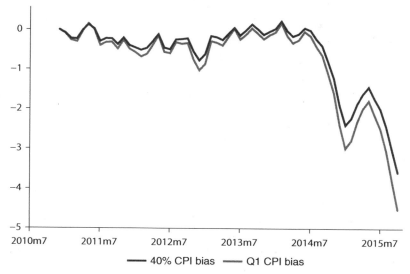

Source: Based on Central Bank of the Dominican Republic data.
Note: Q1 CPI bias = plutocratic bias based on the CPI specific to the poorest 20 percent of households; 40%
CPI bias = plutocratic bias based on the CPI specific to the poorest 40 percent of households.

Poverty Lines and Poverty Incidence

Using the official national poverty line of March 2011 (RD$3,996.80), several poverty lines can be calculated as a function of different price indexes. The general CPI is the price index used to determine the official poverty line and the official poverty incidence. Figure 1.14 depicts the evolution of the official poverty lines adjusted for the different CPIs.[19] As expected, up to September 2014, the poverty lines—calculated as a function of general CPI, for the poorest 20 percent (Q1 CPI, or the first quintile), and the poorest 40 percent (40% CPI)—were almost the same. This means that there was no significant variance of the poverty incidence owing to CPI index differences. From September 2014 to March 2015, the reduction of the general CPI reduced the level of the official poverty line; thus, it diminishes the level of the poverty incidence.

Table 1A.7 (in the annex) presents the results of poverty incidence for each of the poverty lines adjusted by different CPIs, and it also includes their confidence intervals.[20] In September 2015, the poverty incidence obtained using the general CPI was 31.5 percent, with the 95 percent confidence interval ranging from 29.7 percent to 33.3 percent. For the same period, the general poverty incidence using the poorest 40 percent (40% CPI) was 32.6 percent (figure 1.15), which lies within the confidence interval of the poverty incidence calculated using the general CPI. This means that the plutocratic bias created a difference of just 1.1 percentage points in the poverty incidence up to September 2015; but on average, the difference was only 0.15 percentage point from March 2011 to September 2015. Using the index of the poorest 20 percent (Q1 CPI), the general

Figure 1.14 General Poverty Lines—National: CPI, Q1 CPI, and 40% CPI, 2011–15

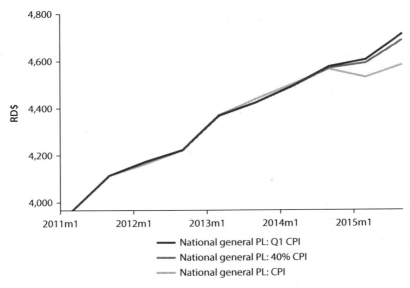

Source: Based on ONE and BCRD data.
Note: CPI = General CPI; Q1 CPI = first quintile, or poorest 20 percent of households; 40% CPI = poorest
40 percent of households; BCRD = Banco Central de la República Dominicana (Central Bank of the
Dominican Republic); ONE = Oficina Nacional de Estadística (National Bureau of Statistics); PL = poverty line.

**Figure 1.15 General Poverty Incidence—National: CPI, 40% CPI, and
Q1 CPI, 2011–15**

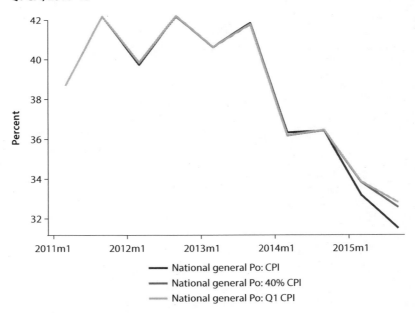

Source: Based on ONE and BCRD data.
Note: CPI = General CPI; Q1 CPI = first quintile, or poorest 20 percent of households; 40% CPI = poorest 40
percent of households; BCRD = Banco Central de la República Dominicana (Central Bank of the Dominican
Republic); ONE = Oficina Nacional de Estadística (National Bureau of Statistics); Po = poverty incidence.

poverty incidence is 32.8 percent. In this case, the plutocratic bias created a difference of 1.3 percentage points in poverty incidence, but the average difference is 0.19 percentage point.

This result suggests that adjusting the poverty lines using a general CPI or a CPI specific to the typical consumption basket for the poor has not distorted—significantly—the measures of poverty incidence in the period under analysis. Similar conclusions can be achieved for the extreme poverty and general poverty (rural and urban) headcounts (figures 1.16–1.18). Thus, the hypothesis that states that using a general CPI has *overestimated* poverty incidence can be rejected. It is worth noting that from March 2015 to October 2015, the negative plutocratic bias (that is, the difference between CPI and the 40% CPI) moved from 1.9 to 3.6; this means that the impact of food and fuel prices movements on CPI and specific CPIs undervalue the level of poverty lines that tend to *underestimate* the poverty incidence in the Dominican Republic in that period. Up to October 2015, the difference between the official poverty line (RD$4,616.19), calculated with the general CPI, and the poverty line calculated with the 40% CPI (RD$4,742.36) is 2.7 percent, almost 1.4 percentage points higher than the difference observed in March 2015. In the case of the bottom 20 percent (Q1 CPI), the difference of poverty lines in October 2015 is 3.4 percent, almost 1.9 percentage points higher than the difference observed in March 2015. This means that the *underestimation* of poverty incidence increased in the second part of 2015.

Figure 1.16 Extreme Poverty Incidence—National: CPI, 40% CPI, and Q1 CPI, 2011–15

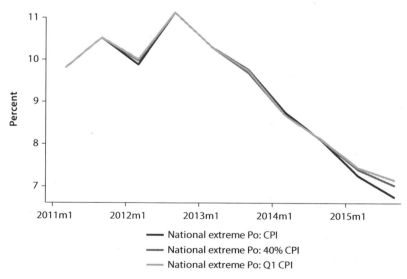

Source: Based on ONE and MEPyD (2015b) and BCRD data.
Note: CPI = General CPI; Q1 CPI = first quintile, or poorest 20 percent of households; 40% CPI = poorest 40 percent of households; BCRD = Banco Central de la República Dominicana (Central Bank of the Dominican Republic); MEPyD = Ministerio de Economía, Planificación y Desarrollo (Ministry of the Economy, Planning and Development); Po = poverty incidence; ONE = Oficina Nacional de Estadística (National Bureau of Statistics).

Figure 1.17 General Poverty Incidence—Urban: CPI, 40% CPI, and Q1 CPI, 2011–15

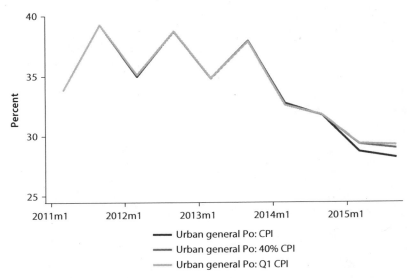

Source: Based on ONE and MEPyD (2015b) and BCRD data.
Note: CPI = General CPI; Q1 CPI = first quintile, or poorest 20 percent of households; 40% CPI = poorest 40 percent of households; BCRD = Banco Central de la República Dominicana (Central Bank of the Dominican Republic); MEPyD = Ministerio de Economía, Planificación y Desarrollo (Ministry of the Economy, Planning and Development); ONE = Oficina Nacional de Estadística (National Bureau of Statistics); Po = poverty incidence.

Figure 1.18 General Poverty Incidence—Rural: CPI, 40% CPI, and Q1 CPI, 2011–15

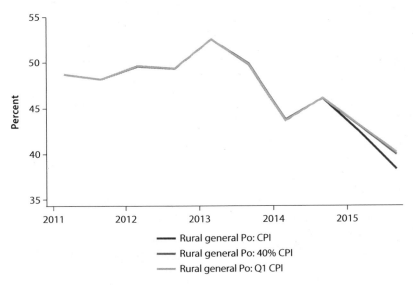

Source: Based on ONE and MEPyD (2015b) and BCRD data.
Note: CPI = General CPI; Q1 CPI = first quintile, or poorest 20 percent of households; 40% CPI = poorest 40 percent of households; Po = poverty incidence; BCRD = Banco Central de la República Dominicana (Central Bank of the Dominican Republic); MEPyD = Ministerio de Economía, Planificación y Desarrollo (Ministry of the Economy, Planning and Development); ONE = Oficina Nacional de Estadística (National Bureau of Statistics).

Conclusion

The results of the analysis in this chapter confirm the conclusion that house-hold surveys in the Dominican Republic could be improved to include more detailed information on the sources of income, mainly income derived from social programs and agricultural activity. Nevertheless, any amounts of income not included in the computation of poverty incidence are not large enough to have a significant impact on poverty measurement.

The results also show that the average difference in the poverty headcount that arises when calculating the poverty line with different CPIs has been insignificant. Even though the general CPI has an implicit consumption pattern very close to the fourth quintile of the population, the changes in prices from March 2011 to September 2015 did not create a large enough bias to distort measures of the poverty headcount. Nevertheless, it has been demonstrated that significant variations in fuel and food prices, like the ones observed since August 2014, could create a negative plutocratic bias that could distort the results of poverty incidence estimations. In this case, the result is an *underestimation* of poverty incidence.

These results could have policy implications. For instance, should public cash transfers (for example, via the food assistance program Comer es Primero) be indexed according to a food price index? Future research should answer this question.

Annex 1A

Table 1A.1 Income Concepts Included in ENIGH 2007 to Calculate Poverty by Quintile

	Total income RD$, MM	Percent
General total		
Total household income	59,536.7	100.0
Total labor income	42,495.5	71.4
Rents income	1,552.0	2.6
National transfers income	6,686.0	11.2
Foreign transfers income	3,724.8	6.3
Imputed rent of homeownership	5,078.4	8.5
First quintile		
Total household income	2,610.8	100.0
Total labor income	1,393.0	53.4
Rents income	31.3	1.2
National transfers income	722.5	27.7
Foreign transfers income	94.2	3.6
Imputed rent of homeownership	369.9	14.2

table continues next page

Table 1A.1 Income Concepts Included in ENIGH 2007 to Calculate Poverty by Quintile *(continued)*

	Total income RD$, MM	*Percent*
Second quintile		
Total household income	4,877.1	100.0
Total labor income	3,210.3	65.8
Rents income	51.6	1.1
National transfers income	939.4	19.3
Foreign transfers income	189.8	3.9
Imputed rent of homeownership	486.1	10.0
Third quintile		
Total household income	7,093.0	100.0
Total labor income	4,882.8	68.8
Rents income	67.2	0.9
National transfers income	1,077.1	15.2
Foreign transfers income	390.1	5.5
Imputed rent of homeownership	675.8	9.5
Fourth quintile		
Total household income	10,803.8	100.0
Total labor income	7,729.3	71.5
Rents income	137.0	1.3
National transfers income	1,382.7	12.8
Foreign transfers income	672.0	6.2
Imputed rent of homeownership	882.8	8.2
Fifth quintile		
Total household income	34,152.0	100.0
Total labor income	25,280.2	74.0
Rents income	1,264.9	3.7
National transfers income	2,564.4	7.5
Foreign transfers income	2,378.7	7.0
Imputed rent of homeownership	2,663.8	7.8

Sources: ENIGH 2007.

Table 1A.2 Income Concepts from ENIGH 2007 Included, Excluded, and Not Considered to Calculate Poverty, by Quintile

	Total income RD$, MM	*Percent*
General total		
Total household income	59,536.7	100.0
Total labor income	42,495.5	71.4
Rents income	1,552.0	2.6
National transfers income	6,686.0	11.2
Foreign transfers income	3,724.8	6.3
Imputed rent of homeownership	5,078.4	8.5
Income excluded from the wellness indicator	890.8	1.5
Income not considered in the wellness indicator	249.9	0.4

table continues next page

Table 1A.2 Income Concepts from ENIGH 2007 Included, Excluded, and Not Considered to Calculate Poverty, by Quintile (continued)

	Total income RD$, MM	Percent
First quintile		
Total household income	2,610.8	100.0
Total labor income	1,393.0	53.4
Rents income	31.3	1.2
National transfers income	722.5	27.7
Foreign transfers income	94.2	3.6
Imputed rent of homeownership	369.9	14.2
Income excluded from the wellness indicator	96.0	3.7
Income not considered in the wellness indicator	4.8	0.2
Second quintile		
Total household income	4,877.1	100.0
Total labor income	3,210.3	65.8
Rents income	51.6	1.1
National transfers income	939.4	19.3
Foreign transfers income	189.8	3.9
Imputed rent of homeownership	486.1	10.0
Income excluded from the wellness indicator	113.2	2.3
Income not considered in the wellness indicator	11.6	0.2
Third quintile		
Total household income	7,093.0	100.0
Total labor income	4,882.8	68.8
Rents income	67.2	0.9
National transfers income	1,077.1	15.2
Foreign transfers income	390.1	5.5
Imputed rent of homeownership	675.8	9.5
Income excluded from the wellness indicator	110.9	1.6
Income not considered in the wellness indicator	22.4	0.3
Fourth quintile		
Total household income	10,803.8	100.0
Total labor income	7,729.3	71.5
Rents income	137.0	1.3
National transfers income	1,382.7	12.8
Foreign transfers income	672.0	6.2
Imputed rent of homeownership	882.8	8.2
Income excluded from the wellness indicator	218.0	2.0
Income not considered in the wellness indicator	30.6	0.3
Fifth quintile		
Total household income	34,152.0	100.0
Total labor income	25,280.2	74.0
Rents income	1,264.9	3.7
National transfers income	2,564.4	7.5

table continues next page

Table 1A.2 Income Concepts from ENIGH 2007 Included, Excluded, and Not Considered to Calculate Poverty, by Quintile (continued)

	Total income RD$, MM	Percent
Foreign transfers income	2,378.7	7.0
Imputed rent of homeownership	2,663.8	7.8
Income excluded from the wellness indicator	352.7	1.0
Income not considered in the wellness indicator	180.6	0.5

Source: ENIGH 2007.

Table 1A.3 Comparable Income Concepts: ENFT versus ENIGH 2007

ENFT	ENIGH
Monetary Labor Income	
Primary occupational income	Primary occupation wage or salary, primary self-employment labor income, primary occupation agricultural earnings
Secondary occupational income	Secondary occupation wage or salary, secondary self-employment labor income, secondary occupation agricultural earnings
Commissions	Primary occupation commissions, secondary occupation commissions
Gratuities	Primary occupation gratuities, secondary occupation gratuities
Overtime hours	Primary occupation overtime hours, secondary occupation overtime hours
Paid holidays	Primary occupation paid holidays, secondary occupation paid holidays
Dividends	Primary occupation other, secondary occupation other
Allowance	Primary occupation allowance, secondary occupation allowance
Christmas bonus	Primary occupation Christmas bonus, secondary occupation Christmas bonus
Corporate profits	Primary occupation corporate profits participation, secondary occupation corporate profits participation
Other benefits	Primary occupation other benefits secondary occupation other benefits
In-kind labor income	
In-kind food payments	Primary occupation food and beverages, food and beverage secondary occupation, primary occupation prepared meals, secondary occupation prepared meals
In-kind household payments	Primary occupation household, secondary occupation household
In-kind fuel or transport payments	Primary occupation passage money or transport, secondary occupation passage money or transport, primary occupation fuel, secondary occupation fuel
In-kind cellphone payments	Primary occupation telephone or cellphone, secondary occupation telephone or cellphone
Other in-kind income	Primary occupation vehicle maintenance, secondary occupation vehicle maintenance, primary occupation other, secondary occupation other

table continues next page

Table 1A.3 Comparable Income Concepts: ENFT versus ENIGH 2007 *(continued)*

ENFT	ENIGH
Self-consumption and self-supply	In-kind business withdrawals or payments through household expenses of industrial workers, trade and services in: primary occupation food, secondary occupation food, primary occupation phone, secondary occupation phone, primary occupation electric energy, secondary occupation electric energy, primary occupation fuel, secondary occupation fuel, primary occupation transport, secondary occupation transport, primary occupation insurance, secondary occupation insurance, primary occupation other goods and services, secondary transport other goods and services. In-kind business withdrawals or payments through household expenses of agricultural workers, trade and services in: primary occupation food, secondary occupation food, primary occupation phone, secondary occupation phone, primary occupation electric energy, secondary occupation electric energy, primary occupation fuel, secondary occupation fuel, primary occupation transport, secondary occupation transport, primary occupation insurance, secondary occupation insurance, primary occupation other goods and services, secondary transport other goods and services.
Domestic transfers (previous month)	
Retirement pension	Retirement pension
Interest or dividends	Interest on loans to third parties, interest from bank deposits, bonds and financial interests or investment certificates.
Lease or rental of property	Rental of residential property (house, apartment, room or other); rental of premises; lease of agricultural land; car rental; other revenues from the property.
Domestic remittances	Child support; cash remittances from other households, relatives or friends of the country, residents in urban areas; cash remittances from other households, relatives or friends of the country, residents in rural areas.
Government transfers	Public aid from Programa Solidaridad ("Comer es primero," school asistance incentive); government public aid such as scholarships, financial aid to aging people.
Domestic transfers (12 months)	
Retirement pension	Retirement pension
Interest or dividends	Interest on loans to third parties, interest from bank deposits, bonds and financial interests or investment certificates.
Lease or rental of property	Rental of residential property (house, apartment, room or other); rental of premises; lease of agricultural land; car rental; other revenues from the property.
Domestic remittances	Child support; cash remittances from other households, relatives or friends of the country, residents in urban areas; cash remittances from other households, relatives or friends of the country, residents in rural areas.
Government transfers	Public aid from Programa Solidaridad ("Comer es primero," school asistance incentive); government public aid such as scholarships, aid to aging people.
In-kind family and nonfamily and institutional assistance (previous month)	In-kind remittances from foreign friends and family, urban area residents; in-kind remittances from foreign friends and family, rural area residents.

table continues next page

Table 1A.3 Comparable Income Concepts: ENFT versus ENIGH 2007 *(continued)*

ENFT	ENIGH
In-kind family and nonfamily and institutional assistance (12 months)	In-kind remittances from foreign friends and family, urban area residents; in-kind remittances from foreign friends and family, rural area residents.
Foreign transfers	
Foreign retirement pension	Foreign retirement pension
Lease or rental of foreign property	Rental of residential property (house, apartment, room or other), rental of premises, lease of agricultural land, car rental, interest on loans to third parties, bank deposits, bonds and financial interests or investment certificates, other revenues the property.
In-kind foreign remittances	In-kind remittances from foreign friends and family.
Foreign remittances	Money remittances

Source: Methodology for the computation of the official monetary poverty measurement in the Dominican Republic. National Statistics Office.

Table 1A.4 Income Concepts Included *or* Not Included in ENFT 2015 Wellness Indicator to Calculate Poverty, by Quintile

	March 2015		September 2015	
	Total income MM RD$	Percent	Total income MM RD$	Percent
General total				
Total household income	96,913.4	100.0	99,720.0	100.0
Total labor income	72,153.7	74.5	77,447.8	77.7
Rents income	1,662.8	1.7	1,038.5	1.0
National transfers income	8,672.2	8.9	7,836.0	7.9
Foreign transfers income	4,616.9	4.8	4,745.0	4.8
Imputed rent of homeownership	9,807.8	10.1	8,652.8	8.7
Income not included in the wellness indicator	553.3	0.6	378.4	0.4
First quintile				
Total household income	6,829.9	100.0	6,810.6	100.0
Total labor income	4,550.3	66.6	4,603.0	67.6
Rents income	26.2	0.4	47.1	0.7
National transfers income	1,287.7	18.9	1,175.3	17.3
Foreign transfers income	198.5	2.9	233.5	3.4
Imputed rent of homeownership	767.1	11.2	751.9	11.0
Income not included in the wellness indicator	113.2	1.7	70.1	1.0

table continues next page

Table 1A.4 Income Concepts Included *or* Not Included in ENFT 2015 Wellness Indicator to Calculate Poverty, by Quintile (continued)

	March 2015		September 2015	
	Total income MM RD$	Percent	Total income MM RD$	Percent
Second quintile				
Total household income	11,248.4	100.0	11,436.2	100.0
Total labor income	8,375.0	74.5	8,463.3	74.0
Rents income	60.9	0.5	132.8	1.2
National transfers income	1,396.3	12.4	1,323.3	11.6
Foreign transfers income	339.8	3.0	348.8	3.0
Imputed rent of homeownership	1,076.5	9.6	1,168.0	10.2
Income not included in the wellness indicator	62.6	0.6	37.4	0.3
Third quintile				
Total household income	15,015.1	100.0	15,468.2	100.0
Total labor income	11,435.5	76.2	11,743.4	75.9
Rents income	152.7	1.0	94.0	0.6
National transfers income	1,429.1	9.5	1,420.1	9.2
Foreign transfers income	579.9	3.9	758.6	4.9
Imputed rent of homeownership	1,417.9	9.4	1,452.1	9.4
Income not included in the wellness indicator	70.0	0.5	50.9	0.3
Fourth quintile				
Total household income	20,871.5	100.0	21,090.6	100.0
Total labor income	16,024.4	76.8	16,164.9	76.6
Rents income	196.1	0.9	136.9	0.6
National transfers income	1,633.0	7.8	1,796.7	8.5
Foreign transfers income	1,147.6	5.5	1,125.0	5.3
Imputed rent of homeownership	1,870.4	9.0	1,867.1	8.9
Income not included in the wellness indicator	95.4	0.5	131.7	0.6
Fifth quintile				
Total household income	42,948.0	100.0	44,914.4	100.0
Total labor income	31,768.4	74.0	36,473.2	81.2
Rents income	1,226.9	2.9	627.7	1.4
National transfers income	2,926.2	6.8	2,120.7	4.7
Foreign transfers income	2,351.1	5.5	2,279.1	5.1
Imputed rent of homeownership	4,675.9	10.9	3,413.8	7.6
Income not included in the wellness indicator	212.0	0.5	88.3	0.2

Source: Based on Central Bank of the Dominican Republic ENFT March 2015 and September 2015 data.

Table 1A.5 Consumption Baskets at the National Level and by Quintile

Groups of goods and services	National	Quintile 1	P-40%	Quintile 2	Quintile 3	Quintile 4	Quintile 5
Food and nonalcoholic beverages	25.10	47.23	42.08	38.12	31.62	24.89	12.36
Alcoholic beverages and tobacco	2.32	2.36	2.32	2.28	2.59	2.93	1.90
Clothing and footwear	4.56	4.05	4.29	4.47	4.98	5.00	4.32
Housing, water, and electricity	11.60	8.28	8.92	9.41	10.94	11.60	13.47
Furniture, household items	6.46	5.74	5.62	5.52	5.70	6.06	7.49
Health	5.21	4.33	4.69	4.97	4.98	5.59	5.42
Transport	17.95	9.49	11.10	12.34	13.72	16.01	24.80
Communications	2.96	1.25	1.54	1.77	2.44	3.09	3.95
Recreation and culture	4.12	3.07	3.10	3.12	3.30	4.24	5.02
Education	3.74	1.25	1.59	1.86	2.82	3.74	5.41
Hotels and restaurants	8.50	5.35	6.99	8.25	9.20	9.50	8.60
Miscellaneous goods and services	7.47	7.63	7.77	7.87	7.71	7.35	7.26

Source: Based on Central Bank of the Dominican Republic data.
Note: P-40% = Poorest 40 percent of households.

Table 1A.6 Poverty Lines and Consumer Price Indexes, 2011–15

General CPI

Period	General	Extreme	General	Extreme	General	Extreme	CPI 2011 = 100
	National		Urban		Rural		
2011, March	3,966.80	1,826.30	4,111.10	1,851.10	3,660.30	1,773.70	100.00
2011, September	4,114.80	1,894.40	4,264.40	1,920.10	3,796.80	1,839.80	103.72
2012, March	4,163.02	1,916.60	4,314.38	1,942.60	3,841.30	1,861.36	104.94
2012, September	4,221.97	1,943.74	4,375.46	1,970.11	3,895.68	1,887.72	106.43
2013, March	4,370.09	2,011.93	4,528.97	2,039.22	4,032.36	1,953.94	110.16
2013, September	4,438.60	2,043.47	4,599.97	2,071.19	4,095.57	1,984.57	111.89
2014, March	4,500.60	2,072.02	4,664.22	2,100.13	4,152.78	2,012.30	113.45
2014, September	4,564.13	2,101.27	4,730.07	2,129.77	4,211.41	2,040.70	115.05
2015, March	4,529.30	2,085.23	4,693.97	2,113.52	4,179.27	2,025.13	114.17
2015, September	4,582.12	2,109.55	4,748.71	2,138.17	4,228.01	2,048.75	115.50

Q1 CPI

Period	General	Extreme	General	Extreme	General	Extreme	Q1 CPI 2011 = 100
	National		Urban		Rural		
2011, March	3,966.80	1,826.30	4,111.10	1,851.10	3,660.30	1,773.70	100.00
2011, September	4,114.40	1,894.26	4,264.07	1,919.98	3,796.50	1,839.70	103.72
2012, March	4,173.93	1,921.66	4,325.77	1,947.76	3,851.43	1,866.32	105.22
2012, September	4,222.78	1,944.15	4,376.39	1,970.55	3,896.50	1,888.16	106.45
2013, March	4,369.31	2,011.61	4,528.25	2,038.93	4,031.71	1,953.68	110.15

table continues next page

Table 1A.6 Poverty Lines and Consumer Price Indexes, 2011–15 *(continued)*

Q1 CPI

Period	General	Extreme	General	Extreme	General	Extreme	Q1 CPI
	National		Urban		Rural		2011 = 100
2013, September	4,423.50	2,036.56	4,584.41	2,064.22	4,081.71	1,977.91	111.51
2014, March	4,492.57	2,068.36	4,655.99	2,096.45	4,145.44	2,008.79	113.25
2014, September	4,574.61	2,106.13	4,741.02	2,134.73	4,221.15	2,045.47	115.32
2015, March	4,603.99	2,119.66	4,771.47	2,148.45	4,248.26	2,058.61	116.06
2015, September	4,713.13	2,169.91	4,884.58	2,199.37	4,348.97	2,107.41	118.81

40% CPI

Period	General	Extreme	General	Extreme	General	Extreme	40% CPI
	National		Urban		Rural		2011 = 100
2011, March	3,966.80	1,826.30	4,111.10	1,851.10	3,660.30	1,773.70	100.00
2011, September	4,113.82	1,893.99	4,263.47	1,919.71	3,795.96	1,839.44	103.71
2012, March	4,171.10	1,920.36	4,322.83	1,946.43	3,848.81	1,865.05	105.15
2012, September	4,221.12	1,943.39	4,374.67	1,969.78	3,894.97	1,887.42	106.41
2013, March	4,366.99	2,010.55	4,525.85	2,037.85	4,029.57	1,952.64	110.09
2013, September	4,422.75	2,036.22	4,583.63	2,063.87	4,081.02	1,977.57	111.49
2014, March	4,490.72	2,067.51	4,654.08	2,095.58	4,143.74	2,007.96	113.21
2014, September	4,568.62	2,103.37	4,734.81	2,131.94	4,215.62	2,042.79	115.17
2015, March	4,590.00	2,113.22	4,756.97	2,141.92	4,235.35	2,052.36	115.71
2015, September	4,686.99	2,157.88	4,857.49	2,187.18	4,324.85	2,095.73	118.16

Source: Based on Central Bank of the Dominican Republic data.

Table 1A.7 Poverty Incidence: National General versus Extreme, by CPI Quintile, 2011–15

General CPI

Period	National, general				National, extreme			
	Rate	SE	[95% CI]		Rate	SE	[95% CI]	
			IL	SL			IL	SL
2011, March	38.67%	0.99296	36.72	40.62	9.80%	0.50246	8.82	10.79
2011, September	42.18%	1.02898	40.16	44.20	10.52%	0.55665	9.43	11.62
2012, March	39.74%	0.99306	37.79	41.69	9.88%	0.55032	8.80	10.96
2012, September	42.20%	1.01145	40.21	44.18	11.13%	0.56169	10.03	12.23
2013, March	40.62%	0.94504	38.76	42.47	10.31%	0.51644	9.30	11.32
2013, September	41.82%	0.95641	39.94	43.69	9.77%	0.49258	8.80	10.74
2014, March	36.32%	0.94587	34.46	38.18	8.76%	0.45939	7.86	9.66
2014, September	36.40%	0.94177	34.55	38.25	8.10%	0.46497	7.18	9.01
2015, March	33.17%	0.93811	31.33	35.02	7.26%	0.45017	6.37	8.14
2015, September	31.51%	0.92640	29.69	33.33	6.75%	0.42294	5.92	7.58
Quintile 1 CPI								
2011, March	38.67%	0.99296	36.72	40.62	9.80%	0.50246	8.82	10.79
2011, September	42.18%	1.02898	40.16	44.20	10.52%	0.55665	9.43	11.62
2012, March	39.85%	0.99425	37.90	41.80	10.00%	0.55126	8.92	11.09

table continues next page

Table 1A.7 Poverty Incidence: National General versus Extreme, by CPI Quintile, 2011–15 *(continued)*

	National, general				National, extreme			
			[95% CI]				[95% CI]	
Period	Rate	SE	IL	SL	Rate	SE	IL	SL
2012, September	42.20%	1.01145	40.21	44.18	11.13%	0.56169	10.03	12.23
2013, March	40.62%	0.94504	38.76	42.47	10.31%	0.51644	9.30	11.32
2013, September	41.76%	0.95626	39.88	43.63	9.75%	0.49220	8.78	10.71
2014, March	36.17%	0.94676	34.32	38.03	8.70%	0.45889	7.80	9.60
2014, September	36.45%	0.94176	34.60	38.30	8.11%	0.46541	7.20	9.03
2015, March	33.85%	0.96124	31.96	35.73	7.45%	0.45373	6.56	8.34
2015, September	32.80%	0.93107	30.97	34.63	7.15%	0.43853	6.29	8.02
40% CPI								
2011, March	38.67%	0.99296	36.72	40.62	9.80%	0.50246	8.82	10.79
2011, September	42.18%	1.02898	40.16	44.20	10.52%	0.55665	9.43	11.62
2012, March	39.83%	0.99409	37.88	41.78	9.98%	0.55062	8.90	11.06
2012, September	42.16%	1.00939	40.18	44.14	11.13%	0.56169	10.03	12.23
2013, March	40.60%	0.94520	38.75	42.46	10.31%	0.51644	9.30	11.32
2013, September	41.74%	0.95660	39.87	43.62	9.69%	0.49014	8.73	10.66
2014, March	36.17%	0.94675	34.31	38.03	8.69%	0.45890	7.79	9.60
2014, September	36.42%	0.94174	34.57	38.27	8.11%	0.46541	7.20	9.02
2015, March	33.81%	0.96083	31.92	35.69	7.41%	0.45184	6.52	8.29
2015, September	32.55%	0.92450	30.74	34.37	7.03%	0.42841	6.19	7.87

General CPI

	Urban general				Urban, extreme			
			[95% CI]				[95% CI]	
Period	Rate	SE	IL	SL	Rate	SE	IL	SL
2011, March	33.79%	1.30064	31.24	36.35	7.12%	0.58556	5.97	8.27
2011, September	39.27%	1.36329	36.59	41.94	8.25%	0.66523	6.94	9.56
2012, March	34.97%	1.31507	32.39	37.56	7.55%	0.66909	6.23	8.86
2012, September	38.74%	1.32564	36.13	41.34	9.02%	0.67693	7.69	10.35
2013, March	34.83%	1.21701	32.43	37.22	7.66%	0.57901	6.52	8.79
2013, September	37.91%	1.27222	35.41	40.41	7.97%	0.58884	6.81	9.13
2014, March	32.72%	1.22725	30.31	35.13	7.06%	0.54872	5.99	8.14
2014, September	31.71%	1.21633	29.32	34.10	5.97%	0.50255	4.98	6.95
2015, March	28.69%	1.26552	26.27	31.90	5.68%	0.54335	3.58	6.94
2015, September	28.20%	1.20218	25.84	30.56	4.88%	0.48434	3.93	5.83
Quintile 1 CPI								
2011, March	33.79%	1.30064	31.24	36.35	7.12%	0.58556	5.97	8.27
2011, September	39.27%	1.36329	36.59	41.94	8.25%	0.66523	6.94	9.56
2012, March	35.11%	1.31677	32.52	37.70	7.64%	0.66961	6.32	8.96
2012, September	38.74%	1.32564	36.13	41.34	9.02%	0.67693	7.69	10.35
2013, March	34.83%	1.21701	32.43	37.22	7.66%	0.57901	6.52	8.79

table continues next page

General CPI

Period	Urban general				Urban, extreme			
			[95% CI]				[95% CI]	
	Rate	SE	IL	SL	Rate	SE	IL	SL
2013, September	37.86%	1.27185	35.36	40.36	7.95%	0.58899	6.80	9.11
2014, March	32.55%	1.22756	30.13	34.96	7.03%	0.54876	5.95	8.11
2014, September	31.76%	1.21657	29.37	34.15	5.98%	0.50325	4.99	6.97
2015, March	29.35%	1.20017	26.98	32.05	5.82%	0.52974	4.10	8.94
2015, September	29.25%	1.22292	26.84	31.65	5.19%	0.49419	4.22	6.16
40% CPI								
2011, March	33.79%	1.30064	31.24	36.35	7.12%	0.58556	5.97	8.27
2011, September	39.27%	1.36329	36.59	41.94	8.25%	0.66523	6.94	9.56
2012, March	35.11%	1.31677	32.52	37.70	7.64%	0.66964	6.32	8.95
2012, September	38.69%	1.32219	36.09	41.29	9.02%	0.67693	7.69	10.35
2013, March	34.80%	1.21727	32.41	37.19	7.66%	0.57901	6.52	8.79
2013, September	37.86%	1.27185	35.36	40.36	7.88%	0.58488	6.73	9.03
2014, March	32.55%	1.22756	30.13	34.96	7.03%	0.54877	5.95	8.11
2014, September	31.72%	1.21654	29.33	34.11	5.98%	0.50326	4.99	6.97
2015, March	29.32%	1.21554	26.99	33.01	5.80%	0.50012	4.04	6.25
2015, September	28.99%	1.21033	26.61	31.37	5.16%	0.49298	4.19	6.12

General CPI

Period	Rural general				Rural, extreme			
			[95% CI]				[95% CI]	
	Rate	SE	IL	SL	Rate	SE	IL	SL
2011, March	48.70%	1.78241	45.56	52.67	15.33%	0.94201	13.95	18.01
2011, September	48.18%	1.43113	45.36	50.99	15.21%	1.00649	13.23	17.19
2012, March	49.56%	1.37352	46.86	52.25	14.69%	0.95199	12.82	16.57
2012, September	49.33%	1.44692	46.49	52.18	15.47%	0.99449	13.52	17.43
2013, March	52.55%	1.43332	49.73	55.37	15.78%	1.03317	13.75	17.81
2013, September	49.87%	1.32460	47.27	52.47	13.48%	0.89601	11.72	15.24
2014, March	43.74%	1.42536	40.94	46.54	12.26%	0.83645	10.62	13.91
2014, September	46.08%	1.42668	43.27	48.88	12.49%	0.97442	10.57	14.40
2015, March	42.42%	1.38385	39.70	45.14	10.50%	0.86737	8.80	12.20
2015, September	38.33%	1.34791	35.68	40.98	10.60%	0.81632	9.00	12.21
Quintile 1 CPI								
2011, March	48.70%	1.82014	46.18	51.28	15.33%	0.92001	13.50	17.85
2011, September	48.18%	1.43113	45.36	50.99	15.21%	1.00649	13.23	17.19
2012, March	49.62%	1.37460	46.92	52.32	14.87%	0.95564	13.00	16.75
2012, September	49.33%	1.44692	46.49	52.18	15.47%	0.99449	13.52	17.43
2013, March	52.55%	1.43332	49.73	55.37	15.78%	1.03317	13.75	17.81
2013, September	49.79%	1.32475	47.19	52.39	13.44%	0.89371	11.68	15.20
2014, March	43.65%	1.42761	40.84	46.45	12.12%	0.83384	10.49	13.76

table continues next page

General CPI

| | Rural general | | | | Rural, extreme | | | |
| | | | [95% CI] | | | | [95% CI] | |
Period	Rate	SE	IL	SL	Rate	SE	IL	SL
2014, September	46.10%	1.42578	43.30	48.90	12.50%	0.97485	10.59	14.42
2015, March	43.12%	1.40104	40.37	45.88	10.81%	0.87619	9.08	12.53
2015, September	40.12%	1.29216	37.58	42.66	11.21%	0.86609	9.50	12.91
40% CPI								
2011, March	48.70%	1.82014	46.18	51.28	15.33%	0.92001	13.50	17.85
2011, September	48.18%	1.43113	45.36	50.99	15.21%	1.00649	13.23	17.19
2012, March	49.56%	1.37352	46.86	52.25	14.80%	0.95240	12.93	16.67
2012, September	49.31%	1.44694	46.47	52.16	15.47%	0.99449	13.52	17.43
2013, March	52.55%	1.43332	49.73	55.37	15.78%	1.03317	13.75	17.81
2013, September	49.75%	1.32674	47.14	52.36	13.44%	0.89371	11.68	15.20
2014, March	43.64%	1.42750	40.83	46.44	12.12%	0.83384	10.49	13.76
2014, September	46.10%	1.42578	43.30	48.90	12.50%	0.97485	10.59	14.42
2015, March	43.06%	1.39866	40.31	45.81	10.79%	0.86814	9.01	12.42
2015, September	39.90%	1.29742	37.35	42.45	10.88%	0.81982	9.27	12.49

Source: Based on Central Bank of the Dominican Republic data.

Note: CI = confidence interval; IL = inferior limit; SL = superior limit.

Notes

1. See Dauhajre and Aristy-Escuder (1996) for a description of the set of structural reforms implemented since the beginning 1990s. Also, see Guzmán and Lizardo (2002) for an analysis of the impact of structural reforms on economic growth.

2. In this chapter, wellness is related to *monetary poverty*, defined as a function of household disposable income. Thus, a higher level of income increases wellness and reduces monetary poverty. Nevertheless, it is well understood that poverty is a multidimensional problem, as stated in the Sustainable Development Goals.

3. The poverty line is determined by the market cost of a basic consumption basket of goods and services. This can be defined as "the minimum income level to not be considered poor." See Ravalion (2016, 191).

4. It is well known that consumption is more stable than income, given that households smooth their consumption when there are occasional movements of income. This means that consumption is more related to permanent income. Also, current consumption is a better indicator than the current income of the standard of living. Nevertheless, some argue for using current income to measure economic welfare and poverty because it allows a good assessment of the distributional impact of taxes and transfers. See Ravallion (2016) and UN-SD (2005).

5. The government also calculates the Quality-of-Life Index, which allows for multidimensional poverty to be measured. This index is used in the individual selection of household beneficiaries by the government social programs. See ONE and MEPyD (2012).

6. Detailed information can be found at National Office of Statistics, Interagency Technical Committee, Estimation of the Basic Baskets and the Poverty Lines, July 2012. https://goo.gl/li3xlo.

7. See table 1A.1 (in the annex) for information on other quintiles.

8. It is worth noting that Deaton and Zaidi (2002) suggest leaving occasional incomes out of the aggregate because they would turn into a noisy measure of averages that are very difficult to measure accurately. Thus, only income received regularly should be included as a source of income for poverty calculations.

9. See table 1A.2 (in the annex) for income concepts from ENIGH 2007.

10. See table 1A.3 (in the annex) for a comparison of income concepts of the ENIGH 2007 and ENFT.

11. Figures for other quintiles are shown in table 1A.4 (in the annex). For all quintiles, except the first, the income not included in the wellness indicator accounts for less than 0.6 percent of total household income.

12. As such, the growth elasticity of poverty would be approximately $-1.1 = -5.6/5.0$.

13. The new Encuesta Nacional Continua de Fuerza de Trabajo (ENCFT) questionnaire details government transfers to households.

14. Central Bank of the Dominican Republic (2011). The CPI is computed using the Laspeyres formula. Only urban prices are considered in computing the general CPI.

15. In 1999, the share of food and nonalcoholic beverages was 30.8 percent.

16. In this case, $d\left(CPI_G, CPI_S\right) = \sqrt{\sum_i \left(w_{Gi} - w_{Si}\right)^2}$, where W_{Gi}, W_{Si} are the weights of different group of goods and services included in the consumption basket for the general CPI (CPI_G) and the specific CPI (CPI_S), which can be the first quintile of the population, or the poorest 40 percent of the population.

17. In 2015, the prices of some important food products (for example, cassava, plantains, chicken, pinto beans, meat beef, red beans, garlic, and coffee) increased considerably, owing to weather conditions. See Central Bank of the Dominican Republic (2015).

18. This is the plutocratic bias presented by Ley (2001).

19. See table 1A.6 in the annex.

20. For estimating the standard errors and confidence intervals for poverty incidence, the *svyset* command in Stata, which allows for the identification of the survey design variables, was used. For the purposes of this study, the strata variable (eft_estrato) and primary sampling unit (eft_upm) were specified to conduct the estimations considering the observations at these levels. Expansion factor (eft_factor_exp) was used as a weight option.

References

Central Bank of the Dominican Republic. 2011. "Metodología índice de precios al consumidor (IPC): Base diciembre 2010." Santo Domingo: Banco Central de la República Dominicana.

———. 2015. "Informe de la economía Dominicana." Enero–septiembre 2016. Santo Domingo: Banco Central de la República Dominicana.

Dauhajre, A., and J. Aristy-Escuder, eds. 1996. *El programa: Programa macroeconómico de mediano plazo para la República Dominicana: 1996–2000*. Santo Domingo: Fundación Economía y Desarrollo.

Deaton, A., and S. Zaidi. 2002. "Guidelines for Constructing Consumption Aggregates for Welfare Analysis." Living Standards Measurement Study Working Paper 135. World Bank, Washington, DC.

Guzmán, R., and M. Lizardo. 2002. *Crecimiento económico, acumulación de factores y productividad en la República Dominicana (1950–2000)*. Serie de Estudios Económicos y Sociales. Washington, DC: Inter-American Development Bank.

Johnson, C. 2013. "Potential Output and Output Gap in Central America, Panama and Dominican Republic." IMF Working Paper WP/13/145, International Monetary Fund, Washington, DC.

Ley, E. 2001. "Whose Inflation? A Characterization of the CPI Plutocratic Bias." IMF Working Paper WP/01/59, International Monetary Fund, Washington, DC.

ONE and MEPyD (Oficina Nacional de Estadística and Ministerio de Economía, Planificación y Desarrollo). 2012. *Metodología para el cálculo de la medición oficial de la pobreza monetaria en la República Dominicana*. Dominican Republic Poverty Committee. Accessible at www.one.gob.do/Multimedia/Download?ObjId=1936.

———. 2015a. "Boletín de Estadísticas Oficiales de Pobreza Monetaria." *Boletín Semestral* Año 1 (1): 1–8.

———. 2015b. "Boletín de Estadísticas Oficiales de Pobreza Monetaria." *Boletín Semestral* Año 1 (2): 1–16.

Ravallion, M. 2016. *The Economics of Poverty. History, Measurement, and Policy*. New York: Oxford University Press.

UN-SD. (United Nations, Statistics Division). 2005. *Handbook on Poverty Statistics: Concepts, Methods and Policy Use*. New York: United Nations.

CHAPTER 2

Comparative Advantage and Labor Demand

Implications for the Dominican Republic

Shushanik Hakobyan and Daniel Lederman

In theory, an abundant labor endowment is associated with specialization in labor-intensive manufacturing, provided trade costs are not prohibitive. China's progress and ability to reduce poverty on a large scale and the East Asian region's quick recovery from the economic crisis of the late 1990s are two examples. In fact, the success of East Asia's most dynamic economies is attributed precisely to their ability to integrate into the world economy through the efficient use of the one factor of production that they had in good supply: labor (World Bank 1993). In that part of the world, macroeconomic trends have been based, primarily, on a model that relies on importing capital and know-how and on exporting goods and services that require a great deal of labor (Gill et al. 2013).

On the other hand, the Dominican Republic is an example of a country where, despite a fast-growing economy and an abundance of labor, poverty and unemployment have remained high. This is a very different story from that of East Asia. It is a story suggesting that some countries might not be using their most abundant factors of production efficiently.

In terms of growth performance, the Dominican Republic has enjoyed one of the strongest growth rates in Latin America and the Caribbean over the

The authors express their gratitude to their collaborators for insightful comments and suggestions—in particular, Francisco Carneiro and the anonymous referees.

Shushanik Hakobyan is assistant professor of economics at Fordham University. She holds a doctorate in economics from the University of Virginia. Please direct correspondence to shakobyan@fordham.edu.

Daniel Lederman is deputy chief economist for the Latin America and the Caribbean Region at the World Bank. He holds a bachelor of arts degree in political science from Yale University and master's and doctoral degrees from the Johns Hopkins University's School of Advanced International Studies. Please direct correspondence to dlederman@worldbank.org.

past 20 years. At the same time, however, analysts from the Dominican Republic and elsewhere seem concerned that fast productivity growth over the past two decades in the economy's key sectors has brought limited employment gains and rising informality. The underlying premise is that most of the jobs created have been of low quality in low-productivity sectors. Moreover, the fact that the faster-expanding sectors have created mostly unskilled jobs (in retail and wholesale trade, hotels and restaurants, and other services) is another pessimistic argument for this viewpoint.

This chapter explores the relationship between factor endowments and comparative advantage. In particular, it tests the null hypothesis that the products exported by labor-abundant countries are not labor-intensive but rather capital-intensive. In this context, Rybczynski coefficients are estimated for the world and for subsets of countries, and they are tested to determine whether they vary across different types of countries.[1] The chapter continues by presenting the economy of the Dominican Republic as a case study to assess whether it has a comparative advantage in capital-intensive versus labor-intensive products.

This chapter studies the factor intensity of tradable industries across countries and over time—an approach that is consistent with two neoclassical theories of international trade, namely, the Ricardian and factor proportions models. Ricardian models rely on the assumption that countries differ in production technologies. In contrast, factor proportions models presume that countries apply similar technologies in production—and thus, an economy's patterns of trade are driven purely by international differences in relative factor abundance.

The analytical approach presented in this chapter relies on the vast academic literature that is relevant to these theories (for example, Fitzgerald and Hallak 2004; Harrigan 1997; Schott 2003), which is briefly reviewed in the second section. The chapter contributes to this literature in at least two ways. First, a large number of countries with considerable heterogeneity in their endowments of capital and skilled and unskilled labor are examined. In contrast, the literature has focused on mostly homogeneous groups of countries, such as the countries that belong to the Organisation for Economic Co-operation and Development (OECD) or a small number of countries, owing to the limited availability of production data. Using trade data, the sample for this analysis has been expanded to include more than 100 countries. Second, the possibility of changes taking place in both export-oriented and import-competing industries is allowed for, thus controlling for potential general equilibrium effects (relying on Leamer 1995).[2]

The empirical strategy and description of the data is presented in the third section, and the results are presented in the fourth. The revealed comparative advantage index for the Dominican Republic is examined in the fifth section, and conclusions for the theoretical and empirical arguments presented in the chapter are drawn in the sixth. Finally, annex 2A details the data set's construction and highlights the limitations on the country and time coverage imposed by data availability.

Review of the Empirical Literature Testing Neoclassical Theories of International Trade

Two strands of the empirical trade literature are related to the Ricardian and factor proportions models. The first strand examines the implications of the factor proportions theory, under the assumption that all countries can access the same technologies. The second assumes Hicks-neutral technological differences across countries.

Under the first strand, Harrigan (1995) focuses on the production side of the factor proportions model and uses data on manufacturing output and factor endowments for 20 OECD countries during 1970–85. The findings strongly suggest that capital abundance and unskilled labor are sources of comparative advantage in most sectors, but the evidence on the effects of skilled labor (and land) is rather weak.

Schott (2003), on the other hand, investigates whether developed and developing countries specialize in different subsets of products owing to their differences in factor endowments—and finds that labor-abundant countries produced relatively few of the most capital-intensive goods. This conclusion was based on 1990 value-added, capital stock, and employment data from UNIDO (United Nations Industrial Development Organization) for up to 45 developed and developing countries across 28 manufacturing industries (aggregated into "Heckscher-Ohlin aggregates" based on input intensity).

Batista and Potin (2014) extend Schott's work to explain the dynamics of industrial specialization over time by examining a panel of 44 developed and developing countries during 1976–2000. They find a substantial Rybczynski effect, in that countries that accumulate capital produce fewer labor-intensive goods and more capital-intensive goods. The authors further find that poor labor-abundant countries that accumulate capital diversify their output by moving away from labor-intensive industries and into capital-intensive industries, while rich capital-abundant countries that accumulate capital specialize in the production of highly capital-intensive goods.

Romalis (2004) uses a factor proportions model to examine whether it could explain the structure of commodity trade by integrating a multicountry version of the Heckscher-Ohlin model featuring a Dornbusch, Fischer, and Samuelson (1980) model with a continuum of goods and a Krugman (1980) model of monopolistic competition and transport costs. Romalis (2004) assumes no factor intensity reversals and fixed factor shares within industries and across countries. His results corroborate two predictions. First, countries tend to capture larger production and trade shares of products that use their abundant factors more intensively. Second, countries that rapidly accumulate a factor see their production and export structures systematically shift toward industries that use that factor intensively.

In the second strand of the empirical trade literature, Harrigan (1997) was the first to empirically test the factor proportions theory, assuming technological differences across countries that are Hicks-neutral and industry-specific. He uses factor endowment data and manufacturing output shares in gross domestic product (GDP) for ten developed countries across seven industries (food, apparel, paper, chemicals, glass, metals, and machinery) for the period 1970–88. His results are roughly consistent with those presented by Leamer (1984), who uses net exports as the proxy for the dependent variable; and by Harrigan (1995), who, instead, uses output. Harrigan's most recent results, published in his 1997 seminal paper, suggest that the abundance of both capital and medium-educated workers are generally associated with larger manufacturing output shares, while nonresidential construction and highly educated workers lead to lower output shares.[3] But whereas this finding improves substantially on previous empirical work, his data show little cross-country variation, as high-income, OECD-member countries have similar factor endowments and sectoral output shares.

Harrigan and Zakrajšek (2000) overcome this drawback and exploit the cross-country variation by expanding the sample to include 28 OECD-member and -nonmember, developed and developing countries and 12 industries over a longer period (1970–92). Their evidence is broadly consistent with the neoclassical theory, in that human and physical capital abundance raise output in heavy industrial sectors, whereas physical capital lowers output in the food and apparel/textile industries.

In a similar vein, Fitzgerald and Hallak (2004) use a cross section of 21 OECD-member countries in 1988 to estimate the effects of factor endowment on the pattern of manufacturing specialization, but allow factor accumulation to respond to productivity. Their results suggest that the failure to control for productivity differences across countries produces biased estimates of the Rybczynski coefficients. Their model generates robust results that explain two-thirds of the observed differences in the pattern of specialization between the poorest and richest OECD-member countries.

Using a similar approach, Redding (2002) concludes that in the short run, common cross-country effects such as technological progress are more important in explaining observed changes in specialization than factor endowments. Over longer periods, factor endowments become relatively more important and account for most of the observed variation in specialization. This evidence is consistent with the idea that changes in relative factor abundance occur gradually and take time to affect the structure of production.

Morrow (2010) builds on Romalis (2004) to augment the model with Ricardian total factor productivity (TFP) differences, and estimates the model using panel data for the period 1985–95 across 20 developed and developing countries, spanning 24 manufacturing industries. Morrow (2010) finds that productivity differences and the interaction of factor abundance with factor intensity both play a role in determining international specialization patterns—with little evidence that relative productivity levels are systematically higher or lower for skilled-labor-abundant countries in skilled-labor-intensive sectors. Furthermore, he finds that differences in factor abundance are more potent than differences in Ricardian productivity in determining patterns of specialization.

Estimation Strategy and Data

The empirical approach used to estimate Rybczynski coefficients and the data used in the estimation are presented in this section. These include net exports and endowments of labor, capital, and arable land.

Econometric Model

The empirical relationship between factor accumulation and exports can be due to the adoption of technologies (which determine factor input requirements in production), the overall level of economic efficiency in an economy, or the rate of factor accumulation (that is, industries employing skilled-labor-intensive technologies will not emerge in economies with insufficient skilled labor). In turn, technology adoption and factor accumulation can be determined by various economic, social, and institutional phenomena. Broadly speaking, the empirical Rybczynski function for a given industry can be specified as shown here in equation 2.1:

$$x_{cit} = \alpha_{i0} + \beta_{i1}K_{ct} + \beta_{i2}SL_{ct} + \beta_{i3}UL_{ct} + \beta_{i4}T_{ct} + \gamma_{it} + \varepsilon_{cit} \tag{2.1}$$

where the subscript c represents countries; i, industries; t, the time period; and K, SL, UL, and T, endowments of capital, skilled labor, unskilled labor, and arable land, respectively. The dependent variable x is for output or exports, γ_t is the year fixed effect, and ε represents the error term.

In equation (2.1), the intercept term captures any other factor of production that is not explicitly included and is industry-specific; that is, it is estimated for each industry separately. The parameters of interest in equation 2.1 are the βs, which can be interpreted as the inverse of technologically determined factor input requirements (that is, the amount of each input required to produce and export one unit of a final good) in a given industry.

To allow for the possibility that changes in the economy take place in both export-oriented and import-competing industries, consumption effects are controlled for by following Leamer (1995), as shown here in equation 2.2:

$$NX_{ci} = A_{ci}^{-1}\left(V_c - s_{ci}V^w\right) \tag{2.2}$$

where NX_{ci} is the net exports of country c in industry i; V_c and V^w are the vectors of endowments in country c and in the world, respectively (which could potentially include different numbers of factors of production); s_{ci} is the consumption share of industry i in country c in total world consumption of that industry; and A is the input-output matrix, with unit factor requirements as its elements. Hence, the estimating equation (2.3) is the following:

$$NX_{cit} = \alpha_{i0} + \beta_{i1}\left(K_{ct} - s_{ci}K^w\right) + \beta_{i2}\left(SL_{ct} - s_{ci}SL^w\right) \\ + \beta_{i3}\left(UL_{ct} - s_{ci}UL^w\right) + \beta_{i4}\left(T_{ct} - s_{ci}T^w\right) + \gamma_{it} + \varepsilon_{cit} \tag{2.3}$$

In this specification, all variables are observable except for consumption shares. The following two approaches are used to estimate consumption shares and construct the independent variables. The first assumes homothetic preferences across countries, so that s_{ci} can be approximated by the ratio of country c's consumption to the world's consumption, $s_{ci} \approx C_c/C_w$. The second approach further allows consumption shares to vary by the country's level of development by assuming that they are a function of country c's GDP per capita in year t.

As with most applied economic analysis, several concerns are worth pointing out. First, the βs can differ across countries within industries owing to differences in technology adoption (Cusolito and Lederman 2009) or to differences in aggregate economic efficiency (or TFP) that can be seen as a scaling factor for the observed factor endowments.

As noted above, one of the key assumptions underlying neoclassical trade models where comparative advantage is driven by factor endowments is that technologies are identical across countries. Of particular importance, this implies that a unit of labor or capital in one country is just as productive as a unit of labor or capital in, for instance, the United States. To address these estimation challenges, the approach taken by Fitzgerald and Hallak (2004) is followed, using existing estimates of aggregate TFP to adjust each country's factor endowments by the TFP differential with respect to the United States, thus netting out productivity differences across countries.

Second, another assumption of neoclassical trade models is that the number of goods equals the number of factors of production. The literature interprets the constant in the empirical equation as capturing the average effect of all omitted factors of production. Consequently, the inclusion of country fixed effects is equivalent to assuming that the number of omitted factors of production can vary across countries. The model is estimated both with and without fixed effects (for discussion, see Fitzgerald and Hallak 2004).

Furthermore, the analysis explores differences in βs between different subsets of countries: (a) high-income versus low-income countries; and (b) countries with capital or skilled-labor abundance versus those with unskilled-labor abundance. To account for a common error structure, all the regressors were interacted with the indicator variable for each such group. This is essentially a test of the assumption that all countries apply the same technologies for each industry (after adjusting for cross-country TFP differentials, as done by Fitzgerald and Hallak 2004), or that belong to the same diversification cone.

Data on Net Exports and on Endowments of Labor, Capital, and Arable Land

The data set used in this chapter contains information on net exports in 28 three-digit ISIC (International Standard Industrial Classification) manufacturing industries, on endowments of capital and arable land, and on the employment of skilled and unskilled workers for a sample of 129 countries over the 1975–2010 period. Moreover, annex 2A details the data set construction, highlighting the limitations on the country and time coverage imposed by data availability.

One such limitation is the availability of educational data in five-year increments. Thus, the data set is a panel of countries by industry over five-year periods, with factor endowments measured at the initial year of each period, and net (gross) exports averaged over the five-year period.

The employment of skilled and unskilled workers is constructed using population and educational attainment data from Barro and Lee (2013). *Skilled labor* refers to workers between the ages of 25 and 64 who completed high school (secondary) education. The data on trade come from UN Comtrade (an international trade statistics database); that on capital stock, TFP, and consumption from the Penn World Tables; and that on arable land from the World Bank's World Development Indicators. (See annex 2A for details.)

Table 2.1 (panel A) reports summary statistics for TFP and for endowments of capital, skilled and unskilled labor, and arable land (unadjusted for productivity differences) in the sample over time. Panels B and C report the same statistics for two subgroups: countries with a high skilled-to-unskilled labor ratio and those with a low ratio in 2000. The sample is split into two subgroups using the median for the skilled-to-unskilled labor ratio in 2000.[4]

The number of countries for which data are available gradually increased, from 45 in 1975 to 107 by 2000; arguably, data for more unskilled,

Table 2.1 Summary Statistics: Endowments and Total Factor Productivity for All Countries and Low- versus High-Skilled Labor-Abundant Countries

Year	TFP	Capital, US$	Skilled labor	Unskilled labor	Arable land, hectares	Number of countries
				(in millions)		
Panel A: All countries						
1975	0.84	0.86	7.29	27.74	13.69	45
	(0.46)	(2.20)	(24.82)	(72.98)	(36.32)	
1980	0.82	0.85	7.06	23.48	11.36	65
	(0.41)	(2.44)	(25.28)	(68.28)	(31.28)	
1985	0.75	0.88	9.62	36.46	12.72	71
	(0.27)	(2.46)	(29.27)	(123.14)	(32.80)	
1990	0.72	0.95	11.08	33.26	11.14	85
	(0.26)	(2.67)	(33.32)	(123.57)	(30.30)	
1995	0.63	1.18	15.27	31.56	12.00	98
	(0.28)	(3.09)	(43.50)	(121.77)	(30.39)	
2000	0.63	1.25	18.33	29.29	10.91	107
	(0.35)	(3.51)	(55.54)	(118.59)	(28.69)	
2005	0.67	1.65	21.76	30.73	11.16	105
	(0.35)	(4.67)	(61.46)	(128.44)	(28.46)	
2010	0.67	2.19	24.55	32.86	11.12	104
	(0.32)	(6.00)	(63.34)	(144.67)	(27.88)	

table continues next page

Table 2.1   Summary Statistics: Endowments and Total Factor Productivity for All Countries and Low- versus High-Skilled Labor-Abundant Countries *(continued)*

Year	TFP	Capital, US$	Skilled labor	Unskilled labor	Arable land, hectares	Number of countries
		(in millions)				
Panel B: Relatively high-skilled, labor-abundant countries						
1975	0.80	1.12	10.17	16.50	12.03	29
	(0.21)	(2.69)	(30.64)	(23.83)	(35.29)	
1980	0.83	1.32	11.45	14.64	11.01	34
	(0.23)	(3.27)	(34.43)	(20.74)	(33.18)	
1985	0.75	1.29	13.09	14.43	10.74	36
	(0.21)	(3.35)	(37.31)	(19.91)	(32.23)	
1990	0.76	1.32	13.34	11.53	8.93	45
	(0.22)	(3.54)	(37.39)	(17.17)	(28.71)	
1995	0.66	1.65	17.42	10.76	11.29	52
	(0.25)	(4.04)	(41.74)	(15.74)	(31.15)	
2000	0.68	1.72	19.66	8.93	10.63	54
	(0.31)	(4.58)	(46.12)	(12.96)	(29.78)	
2005	0.72	2.13	22.58	8.08	10.72	52
	(0.29)	(5.77)	(50.50)	(11.56)	(29.08)	
2010	0.70	2.48	24.28	7.30	10.20	53
	(0.23)	(6.25)	(54.36)	(10.35)	(27.95)	
Panel C: Relatively low-skilled, labor-abundant countries						
1975	0.92	0.38	2.08	48.10	16.70	16
	(0.73)	(0.58)	(3.18)	(117.81)	(39.11)	
1980	0.82	0.33	2.25	33.17	11.74	31
	(0.54)	(0.58)	(3.76)	(96.37)	(29.60)	
1985	0.75	0.45	6.05	59.13	14.75	35
	(0.33)	(0.73)	(17.47)	(172.54)	(33.72)	
1990	0.68	0.53	8.53	57.70	13.61	40
	(0.30)	(0.93)	(28.32)	(177.20)	(32.18)	
1995	0.60	0.66	12.85	55.07	12.79	46
	(0.30)	(1.25)	(45.75)	(174.98)	(29.83)	
2000	0.58	0.77	16.98	50.05	11.18	53
	(0.37)	(1.82)	(64.16)	(166.21)	(27.83)	
2005	0.62	1.17	20.96	52.96	11.59	53
	(0.40)	(3.23)	(71.08)	(178.46)	(28.11)	
2010	0.63	1.88	24.82	59.43	12.08	51
	(0.39)	(5.77)	(72.05)	(203.94)	(28.04)	

Sources: Penn World Tables, World Development Indicators, and World Bank calculations.

Note: TFP = total factor productivity. The TFP values are relative to U.S. TFP (U.S. value = 1 in all years). Standard deviations are reported in parentheses. Panel A reports summary statistics for endowments of capital, land, and labor (skilled and unskilled) by year for all countries in the sample. Panels B and C report the same statistics for countries with a skilled-to-unskilled labor ratio above and below the median in the year 2000, respectively.

labor-abundant countries became available in later years. Yet, the summary statistics show that the average number of skilled labor stock exploded over this period. Keeping in mind the changing set of countries over the years, the skilled-labor endowment for an average country increased from 7.3 to 25 million, while the unskilled-labor endowment of an average country hovered at about 30 million. A similar pattern, albeit less striking, is observed for capital endowment, which for an average country was at US$0.9 and $2.2 million in 1975 and 2010, respectively. Comparing panels B and C, we see that even though relatively high-skilled, labor-abundant countries tend to have, on average, larger endowments of skilled labor and smaller endowments of unskilled labor (by construction), many of the changes in skilled labor endowment over time were driven by the group of relatively low-skilled, labor-abundant countries. Skilled labor endowment for an average country in the latter group increased from 2.1 million in 1975 to 14 million in 2010, compared to the same statistic for the group of relatively high-skilled, labor-abundant countries, which changed only from 10 million to 24 million.

Table 2.2 summarizes sectoral net exports in millions of U.S. dollars and as a share of GDP in 1975 and 2010. It shows significant variation in the sectoral trade patterns within industries and across industries within countries.

Table 2.2 Summary Statistics: Net Exports in U.S. Dollars and as a Share of GDP, 1975 versus 2010

| Sector | Description | US$ (millions) | | | | Share of GDP (%) | | | |
| | | 1975 | | 2010 | | 1975 | | 2010 | |
		Mean	SD	Mean	SD	Mean	SD	Mean	SD
311	Food manufacturing	−36.3	1,537.7	538.8	7,757.3	0.30	1.23	−0.32	2.34
313	Beverages	9.4	487.4	38.0	2,127.7	0.00	0.16	0.01	0.35
314	Tobacco manufactures	24.5	145.9	−3.2	764.5	0.00	0.10	−0.03	0.18
321	Textiles	−1.4	520.9	335.5	7,117.2	−0.21	0.68	−0.28	0.44
322	Apparel	−84.1	889.2	−80.9	13,746.3	0.18	0.93	−0.02	0.79
323	Leather products	−8.5	111.7	−32.0	2,752.4	−0.01	0.06	−0.06	0.27
324	Footwear	−35.2	536.9	−76.9	2,915.3	0.01	0.13	−0.05	0.18
331	Wood products	−125.9	658.3	45.6	1,617.9	0.07	0.40	0.07	0.57
332	Furniture	−20.8	281.9	60.5	5,346.0	−0.01	0.08	−0.02	0.38
341	Paper products	7.0	1,035.9	6.5	2,287.9	0.02	0.64	−0.13	0.65
342	Printing and publishing	5.7	179.8	27.4	747.9	−0.04	0.07	−0.04	0.27
351	Industrial chemicals	133.3	1,442.4	−755.6	9,930.6	−0.28	0.79	−0.40	2.37
352	Other chemical products	73.3	606.0	44.6	7,605.8	−0.13	0.22	−0.33	2.54
353	Petroleum refineries	−285.6	1,836.8	951.1	12,567.6	0.27	2.76	−1.03	5.22
354	Miscellaneous petroleum and coal products	8.3	189.9	−0.5	337.3	−0.01	0.04	−0.02	0.04

table continues next page

Table 2.2 Summary Statistics: Net Exports in U.S. Dollars and as a Share of GDP, 1975 versus 2010 *(continued)*

| | | US$ (million) | | | | Share of GDP (%) | | | |
| | | 1975 | | 2010 | | 1975 | | 2010 | |
Sector	Description	Mean	SD	Mean	SD	Mean	SD	Mean	SD
355	Rubber products	6.4	267.7	18.1	2,067.8	−0.04	0.08	−0.12	0.29
356	Plastic products	−15.8	207.1	42.6	4,903.0	−0.01	0.11	−0.18	0.27
361	Pottery, china, earthenwear	−3.0	117.6	25.6	853.0	−0.02	0.03	−0.02	0.04
362	Glass products	1.5	107.1	15.1	987.6	−0.04	0.07	−0.06	0.12
369	Nonmetallic mineral products	19.1	268.4	107.8	1,917.7	−0.04	0.18	−0.15	0.27
371	Iron and steel	241.4	2,140.5	83.8	5,122.7	−0.19	0.66	−0.34	0.80
372	Nonferrous metals	−143.6	737.2	−224.1	9,213.6	0.15	0.65	0.67	2.76
381	Fabricated metal products	114.6	830.8	181.5	9,566.3	−0.18	0.30	−0.42	0.52
382	Machinery except electrical	705.0	4,304.6	88.6	29,106.5	−0.75	1.08	−1.45	2.19
383	Electrical machinery	203.2	2,107.2	−2,664.9	26,089.3	−0.23	0.41	−1.08	4.99
384	Transport equipment	508.7	4,448.5	1,092.7	28,773.0	−0.70	0.94	−1.28	2.57
385	Professional and scientific equipment	−10.4	603.6	−42.2	5,373.8	−0.08	0.24	−0.09	1.24
390	Other manufacturing	−83.3	535.5	18.9	8,691.0	−0.05	0.14	0.04	1.83
Number of countries		45		103		45		103	

Sources: World Bank calculations based on data from UN Comtrade and Penn World Tables.
Note: SD = standard deviation.

Results

Table 2.3 contains the first set of results, which correspond to the unadjusted Rybczynski equations, sector by sector for each of the 28 sectors. The dependent variable is net exports, with independent variables constructed as in equation 2.3. In turn, table 2.4 shows the results from the productivity-adjusted Rybczynski equations in which the independent variables are constructed using raw factor endowments multiplied by TFP, as done by Fitzgerald and Hallak (2004).

To assess how the productivity adjustment affects the estimated coefficients, industries were ranked by factor intensity (from most factor intensive to least) and rank correlations were then computed for the specification that includes both country and year fixed effects (from tables 2.3 and 2.4). Little correlation is found between the ranking of industries by skilled and unskilled labor intensity (0.33 and 0.58, respectively), whereas the ranking of industries by capital intensity is almost reversed (−0.64), suggesting that adjusting for productivity makes a difference.[5] Therefore, the discussion of results below focuses on the estimates presented in table 2.4.

Three sets of results are reported in table 2.4, controlling for only year fixed effects, only country fixed effects, and both country and year fixed effects. Country fixed effects are included to allow for the possibility that the number of omitted factors of production varies across countries. The year fixed effects

Table 2.3 Unadjusted Rybczynski Equations for Net Exports

Dependent variable: Net exports	Year fixed effect				Country fixed effect				Country and year fixed effects			
	Capital	Skilled Labor	Unskilled Labor	Land	Capital	Skilled Labor	Unskilled Labor	Land	Capital	Skilled Labor	Unskilled Labor	Land
Food	-1.36***	-0.04	-5.19	0.52***	-0.86**	4.03	24.40	0.33	-0.86**	4.55	24.59	0.38
Beverages	0.45*	-1.22	4.34**	0.02	0.37***	17.31***	-3.34	0.24**	0.37***	17.51***	-3.58	0.25**
Tobacco	-0.27***	6.30**	-1.85**	-0.01	-0.12	4.72	-1.09	-0.11	-0.12	4.72	-1.11	-0.11
Textiles	1.40*	5.77	23.96***	-0.78***	2.11***	-9.88	64.41***	-3.40***	2.10***	-10.97	65.83***	-3.45***
Apparel	2.92**	53.19	52.44***	-1.06**	4.33***	52.36*	122.32***	-5.24***	4.32***	49.91*	125.14***	-5.36***
Leather and leather products	0.57*	1.20	8.58***	-0.15	0.78***	0.08	24.55***	-0.96***	0.78***	-0.47	25.18***	-0.99***
Footwear	0.87***	5.67	13.21***	-0.22***	0.94***	11.81**	23.30***	-0.91***	0.94***	11.30**	23.87***	-0.93***
Wood and wood products	0.21	10.59*	1.93	0.24***	0.20	14.47**	10.52	0.00	0.20	14.53**	10.47	0.01
Furniture and fixtures	1.57***	13.86	17.80***	-0.37**	2.07***	23.76	32.24**	-1.80***	2.06***	23.05	33.08**	-1.83***
Paper and paper products	-0.06	-10.13**	-4.89***	0.35***	-0.27***	-10.99**	-1.04	0.72***	-0.27***	-10.70**	-1.32	0.74***
Printing and publishing	0.11***	-1.40	1.20***	-0.11***	0.16***	-1.86	-0.13	-0.06	0.16***	-1.85	-0.14	-0.06
Industrial chemicals	0.35	-4.19	-25.61**	0.57	-0.67	2.24	-74.07***	3.54***	-0.65	3.07	-75.00***	3.56***
Other chemical products	0.19	9.51	4.83	-0.42***	0.60	44.02***	-27.33*	0.42	0.60	45.02***	-28.29*	0.47
Petroleum refineries	-0.51	84.42**	-17.74*	1.01***	-2.76**	70.16*	-25.13	-0.46	-2.76**	70.53*	-25.46	-0.44
Misc. petroleum, coal products	-0.04	-1.61**	-0.45**	-0.01	-0.06**	-2.76**	-0.60	0.09***	-0.06**	-2.73**	-0.63	0.09***

table continues next page

Table 2.3 Unadjusted Rybczynski Equations for Net Exports *(continued)*

Dependent variable: Net exports	Year fixed effect				Country fixed effect				Country and year fixed effects			
	Capital	Skilled Labor	Unskilled Labor	Land	Capital	Skilled Labor	Unskilled Labor	Land	Capital	Skilled Labor	Unskilled Labor	Land
Rubber products	0.82***	1.68	6.89***	−0.23***	0.84***	7.85*	0.61	−0.52***	0.84***	7.77**	0.72	−0.52***
Plastic products	1.13**	1.93	17.47***	−0.50***	1.58***	−3.55	35.46***	−1.88***	1.57***	−4.33	36.40***	−1.91***
Pottery, china, and earthenwear	0.24***	−0.28	3.67***	−0.10***	0.26***	−1.62	7.62***	−0.31***	0.26***	−1.75	7.77***	−0.32***
Glass and glass products	0.33***	−2.53	3.45***	−0.12***	0.36***	−4.62**	8.14***	−0.30***	0.36***	−4.73**	8.28***	−0.30***
Other nonmetal mineral products	0.67***	−2.26	7.35***	−0.19***	0.75***	0.84	14.28***	−0.58***	0.75***	0.70	14.45***	−0.58***
Iron and steel	2.47***	7.07	11.90***	−0.22	1.51***	1.09	18.22*	−1.16***	1.50***	0.27	19.14**	−1.21***
Nonferrous metals	0.23	−1.16	−18.70**	1.19***	−0.54	−2.38	−44.70***	3.85***	−0.53	−1.69	−45.93***	3.89***
Fabricated metal products	3.00***	4.88	34.19***	−1.11***	3.72***	1.17	61.50***	−3.49***	3.71***	−0.12	63.04***	−3.56***
Machinery	12.65***	1.69	96.88***	−4.22***	14.34***	53.83	50.89	−7.33***	14.33***	51.86	53.33	−7.43***
Electrical machinery	9.27***	43.11	76.89***	−2.33***	9.36***	117.51*	34.16	−5.25***	9.37***	114.06*	37.81	−5.47***
Transport equipment	11.36***	46.41	56.18*	−2.49***	9.35***	214.98***	−200.72***	2.34	9.37***	218.34***	−204.95***	2.52
Professional scientific equipment	0.50	−4.39	−2.16	−0.15	0.18	7.35	−36.34**	1.21***	0.18	7.92	−36.99***	1.24***
Other manufacturing	2.31***	35.87**	31.88***	−0.59***	2.61***	44.55**	65.48***	−2.75***	2.60***	43.01**	67.27***	−2.82***

Note: Coefficients on capital and land are divided by 1,000 and 100, respectively.
***, **, and * indicate significance at the 1 percent, 5 percent and 10 percent levels, respectively.

Table 2.4 Productivity-Adjusted Rybczynski Equations for Net Exports

Dependent variable:	Year fixed effect				Country fixed effect				Country and year fixed effect			
		Skilled Labor	Unskilled			Skilled Labor	Unskilled			Skilled Labor	Unskilled	
Net exports	Capital	Labor		Land	Capital	Labor		Land	Capital	Labor		Land
Food	−1.83**	−80.08**	−35.88**	1.55***	−1.63	−23.10	−18.84	0.87	−1.89	−33.19	−25.31	1.09
Beverages	0.53	−0.15	22.69***	−0.04	−0.44	34.95**	−17.06	0.11	−0.47	33.65**	−17.94	0.14
Tobacco	−0.44***	6.14	−10.91***	0.03	−0.52***	−2.37	−11.30***	0.17	−0.54***	−3.16	−11.88***	0.19
Textiles	−2.61*	−67.85	−25.40	−0.97***	−2.23***	−115.74	80.22**	−3.48***	−2.33***	−119.60	77.99***	−3.43***
Apparel	−6.96***	−176.05	−45.51	−1.13***	−6.95***	−92.01	40.58	−6.29***	−6.96***	−92.45	40.53	−6.33***
Leather and leather products	−1.06**	−44.10	−8.98	−0.13*	−1.39***	−48.03	6.56	−0.79***	−1.40***	−48.42	6.38	−0.79***
Footwear	−1.00***	−40.79*	3.15	−0.31***	−1.21***	−8.72	7.11	−1.30***	−1.19***	−7.99	7.62	−1.32***
Wood and wood products	−0.74***	−24.29	0.03	0.51***	−0.77***	27.40	−9.50	−0.28	−0.81***	25.84	−10.53	−0.25
Furniture and fixtures	−2.05***	−62.07	−12.29	−0.53***	−2.66***	−29.80	0.04	−2.20***	−2.70***	−31.36	−0.91	−2.18***
Paper and paper products	0.51**	−17.31	4.70	0.65***	0.75**	8.58	0.22	0.52*	0.74**	8.29	0.03	0.53*
Printing and publishing	0.10	6.33	1.09	−0.22***	0.07	−2.58	1.24	−0.12	0.07	−2.84	1.08	−0.12
Industrial chemicals	4.73***	184.65***	58.47**	−0.26	4.44***	148.21***	−24.88	2.65**	4.70***	158.23***	−18.62	2.45**
Other chemical products	1.32*	106.31***	37.52***	−1.03***	−0.08	125.83***	−23.64	−0.31	−0.24	120.31***	−27.35	−0.18
Petroleum refineries	1.72*	261.67***	80.46***	1.04***	1.12	187.00*	134.22	3.62	1.01	182.15*	131.20	3.72
Misc. petroleum, coal products	0.13***	2.38	0.90	−0.02*	0.17***	−1.38	1.12	0.08*	0.18***	−1.23	1.22	0.07*

table continues next page

61

Table 2.4 Productivity-Adjusted Rybczynski Equations for Net Exports (continued)

Dependent variable: Net exports	Year fixed effect				Country fixed effect				Country and year fixed effect			
	Capital	Skilled Labor	Unskilled	Land	Capital	Skilled Labor	Unskilled	Land	Capital	Skilled Labor	Unskilled	Land
Rubber products	-0.06	4.68	7.43	-0.53***	-0.23	0.42	10.78	-0.72**	-0.24	0.13	10.61	-0.72**
Plastic products	-1.97**	-72.03	-20.93	-0.64***	-2.00***	-79.68	10.21	-1.99***	-2.04***	-81.34	9.23	-1.98***
Pottery, China and earthenware	-0.33***	-14.12	-2.41	-0.15***	-0.31***	-15.25	4.10	-0.33***	-0.31***	-15.53	3.94	-0.33***
Glass and glass products	-0.10	-8.18	0.33	-0.21***	-0.13	-21.45	11.89**	-0.21	-0.14	-21.63	11.81**	-0.21
Other non-metal mineral prod.	-0.22	-19.34	4.32	-0.29***	-0.32	-6.75	16.43	-0.99***	-0.34	-7.64	15.91	-0.98***
Iron and steel	-0.14	-7.82	16.06	-1.07***	-1.04	-77.88	51.01*	-0.06	-0.99	-76.08	52.28*	-0.12
Non-ferrous metals	0.13	-73.29	-15.33	1.74***	-0.38	43.38	-217.30***	3.75***	-0.34	44.56	-216.73***	3.76***
Fabricated metal products	-2.78	-93.09	-21.02	-1.81***	-3.12**	-117.71	42.59	-4.25***	-3.19**	-120.46	41.02	-4.22***
Machinery	-2.35	-32.30	13.27	-8.98***	-5.14	-129.43	35.59	-12.81***	-5.30	-134.71	32.66	-12.78***
Electrical machinery	-4.17	-37.01	20.81	-5.85***	-8.51	-12.97	-68.06	-7.84**	-8.04	5.83	-56.47	-8.26**
Transport equipment	9.06**	515.14***	270.61***	-8.31***	5.31	691.38***	-77.54	-6.89	5.21	687.06**	-80.16	-6.80
Professional scientific equipment	1.83***	87.10***	29.66***	-0.86***	1.31*	56.84*	-24.72	1.06	1.32*	57.24*	-24.55	1.06
Other manufacturing	-2.89***	-39.73	7.56	-1.07***	-3.46***	1.81	43.08	-3.45***	-3.43***	3.02	44.06	-3.52***

Note: Coefficients on capital and land are divided by 1,000 and 100, respectively.

***, **, and * indicate significance at the 1 percent, 5 percent and 10 percent levels, respectively.

are included to capture any time-varying factors common to all countries, such as common shocks in any given year or common changes in price levels over time. Rank correlations were used to assess the importance of the inclusion of country and year fixed effects. The coefficient estimates from table 2.4 suggest that the inclusion of year fixed effects does not alter the ranking of industries by their factor intensity because the rank correlation between the two sets of estimates is close to 0.99. However, the omission of country fixed effects changes the ranking of industries quite a bit. In particular, the rankings are completely independent when industries are ranked by unskilled labor intensity. A quick glance at the estimates from specifications with country fixed effects and with country and year fixed effects in table 2.4 also reveals that the two sets of estimates are qualitatively the same, and the discussion below thus focuses on the latter.

A positive estimated coefficient on, for example, skilled labor for a particular industry means that skilled-labor abundance is associated with net exports of that industry or is a source of comparative advantage. Likewise, a negative coefficient on skilled labor indicates that skilled labor abundance is a source of comparative disadvantage or is associated with net imports in that industry.

In general, the only strong inference is that capital and land are found to be a source of comparative disadvantage in most industries. The coefficients on capital are statistically significant and negative for 11 industries and positive for only 4 industries, with coefficients for the remaining industries being imprecisely estimated. The coefficients on land are statistically significant and negative for 13 industries and positive for 4 industries. The effect of skilled labor is always positive whenever statistically significant, suggesting that skilled-labor abundance is a source of comparative advantage for six industries. The effect of unskilled labor is difficult to sign because of imprecisely estimated effects with large standard errors. These results are consistent with findings by Fitzgerald and Hallak (2004) that, after adjusting for productivity differences, the coefficient on capital is more often negative than positive.

The results described above are based on the assumption of homothetic preferences across countries and the imputed consumption shares. It is further assumed that consumption shares may vary by the income level of countries, and GDP per capita is included in the preferred specification. Table 2.5 reports the results from the productivity-adjusted Rybczynski equations that control for country income level. The estimates are qualitatively the same as in table 24, and hence, the preferred specification is used in all estimations below.

To allow for the possibility of more than one diversification cone, an indicator variable for countries with a high skilled-to-unskilled labor ratio in 2000 is interacted with factor endowment measures.[6] The main regression is augmented with these four interaction terms, with the results reported in table 2.6. All the regressions include country and year fixed effects. The last two columns indicate whether the difference between estimated coefficients for capital and skilled labor are statistically different from zero across the two groups of countries. For most industries, the estimated coefficients on skilled labor are statistically different

Table 2.5 Productivity-Adjusted Rybczynski Equations for Net Exports, Controlling for GDP per Capita

Dependent variable:	Year fixed effects				Country fixed effects				Country and year fixed effects			
		Labor				Labor				Labor		
Net exports	Capital	Skilled	Unskilled	Land	Capital	Skilled	Unskilled	Land	Capital	Skilled	Unskilled	Land
Food	−1.89**	−80.62**	−36.33**	1.56***	−1.78	−26.75	−20.96	0.95	−1.84	−32.46	−24.95	1.08
Beverages	0.53	−0.17	22.67***	−0.04	−0.47	34.25**	−17.46	0.13	−0.48	33.56**	−17.98	0.14
Tobacco	−0.47***	5.93	−11.08***	0.04	−0.56***	−3.42	−11.91***	0.19	−0.57***	−3.63	−12.12***	0.20
Textiles	−2.76*	−69.02	−26.37	−0.94***	−2.50***	−122.33	76.40**	−3.33***	−2.47***	−121.79	76.89***	−3.38***
Apparel	−7.14***	−177.49	−46.70	−1.10***	−7.16***	−97.12	37.62	−6.18***	−7.10***	−94.63	39.44	−6.28***
Leather and leather products	−1.07**	−44.21	−9.07	−0.12*	−1.43***	−48.89	6.07	−0.77***	−1.42***	−48.65	6.27	−0.78***
Footwear	−1.01***	−40.87*	3.08	−0.30***	−1.23**	−9.06	6.91	−1.29***	−1.21***	−8.27	7.48	−1.32***
Wood and wood products	−0.78***	−24.63	−0.25	0.52***	−0.80**	26.64	−9.94	−0.26	−0.82**	25.83	−10.53	−0.24
Furniture and fixtures	−2.10**	−62.48	−12.63	−0.52***	−2.78***	−32.68	−1.63	−2.14***	−2.77***	−32.42	−1.44	−2.16***
Paper and paper products	0.45*	−17.85	4.25	0.67***	0.79**	9.49	0.75	0.50*	0.78**	8.85	0.31	0.51*
Printing and publishing	0.12	6.45	1.19	−0.22***	0.06	−2.81	1.11	−0.12	0.06	−2.88	1.06	−0.12
Industrial chemicals	4.68***	184.23**	58.12**	−0.25	4.42***	147.69***	−25.18	2.66**	4.47***	154.75***	−20.37	2.53**
Other chemical products	1.03	103.95***	35.58***	−0.97***	−0.63	112.58***	−31.32	−0.01	−0.65	114.07***	−30.49	−0.03
Petroleum refineries	1.33	258.54***	77.89***	1.11**	0.49	171.69	125.35	3.96	0.52	174.82	127.52	3.89
Misc. petroleum, coal products	0.14***	2.43	0.94	−0.02*	0.19***	−1.04	1.32	0.07*	0.19***	−1.08	1.30	0.07*

table continues next page

Table 2.5 Productivity-Adjusted Rybczynski Equations for Net Exports, Controlling for GDP per Capita *(continued)*

Dependent variable:	Year fixed effects				Country fixed effects				Country and year fixed effects			
	Capital	Skilled Labor	Unskilled Labor	Land	Capital	Skilled Labor	Unskilled Labor	Land	Capital	Skilled Labor	Unskilled Labor	Land
Net exports												
Rubber products	−0.04	4.80	7.53	−0.53***	−0.25	−0.06	10.50	−0.71**	−0.25	−0.03	10.53	−0.72**
Plastic products	−2.06**	−72.71	−21.49	−0.63***	−2.14***	−83.12	8.21	−1.92***	−2.13***	−82.63	8.59	−1.94***
Pottery, china, and earthenware	−0.33**	−14.17	−2.46	−0.15***	−0.33***	−15.67	3.86	−0.32***	−0.32***	−15.65	3.88	−0.32***
Glass and glass products	−0.09	−8.16	0.34	−0.21***	−0.13	−21.46	11.89**	−0.21	−0.13	−21.53	11.86**	−0.21
Other nonmetal mineral products	−0.22	−19.37	4.29	−0.29***	−0.33	−7.11	16.22	−0.99***	−0.33	−7.50	15.98	−0.98***
Iron and steel	−0.16	−7.93	15.96	−1.06***	−1.05	−78.09	50.89*	−0.06	−1.02	−76.50	52.07*	−0.11
Nonferrous metals	0.24	−72.38	−14.58	1.72***	−0.11	50.02	−213.45***	3.60***	−0.13	47.68	−215.16***	3.68***
Fabricated metal products	−2.89	−94.02	−21.79	−1.78***	−3.32**	−122.72	39.69	−4.13***	−3.30**	−122.10	40.20	−4.18***
Machinery	−2.50	−33.51	12.28	−8.95***	−5.70	−142.88	27.80	−12.51**	−5.63	−139.74	30.13	−12.66***
Electrical machinery	−3.99	−35.50	22.04	−5.89***	−8.24	−6.51	−64.32	−7.99**	−8.16	4.06	−57.36	−8.22**
Transport equipment	9.46**	518.34***	273.25***	−8.38***	5.33	691.76**	−77.32	−6.90	5.33	688.89***	−79.25	−6.84
Professional scientific equipment	1.87***	87.39***	29.90***	−0.87***	1.31*	56.79*	−24.75	1.07	1.30	56.96*	−24.69	1.07
Other manufacturing	−2.91***	−39.90	7.41	−1.07***	−3.46***	1.91	43.14	−3.45***	−3.42***	3.22	44.16	−3.52***

Note: Coefficients on capital and land are divided by 1,000 and 100, respectively.

***, **, and * indicate significance at the 1 percent, 5 percent, and 10 percent levels, respectively.

65

Table 2.6 Productivity-Adjusted Rybczynski Equations for Net Exports by Low- versus High-Skilled-to-Unskilled Labor Ratio Country Groups

Dependent variable: Net exports	Countries with low skilled-to-unskilled labor ratio				Countries with high skilled-to-unskilled labor ratio				Difference significant?	
	Capital	Skilled Labor	Unskilled Labor	Land	Capital	Skilled Labor	Unskilled Labor	Land	Capital	Skilled labor
Food	−5.58*	−118.02	−103.50*	5.80*	−1.56	−44.46	28.56	−0.73		***
Beverages	0.26	12.58*	0.26	−0.12	−0.27	83.49***	0.42	−0.13		
Tobacco	−0.37***	−14.76***	−3.00	0.44***	−0.62***	6.25	−23.79	−0.06		
Textiles	−2.24***	−175.91***	106.51***	−6.70***	−0.12	104.33***	18.76	−0.99***	**	***
Apparel	−6.05***	−297.17***	86.60**	−10.30***	−2.07	457.34***	164.17**	−4.56***	**	***
Leather and leather products	−1.20***	−83.97***	19.90***	−1.54***	−0.62**	46.00***	5.37	−0.39*	*	***
Footwear	−1.13***	−45.39***	10.46	−2.15***	−0.15	99.39***	47.27**	−0.92***	**	***
Wood and wood products	−0.48**	−14.55	−3.76	−0.41	−0.13	113.83***	42.44*	−0.51		***
Furniture and fixtures	−2.16***	−162.36***	33.86***	−3.22***	−0.44	256.17***	42.47	−2.01***	*	***
Paper and paper products	0.23	−3.17	−12.59	1.13**	0.84*	9.49	16.65	0.28		
Printing and publishing	−0.06	−10.07***	1.68	−0.34***	0.30***	18.27**	−7.92	0.13	***	***
Industrial chemicals	6.34***	115.91	17.94	4.03	4.02***	176.69***	30.90	0.26		
Other chemical products	−0.14	33.33	12.03	0.65	0.20	234.31***	−117.52	−0.66		**
Petroleum refineries	5.09***	318.61***	234.15***	−3.35*	0.58	170.86	−56.27	7.54		
Misc. petroleum, coal products	0.07	4.00**	−2.61***	0.07	0.15*	−10.41***	2.06	0.13**		***
Rubber products	−0.10	−29.31***	23.44***	−1.45***	0.44	80.85***	−2.32	−0.26		***
Plastic products	−1.87***	−145.18***	32.91**	−3.72***	−0.41	101.89***	−10.69	−0.82*	**	***
Pottery, china, and earthenware	−0.33***	−27.83***	6.29**	−0.58***	−0.01	17.43***	5.74**	−0.16***	***	***
Glass and glass products	−0.22***	−31.50***	12.77***	−0.76***	0.31***	18.37***	10.33	0.23*	***	***

table continues next page

Table 2.6 Productivity-Adjusted Rybczynski Equations for Net Exports by Low- versus High-Skilled-to-Unskilled Labor Ratio Country Groups (continued)

| Dependent variable: | Countries with low skilled-to-unskilled labor ratio | | | | Countries with high skilled-to-unskilled labor ratio | | | | Difference significant? | |
| | | Skilled labor | Unskilled | | | Skilled | Unskilled | | | |
Net exports	Capital	Labor	Labor	Land	Capital	Labor	Labor	Land	Capital	Skilled labor
Other non-metal mineral products	−0.06	−37.04***	27.93***	−2.06***	0.54***	89.92***	25.63**	−0.41**		***
Iron and steel	−1.05	−115.18***	59.90**	−2.51***	0.81	91.87**	59.83	1.58*		***
Nonferrous metals	1.94**	39.11	−218.27***	4.30***	−0.48	67.61*	61.75**	1.32	**	
Fabricated metal products	−3.08***	−288.21***	91.21***	−7.84***	0.79	326.38***	5.70	−1.75	**	***
Machinery	−8.50***	−885.79***	181.77**	−19.38***	8.79	1,485.95***	−199.38	−6.58	**	***
Electrical machinery	−3.94**	−615.09***	167.00***	−9.78***	−0.08	1,210.54***	16.64	−10.27**	**	***
Transport equipment	0.03	41.24	39.25	−3.31	12.69	1,686.22***	−546.89	−6.05		***
Professional scientific equipment	0.95	−9.88	−1.56	2.77***	1.22	101.63*	−111.89	0.20		*
Other manufacturing	−2.70***	−126.35***	82.85***	−6.34***	−0.34	358.19***	91.81*	−2.15***	*	***

Note: The low skilled-to-unskilled labor ratio and the high skilled-to-unskilled labor ratio are computed for 54 country groups. The regressions include country and year fixed effects. Coefficients on capital and land are divided by 1,000 and 100, respectively.

***, **, and * indicate significance at the 1 percent, 5 percent, and 10 percent levels, respectively.

between the two groups of countries, while the difference in the estimated coefficients on capital are only statistically different from zero for about half of the industries.

To summarize the results so far, the effects of capital and skilled/unskilled labor abundance on net exports is strikingly heterogeneous across countries with either high or low skilled-to-unskilled labor ratios. A variety of reasons could explain such heterogeneity. First, countries with high or low skilled-to-unskilled labor ratios possibly produce different varieties within the same commodity categories, with the former using more capital-intensive technologies than the latter, leading to the patterns of comparative advantage observed in the data. This is consistent with the findings of Schott (2003).

Second, the restrictions on capital mobility have been gradually removed over time, whereas the restrictions on labor mobility persist. Thus, capital might have possibly become more mobile over time, flowing to countries where it could complement abundant unskilled labor.[7] This would lead the coefficient on capital to become similar across two groups of countries, as is the case in half of the industries in the sample. Figure 2.1 shows the ratio of foreign direct investment to gross capital formation in high-income and

Figure 2.1 Ratio of Foreign Direct Investment to Gross Capital Formation in High-Income and Low-to-Middle-Income Countries, 1975–2014

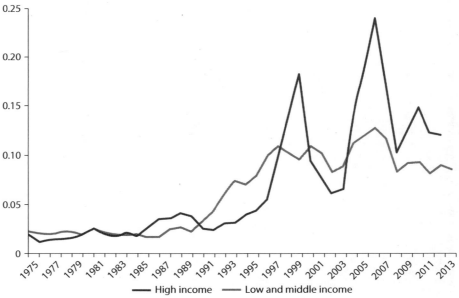

Source: Based on the World Bank's World Development Indicators data.
Note: Both foreign direct investment inflows and gross capital formation are used as a share of GDP to construct the ratio plotted above. The World Bank classification is used to group countries into *high-income* and *low-and-middle-income* subgroups.

low-to-middle-income countries over the past 40 years. This ratio was relatively stable for both groups of countries up until the early 1990s but has grown significantly since then. Additionally, it has been much more volatile for the high-income group relative to the low-to-middle-income group. A structural break in the series seems to have appeared in the early 1990s. To account for the potential changes in capital mobility across countries, the preferred specification is estimated using pre- and post-1995 subsamples. The coefficient estimates on capital and skilled labor for two sets of countries with high or low skilled-to-unskilled labor ratios before and after 1995 are reported in table 2.7.

Before 1995, capital was a source of comparative disadvantage in all industries of countries with a low skilled-to-unskilled labor ratio (estimates for 10 industries are statistically significant and negative), while it was a source of comparative advantage in a handful of industries in countries with a high skilled-to-unskilled labor ratio (out of 14 statistically significant coefficients on capital, 9 are positive). Furthermore, the difference between the estimates on capital of the two groups of countries is statistically different from zero for all industries, with positive and statistically significant coefficients on capital. However, while the number of industries with a negative coefficient on capital has not changed in countries with a low skilled-to-unskilled labor ratio after 1995 (estimates for 9 industries are statistically significant and negative), there are now four industries in which capital is found to be a source of comparative advantage. In contrast, after 1995 the results are more mixed for countries with a high skilled-to-unskilled labor ratio; in about half of the industries for which the estimates are statistically significant, capital is a source of comparative advantage, and in the other half, it appears to be a source of comparative disadvantage. Additionally, the differences between the two groups of countries are no longer as significantly different as before 1995, providing some support for increased capital mobility in later decades.

Yet, the pattern of comparative advantage based on skilled labor became increasingly different across these two groups of countries over time. Before 1995, skilled labor was a source of comparative advantage in almost all industries with statistically significant coefficients across both subsets of countries. Since 1995, it has continued to be a source of comparative advantage in countries with a high skilled-to-unskilled labor ratio, but becomes a source of comparative disadvantage in many industries in countries with a low skilled-to-unskilled labor ratio.

Revealed Comparative Advantage for the Dominican Republic

After estimating the Rybczynski coefficients for a broad set of products, the coefficients on products for which the Dominican Republic has a comparative advantage are examined. The term *comparative advantage* is defined by constructing a revealed comparative advantage index proposed by Vollrath (1991), namely, the difference between the log of export concentration and the log of import

Table 2.7 Productivity-Adjusted Rybczynski Equations for Net Exports by Low- versus High-Skilled-to-Unskilled Labor Ratio Country Groups, 1975–90 versus 1995–2010

Dependent variable: Net exports	Low skilled-to-unskilled labor ratio				High skilled-to-unskilled labor ratio				Difference significant?			
	1975–1990		1995–2010		1975–1990		1995–2010		Capital		Skilled labor	
	Capital	Skilled labor	Capital	Skilled labor	Capital	Skilled labor	Capital	Skilled labor	1975–1990	1995–2010	1975–1990	1995–2010
Food	-1.59***	205.08***	-6.39	-108.23	-3.32**	-305.19***	1.76***	341.88***		**	***	***
Beverages	-0.05	-18.23	0.47**	11.04	-0.59	0.36	-0.73	41.79		*	***	
Tobacco	0.01	-9.47	-0.22*	-14.00**	-0.39	-113.87**	-0.57***	76.62***		*	*	***
Textiles	-0.59**	175.19***	-2.26**	-138.61**	0.38	120.15	-1.24***	38.70*				***
Apparel	-1.17**	397.64***	-4.60**	-261.08***	-3.54**	287.20*	-4.27***	175.43**				***
Leather and leather products	-0.05	44.18***	-0.91***	-75.56***	-0.36	72.26**	-0.95***	-0.30			***	***
Footwear	-0.11	143.29***	-0.83**	-50.07***	-0.27	154.08**	-0.89***	8.51				**
Wood and wood products	-0.82**	141.24**	0.09	-0.38	-1.36*	-97.03**	0.88***	110.08***		*	***	***
Furniture and fixtures	-0.37***	56.35***	-1.71***	-149.51***	-0.07	13.71	-2.39***	163.75***				***
Paper and paper products	-0.22	86.61	-0.02	2.98	0.46	-36.93	1.90***	74.30**		***		**
Printing and publishing	-0.01	-8.52	-0.18*	-12.05***	0.31*	-20.06	0.34*	32.16*	*	***		**
Industrial chemicals	-1.25	-61.88	6.78**	29.22	1.55	-174.59	4.36***	217.41				
Other chemical products	0.10	-64.66	-0.15	43.16*	0.69	-8.68	-0.39	419.56**				*
Petroleum refineries	-1.13	-173.51**	7.16***	452.72***	-1.23**	-119.16**	3.63	600.83*				
Misc. petroleum, coal products	-0.03	0.79	0.06	4.96**	-0.10	-10.86	0.35***	2.69		***		

table continues next page

Table 2.7 Productivity-Adjusted Rybczynski Equations for Net Exports by Low- versus High-Skilled-to-Unskilled Labor Ratio Country Groups, 1975–90 versus 1995–2010 *(continued)*

Dependent variable: Net exports	Low skilled-to-unskilled labor ratio				High skilled-to-unskilled labor ratio				Difference significant?			
	1975–1990		1995–2010		1975–1990		1995–2010		Capital		Skilled labor	
	Capital	Skilled labor	Capital	Skilled labor	Capital	Skilled labor	Capital	Skilled labor	1975–1990	1995–2010	1975–1990	1995–2010
Rubber products	0.10	26.46***	−0.28	−34.04***	0.80***	80.07***	−0.91	−10.15	***			
Plastic products	−0.18	128.18***	−1.17**	−149.16***	0.18	71.38**	−1.18**	76.57*			***	***
Pottery, china, and earthenwear	−0.05	12.55	−0.18**	−29.89***	0.12*	28.99***	−0.11***	10.85***	**			***
Glass and glass products	−0.15***	23.29***	−0.17	−29.16***	0.43***	25.31***	0.05	−4.41	***			*
Other nonmetal mineral products	−0.57	6.47	0.02	−35.29**	0.46	14.76	0.28**	92.67***	*			***
Iron and steel	0.42	−118.21**	−0.25	−65.96	−0.69	16.86	−0.72	−157.57***			*	
Nonferrous metals	0.66	19.01	2.90**	−57.63	−1.89**	−230.14***	−0.28	146.61	***	**	***	*
Fabricated metal products	−1.65***	125.06***	−2.13	−268.27***	1.66***	170.35***	−1.49	264.24**	***		***	***
Machinery	−1.30	−244.39	−7.43	−785.50***	24.57***	1,518.48***	−5.73	701.34	***		***	**
Electrical machinery	−2.59***	108.65**	−2.42	−621.19***	16.14***	1,804.55***	−14.93***	511.37	***	**	***	***
Transport equipment	−0.55	35.74	1.64	50.75	22.53***	1,848.37***	−2.70	304.45	***		***	
Professional scientific equipment	−0.60*	23.73	1.46	−48.96	2.03*	−65.55	0.68	162.81	**			
Other manufacturing	−0.91*	339.37***	−1.45	−104.00	−0.20	353.55***	−2.07***	138.73*				**

Note: The low skilled-to-unskilled labor ratio and the high skilled-to-unskilled labor ratio are computed for 54 country groups. The regressions include country and year fixed effects. Coefficients on capital and land are divided by 1,000 and 100, respectively.

***, **, and * indicate significance at the 1 percent, 5 percent, and 10 percent levels, respectively.

concentration in a given industry. More formally, the measure shown in equation 2.4 was computed for each of 28 industries:

$$RCA_{it} = ln\left(\frac{X_{it}/X_t}{X_{it}^w/X_t^w}\right) - ln\left(\frac{M_{it}/M_t}{M_{it}^w/M_t^w}\right) \tag{2.4}$$

where X_{it} (M_{it}) are the Dominican exports (imports) of product i in year t, X_t (M_t) are the total exports (imports) by the Dominican Republic in year t, and X_{it}^w (M_{it}^w) and X_t^w (M_t^w) refer to world exports (imports) of product i and total world exports (imports) in year t. Positive values reveal a comparative advantage, while negative values indicate a comparative disadvantage.

Table 2.8 reports the revealed comparative advantage index for the Dominican Republic for 2005–14, suggesting that the Dominican Republic had

Table 2.8 Revealed Comparative Advantage Index for the Dominican Republic, 2005–14

Industries	2005	2006	2007	2008	2009	2010	2011	2012	2013	2014
Food	−0.69	−0.53	−0.68	−0.57	−0.17	0.09	−0.04	−0.19	−0.26	−0.22
Beverages	*−0.08*	*0.17*	*0.43*	*0.51*	*0.84*	*1.03*	*0.30*	*0.69*	*0.31*	*0.04*
Tobacco	*4.62*	*4.54*	*4.77*	*5.00*	*4.42*	*3.45*	*3.55*	*3.25*	*3.05*	*2.28*
Textiles	−2.63	−1.87	−0.52	−0.24	0.05	0.15	−0.17	−0.29	−0.04	−0.49
Apparel	*1.20*	*1.32*	*1.49*	*1.69*	*2.23*	*1.82*	*1.80*	*1.98*	*1.46*	*1.67*
Leather and leather products	0.75	−0.07	−1.62	−1.41	−1.08	−0.72	−0.84	−0.83	−0.91	−0.82
Footwear	*1.71*	*1.53*	*1.55*	*1.67*	*1.73*	*2.05*	*2.10*	*2.07*	*1.93*	*2.12*
Wood and wood products	−3.14	−3.43	−2.70	−1.97	−2.30	−2.33	−2.41	−2.00	−2.59	−2.27
Furniture and fixtures	−0.96	−1.03	−1.49	−1.24	−0.93	−0.90	−1.28	−1.13	−1.24	−1.17
Paper and paper products	−0.08	0.08	−0.06	−0.23	0.14	0.19	−0.05	−1.17	−1.25	−1.06
Printing and publishing	−2.04	−1.73	−2.33	−1.61	−1.49	−1.17	−1.22	0.51	−1.15	−1.09
Industrial chemicals	−1.75	−1.62	−1.52	−1.21	−0.98	−0.74	−0.85	−1.04	−1.02	−1.05
Other chemical products	−1.58	−1.65	−1.52	−1.29	−1.08	−0.70	−0.80	−0.05	−0.40	−0.50
Petroleum refineries	1.58	−4.78	1.57	1.85	−6.03	−5.34	−1.79	−1.03	−2.32	−0.93
Misc. petroleum, coal products	−7.64	−7.61	−8.15	−6.16	−3.51	−5.58	−3.85	−4.63	−5.24	−5.27
Rubber products	−2.82	−2.58	−2.52	−2.57	−1.54	−2.13	−1.62	−1.69	−1.64	−1.60
Plastic products	−0.63	−0.17	0.09	0.06	−0.45	−0.03	0.22	0.38	0.01	−0.16
Pottery, china, and earthenwear	*0.58*	*0.61*	*0.44*	*0.38*	*0.39*	*0.38*	*−0.39*	*0.20*	*−1.00*	*−1.54*
Glass and glass products	−3.22	−4.55	−2.75	−3.81	−2.42	−2.96	−3.31	−3.19	−3.60	−2.91
Other nonmetal mineral products	*−1.98*	*−0.68*	*−0.12*	*0.31*	*0.69*	*0.84*	*0.41*	*0.63*	*0.56*	*0.39*
Iron and steel	*0.54*	*1.09*	*1.43*	*0.52*	*−0.23*	*−0.40*	*0.90*	*0.55*	*0.19*	*−0.95*
Nonferrous metals	*−0.52*	*−1.30*	*−1.73*	*−0.23*	*0.34*	*0.79*	*0.62*	*1.17*	*2.68*	*2.68*
Fabricated metal products	−2.02	−2.06	−1.53	−1.64	−1.35	−1.44	−1.52	−1.57	−1.19	−1.41
Machinery	−0.62	−1.41	−3.17	−3.26	−2.37	−2.73	−2.53	−1.44	−1.77	−1.82
Electrical machinery	*0.10*	*0.05*	*0.38*	*0.06*	*0.20*	*0.22*	*0.11*	*0.00*	*0.00*	*0.05*
Transport equipment	−5.67	−5.38	−5.12	−4.41	−3.60	−3.31	−2.98	−3.43	−3.29	−3.43
Professional scientific equipment	*1.72*	*1.72*	*−0.79*	*1.37*	*2.36*	*2.34*	*1.98*	*1.60*	*1.91*	*1.71*
Other manufacturing	2.68	1.78	1.55	1.22	1.17	1.33	1.10	0.55	0.84	0.48

Note: The revealed comparative advantage (RCA) index is constructed following Vollrath (1991). Industries in which the Dominican Republic has a comparative advantage (RCA > 0) are in italic. Industries in bold and italic are those mentioned in the text.

a comparative advantage in tobacco, beverages, apparel, footwear, electrical machinery, and professional scientific equipment manufacturing. In turn, the goodness of fit of the preferred estimations is evaluated for the Dominican Republic and two subsamples: low human capital countries and high human capital countries.

The results from this exercise are reported in table 2.9. The first set of columns reports the results for the Dominican Republic, followed by the low-skill and the high-skill samples. For each group, the table shows the observed average net exports for each industry category, the mean residual of the estimations reported in table 2.6 for each group of countries, and the ratio of the mean residual divided by the observed net exports.

An important caveat to keep in mind is that the estimations for the Dominican Republic are expected to be less precise than those for the samples of high- and low-skill economies, primarily because the data set includes only three five-year observations for this country. Hence, the residuals for a single economy are expected to be relatively larger than the residuals averaged across a large number of observations.

This said, the estimates for the Dominican Republic are adequate, according to table 2.9. First, the ratio of the average industry-specific residual divided by the observed average net exports is about −0.05 percent for this country, which compares quite favorably with the corresponding ratio of 0.09 percent for the sample of low-skill economies. This is an appropriate comparison because the Dominican Republic is classified as a *low-skill economy*. In other words, the estimation errors for the Dominican economy are small relative to the observed data, even when the absolute values of the errors are higher for the Dominican Republic than for its comparable sample average. The corresponding statistic for the sample of high-skill economies is even higher, at 0.61 percent.

However, as expected, the average ratio of the estimation error over the observed net exports is notably higher—that is, 1.19 percent—for those sectors in which the Dominican Republic seems to have a revealed comparative advantage. Still, given that this ratio is computed from a very small sample (that is, seven, representing the number equal to three times the number of industries in which the Dominican Republic has a revealed comparative advantage), it is unsurprising that this ratio is higher. Yet, it seems low given the small sample. To conclude, the model with heterogeneous Rybczynski coefficients seems to provide an acceptable set of predictions, for both subsamples and for the Dominican Republic itself.

After estimating the Rybczynski coefficients with proper adjustments for Hicks-neutral international technological differences and documenting systematic heterogeneity across countries that differ in terms of their relative endowments of skilled labor, it is important to reexamine the issues concerning the Dominican economy—namely, whether the growth associated with comparative advantage in certain manufacturing industries could help explain why its labor markets have not delivered growth with equity. Simply put, the findings in this chapter suggest that trade specialization is unlikely to provide a full explanation

Table 2.9 Average Net Exports and Mean Residuals for the Dominican Republic and Low- versus High-Skill Economies

Industry	Dominican Republic			Low-skill economies			High-skill economies		
	Net exports (mln $)	Mean res	Ratio (%)	NX (mln $)	Mean res	Ratio	NX (mln $)	Mean res	Ratio
Food	−530.7	18.67	−3.52%	265.6	−1.12	−0.42%	64.1	2.02	3.15%
Beverages	−26.6	−0.33	1.25%	52.7	0.01	0.02%	−23.8	−0.03	0.12%
Tobacco	*283.7*	*1.33*	*0.47%*	2.5	0.15	5.91%	28.6	−0.45	−1.57%
Textiles	−376.5	5.33	−1.42%	358.2	0.00	0.00%	−215.7	−1.04	0.48%
Apparel	*521.4*	*−1.33*	*−0.26%*	1,009.7	1.60	0.16%	−1,192.4	2.59	−0.22%
Leather and leather products	−64.0	1.25	−1.95%	137.0	−0.99	−0.72%	−222.5	−0.48	0.22%
Footwear	*121.4*	*0.33*	*0.27%*	220.3	0.94	0.43%	−311.9	−0.01	0.00%
Wood and wood products	−123.5	1.33	−1.08%	7.2	0.02	0.33%	−46.4	−0.19	0.40%
Furniture and fixtures	−53.8	−0.09	0.17%	234.0	−0.29	−0.12%	−232.4	0.48	−0.21%
Paper and paper products	−180.1	1.33	−0.74%	−299.4	0.57	−0.19%	245.2	−0.30	−0.12%
Printing and publishing	−63.7	0.33	−0.52%	−0.6	−0.01	1.21%	4.0	−0.11	−2.84%
Industrial chemicals	−539.2	1.33	−0.25%	−1,368.4	−2.87	0.21%	629.0	3.97	0.63%
Other chemical products	−419.4	0.00	0.00%	−318.2	0.87	−0.27%	372.2	2.42	0.65%
Petroleum refineries	−843.5	21.33	−2.53%	223.2	1.03	0.46%	65.3	10.38	15.90%
Misc. petroleum, coal products	−7.6	−0.02	0.27%	−22.9	0.06	−0.27%	21.4	−0.20	−0.92%
Rubber products	−104.6	−0.33	0.32%	13.9	−0.30	−2.13%	−2.4	0.08	−3.29%
Plastic products	−167.3	0.00	0.00%	142.3	0.33	0.23%	−228.0	−0.40	0.17%
Pottery, china, and earthenware	−3.4	−0.04	1.23%	56.8	−0.12	−0.21%	−47.4	−0.17	0.36%
Glass and glass products	−63.8	0.08	−0.13%	15.0	0.10	0.67%	−1.1	−0.11	9.77%
Other nonmetal mineral products	−60.8	0.50	−0.82%	125.4	0.19	0.15%	−62.5	−0.27	0.43%
Iron and steel	*12.7*	*0.67*	*5.25%*	−149.6	1.80	−1.20%	224.6	−0.15	−0.07%
Nonferrous metals	*128.3*	*2.67*	*2.08%*	−456.1	−4.35	0.95%	102.4	−4.32	−4.22%
Fabricated metal products	−282.2	0.33	−0.12%	192.3	−1.78	−0.92%	−170.7	0.14	−0.08%
Machinery	−761.5	−10.67	1.40%	−726.7	2.33	−0.32%	828.3	7.37	0.89%

table continues next page

Table 2.9 Average Net Exports and Mean Residuals for the Dominican Republic and Low- versus High-Skill Economies *(continued)*

Industry	Dominican Republic			Low-skill economies			High-skill economies		
	Net exports (mln $)	Mean res	Ratio (%)	NX (mln $)	Mean res	Ratio	NX (mln $)	Mean res	Ratio
Electrical machinery	−382.2	0.00	0.09%	−444.3	3.94	−0.89%	−1,054.2	1.79	−0.17%
Transport equipment	−806.7	10.67	−1.32%	−604.0	3.00	−0.50%	1,772.3	−15.23	−0.86%
Professional scientific equipment	*369.8*	*−2.67*	*−0.72%*	−438.5	0.57	−0.13%	286.6	−4.45	−1.55%
Other manufacturing	219.5	2.67	1.21%	478.2	0.47	0.10%	−759.1	0.42	−0.05%
Average across industries	N.A.	1.95	−0.05%	N.A.	0.22	0.09%	N.A.	0.13	0.61%
Average for DR RCA>1	236.7	0.52	1.19%	N.A.	N.A.	N.A.	N.A.	N.A.	N.A.
Correlation between NX and mean residuals	−0.43			0.08			−0.38		
Number of country observations	3			318			357		

Note: n.a. = not applicable; NX = net exports; RCA = revealed comparative advantage. Dominican industries in which the revealed comparative advantage index is greater than one in at least one year during the period 2005–14 are shown in italics.

of these stylized facts for the following reason: econometric evidence indicates that the industries in which the Dominican Republic developed a comparative advantage are actually those in which the endowments of skilled labor are not a source of comparative advantage in economies with low ratios of skilled over unskilled labor endowments. Furthermore, these results are probably associated with the rise of international equity capital flows to developing economies since the 1990s.

Conclusion

In this chapter, the authors make two contributions to the literature. First, they extend the empirical literature on the estimation of factor proportions as determinants of international trade patterns to a large set of diverse economies, including developing countries. By relying on trade data, rather than on production data, and by following Leamer (1995), they expand the estimation sample to include more than one hundred countries. In turn, this provides richer evidence than that produced by the existing literature, which relies predominantly on data from high-income economies.

Second, the authors focus not only on the role of Hicks-neutral international technological differences but also on the role of systematic technological differences across countries with different relative factor endowments. More specifically, they provide evidence on the differences in Rybczynski coefficients across countries with low and high ratios of skilled labor over unskilled labor.

The resulting evidence seems relevant for understanding global patterns of trade specialization. As found by Fitzgerald and Hallak (2004), the authors find that controlling for Hicks-neutral technological differences across countries is quite important. In particular, capital does not seem to be a "friend" of manufacturing after controlling for international TFP differences that affect the productivity of all factors of production equally. However, skilled labor seems to play an important, favorable role, on average, when one assumes that there are no systematic technological differences across countries.

However, the evidence also suggests that allowing for differences in the Rybczynski coefficients across countries changes the picture significantly. Developing economies, with relatively lower endowments of skilled labor, exhibit statistically significantly different coefficients than their high-skill counterparts within industries. In addition, these differences could be associated with the rise of foreign direct investment since the 1990s, when its importance relative to domestic investment rose, particularly in low- and middle-income countries. From the viewpoint of economies such as the Dominican Republic, which developed comparative advantage in several manufacturing industries, the evidence implies that export-oriented manufacturing industries do require substantial numbers of unskilled workers relative to skilled workers. In turn, the authors conjecture that specializing in manufacturing exports that are in part driven by foreign direct investment is unlikely to raise the skilled-labor premium, precisely because these industries seem to be relatively intensive in the use of unskilled labor in economies with relatively low numbers of skilled workers.

Annex 2A

Exports and Imports

The data on trade come from UN Comtrade and cover 129 countries and 28 ISIC manufacturing industries over the 1976–2014 period.[8] Five-year average exports and imports are constructed for each country-industry pair. For the first period in the data set, the average is available for 4 years of data (1976–79). The resulting data set contains average exports and imports by country and industry over eight five-year periods (1976–79, 1980–84, 1985–89, 1990–94, 1995–99, 2000–2004, 2005–09, and 2010–14). The panel is balanced for 49 countries and unbalanced for the rest due to insufficient time or industry coverage. For example, data for Albania, Armenia, Estonia, the Islamic Republic of Iran, Kazakhstan, and the Kyrgyz Republic are available starting in 1995; and for Bulgaria, the Czech Republic, Croatia, Hungary, Latvia, and Lithuania, among others, starting in 1990. Trade data impose the main constraint on country coverage of the final sample.

Stock of Skilled and Unskilled Labor

The data on international educational attainment come from Barro and Lee (2013). Secondary and tertiary completion ratios and population data for each age group are used to compute the stock of skilled and unskilled labor between ages 25 and 64. These data are available for 146 countries in five-year increments between 1950 and 2010. Educational attainment data availability imposes the main constraint on the time coverage of the sample. For this reason, the data set is constructed to include five-year averages of trade data and initial factor endowments at the beginning of each five-year period.

Capital Stock

The data on capital stock and TFP come from the Penn World Tables, and are available for 166 countries from 1950 to 2011. Capital stock and TFP in 1975, 1980, 1985, 1990, 1995, 2000, 2005, and 2010 are used as initial values for each five-year period. For 142 countries, the capital stock data are available for all years. For 24 countries (primarily former Soviet republics and Eastern European countries), the capital stock data are available since 1990. TFP data are missing for about 56 countries.

Arable Land

The data on arable land are derived from World Bank's World Development Indicators (WDI) and span 205 countries over 1975–2010. For each five-year period, data for the following years are used as initial values: 1975, 1980, 1985, 1990, 1995, 2000, 2005, and 2010.

Table 2A.1 Data Availability, by Country and Year Span

Country code (ISO)	Year(s)	Country code (ISO)	Year(s)	Country code (ISO)	Year(s)
ARG	1980–2010	IDN	1975–2010	RUS	1995–2010
ARM	1995–2010	IND	1975–2010	RWA	1995–2010
AUS	1975–2010	IRL	1975–2010	SAU	1975–2010
AUT	1975–2010	IRN	1995–2010	SEN	1975–2010
BDI	1990–2010	IRQ	2000–10	SGP	1975–2010
BEN	1990–2010	ISL	1975–2010	SLE	1980, 2000
BGR	1990–2010	ISR	1980–2010	SRB	1990–2010
BHR	1990–2010	ITA	1975–2010	SVK	1990–2010
BLX	1975–2010	JAM	1975–2010	SVN	1990–2010
BOL	1975–2010	JOR	1980–2010	SWE	1975–2010
BRA	1980–2010	JPN	1975–2010	SWZ	2000–2005
BRB	1980–2010	KAZ	1995–2010	TGO	1975–2010
BWA	2000–2010	KEN	1980–2010	THA	1975–2010
CAF	1980–2010	KGZ	1995–2010	TJK	2000
CAN	1975–2010	KOR	1975–2010	TTO	1975–2010
CHE	1975–2010	KWT	1985–2010	TUN	1980–2010
CHL	1980–2010	LKA	1975–2010	TUR	1985–2010
CHN	1985–2010	LSO	2000–2010	TZA	1995–2010
CIV	1975–85, 1995–2010	LTU	1990–2010	UKR	1995–2010
CMR	1975–2010	LVA	1990–2010	URY	1980–2010
COL	1975–2010	MAR	1975–2010	USA	1975–2010
CRI	1985–2010	MDA	1990–2010	VEN	1980–2010
CYP	1975–2010	MEX	1985–2010	ZAF	1975–2010
CZE	1990–2010	MLT	1990–2010	ZWE	1980–2010
DEU	1975–2010	MNG	1995–2010		
DNK	1975–2010	MOZ	1990–2010		
DOM	1990–2010	MRT	1995–2010		
ECU	1975–2010	MUS	1980–2010		
EGY	1980–2010	MYS	1975–2010		
ESP	1975–2010	NAM	2000–2010		
EST	1995–2010	NER	1975–80, 1995–2010		
FIN	1975–2010	NLD	1975–2010		
FJI	1980–90, 2000–10	NOR	1975–2010		
FRA	1975–2010	NZL	1975–2010		
GAB	1980, 1990–2005	PAN	1985–2010		
GBR	1975–2010	PER	1975–2010		
GRC	1975–2010	PHL	1975–2010		
GTM	1985–2010	POL	1980–2010		
HKG	1975–2010	PRT	1975–2010		
HND	1985–2010	PRY	1980–2010		
HRV	1990–2010	QAT	1980–2010		
HUN	1990–2010	ROM	1985–2010		

Note: ISO = International Organization for Standardization.

Final Sample

The final sample contains data on exports and imports for 28 ISIC manufacturing industries over the period 1975–2010 in five-year averages, as well as TFP, capital stock, stock of skilled and unskilled labor, and endowment of arable land at the beginning of each five-year period (1975–2010) for 108 countries. The data availability by country and year is reported in table A.1.

Notes

1. Rybczynksi equations relate commodity outputs to factor endowments. When the stock of one factor increases, the output of the good that is intensive in that factor rises.

2. Leamer (1995) shows that in an open economy with limited influence over world prices, the demand curve for every sector is horizontal, at a wage level defined by the price of goods set by the equally horizontal world (excess) demand for its products. In this context, output and trade volumes no longer shift this infinitely elastic labor demand curve, and many of the most familiar types of technological change do not either.

3. Harrigan (1995) assumes that all countries can access the same technologies, whereas Harrigan (1997) assumes Hicks-neutral technological differences across countries.

4. The authors have chosen the year 2000 because of data availability. They have also ranked countries by the skilled–unskilled labor ratio for each of the available years, and the rank correlation across different years is above 0.98.

5. The ranking by land intensity is the least affected ranking by the productivity adjustment, with the rank correlation standing at 0.75.

6. The authors also explored the possibility of more than one diversification cone by splitting the sample by the capital–unskilled labor ratio. The set of countries is similar to that grouped by skilled-to-unskilled labor ratio, and most important, the Rybczynski coefficients are qualitatively the same. These results are available on request.

7. See Jones (2000) for the theory of internationally mobile productive input.

8. Data may be accessed through the World Integrated Trade Solution (WITS) at http://wits.worldbank.org/.

References

Barro, R. and J.-W. Lee. 2013. "A New Data Set of Educational Attainment in the World, 1950–2010." *Journal of Development Economics* 104: 184–98.

Batista, C., and J. Potin. 2014. "Stages of Diversification in a Neoclassical World." *Economics Letters* 122 (2): 276–84.

Cusolito, A. P., and D. Lederman. 2009. "Technology Adoption and Factor Proportions in Open Economies: Theory and Evidence from the Global Computer Industry." World Bank Policy Research Working Paper 5043, World Bank, Washington, DC.

Djankov, S., C. Freund, and C. S. Pham. 2010. "Trading on Time." *Review of Economics and Statistics* 92 (1): 166–73.

Dornbusch, R., S. Fischer, and P. A. Samuelson. 1980. "Heckscher-Ohlin Trade Theory with a Continuum of Goods." *Quarterly Journal of Economics* 95 (2): 203–24.

Fitzgerald, D., and J. C. Hallak. 2004. "Specialization, Factor Accumulation and Development." *Journal of International Economics* 64 (2): 277–302.

Gill, I., I. Izvorski, W. van Eeghen, and D. de Rosa. 2013. *Diversified Development: Making the Most of Natural Resources in Eurasia.* Washington, DC: World Bank.

Harrigan, J. 1995. "Factor Endowments and the International Location of Production: Econometric Evidence for the OECD, 1970–1985." *Journal of International Economics* 39 (1–2): 123–41.

———. 1997. "Technology, Factor Supplies and International Specialization: Estimating the Neoclassical Model." *American Economic Review* 87 (4): 475–94.

Harrigan, J., and E. Zakrajšek. 2000. "Factor Supplies and Specialization in the World Economy." National Bureau of Economic Research Working Paper 7848 (August), Cambridge, MA, and Federal Reserve Bank of New York Staff Report 107 (August), New York.

Helpman, E., M. Melitz, and Y. Rubinstein. 2008. "Estimating Trade Flows: Trading Partners and Trading Volumes." *Quarterly Journal of Economics* 123 (2): 441–87.

Jones, R. W. 2000. *Globalization and the Theory of Input Trade.* Cambridge, MA: MIT Press.

Krugman, P. R. 1980. "Scale Economies, Product Differentiation, and the Pattern of Trade." *American Economic Review* 70 (5): 950–59.

Leamer, E. E. 1984. Sources of Comparative Advantage: Theories and Evidence. Cambridge, MA: MIT Press.

———. 1995. *The Heckscher-Ohlin Model in Theory and Practice.* Vol. 77 of Princeton Studies in International Finance. Princeton, NJ: Princeton University, Department of Economics, International Finance Section.

Morrow, P. M. 2010. "Ricardian–Heckscher–Ohlin Comparative Advantage: Theory and Evidence." *Journal of International Economics* 82 (2): 137–51.

Redding, S. 2002. "Specialization Dynamics." *Journal of International Economics* 58 (2): 299–334.

Romalis, J. 2004. "Factor Proportions and the Structure of Commodity Trade." American Economic Review 94 (1): 67–97.

Schott, P. 2003. "One Size Fits All? Heckscher-Ohlin Specialization in Global Production." *American Economic Review* 93 (3): 686–708.

Vollrath, T. 1991. "A Theoretical Evaluation of Alternative Trade Intensity Measures of Revealed Comparative Advantage." *Review of World Economics* 127 (2): 265–80.

World Bank. 1993. *The East Asian Miracle: Economic Growth and Public Policy.* New York: Oxford University Press.

CHAPTER 3

Labor Income Share and Biased Technical Change

The Case of the Dominican Republic

Javier E. Baez, Andrés García-Suaza, and Liliana D. Sousa

Even as the Dominican Republic's economy has experienced a healthy period of growth, averaging 4.6 percent per year between 2000 and 2014, poverty reduction has been modest. At 41.8 percent, official poverty in 2013 remained above the level recorded in the year 2000—32.6 percent. A central factor underlying this country's lack of inclusive growth is an apparent disconnect between labor productivity and labor earnings. In line with its very strong output growth, the Dominican Republic also recorded high rates of labor productivity between 2000 and 2013. Commonly cited estimates indicate that productivity increased by 39 percent during this period. However, real wages followed an opposite trend, falling between the late 1990s and 2004—a trend intensified by the

The authors express their gratitude to collaborators for their useful comments on data analysis and interpretation—namely, Maritza Garcia, Ramón González Hernández, Magdalena Lizardo, Antonio Morillo, Dagmar Romero (Ministerio de Economía, Planificación y Desarrollo, MEPyD), and Elina Rosario (Central Bank of the Dominican Republic). Also to McDonald Benjamin, Oscar Calvo-González, Francisco Carneiro, Gabriela Inchauste, Cecile Niang, Juan Carlos Parra, Mateo Salazar, Diana Sanchez, and Miguel Sanchez (all of the World Bank). This chapter builds on the analysis included in "Do Labor Markets Limit the Inclusiveness of Growth in the Dominican Republic?" a World Bank 2017 publication.

Javier E. Baez is a senior economist with the Poverty and Equity Global Practice for the Africa Region at the World Bank. He holds bachelor of arts and master of science degrees in economics from Universidad de los Andes, a master of arts degree in development economics from Harvard University, and a doctorate in economics from Syracuse University. Please direct correspondence to jbaez@worldbank.org.

Andrés García-Suaza is professor of economics at Universidad del Rosario in Bogotá. He holds a master of science degree in economics from Universidad del Rosario and a doctorate in economics from Universidad Carlos III de Madrid. Please direct correspondence to andres.garcia@urosario.edu.co.

Liliana D. Sousa is an economist with the Poverty and Equity Global Practice for the Latin America and the Caribbean Region at the World Bank. She holds a doctorate in economics from Cornell University. Please direct correspondence to lsousa@worldbank.org.

2003–04 banking crisis—and largely stagnating through 2013. As a result, per-hour real earnings both for wage earners in the private sector and for self-employed wage workers were about 26 percent lower in 2013 than in 2000.

One possible explanation for why growth has not translated into wage increases is the presence of capital-biased technical change. Intuitively, *biased technical change* refers to changes in the relative factor productivity that affect the relative demand for productive factors and their income distribution. Specifically, if technology increases the productivity of capital disproportionately, given the level of substitution between factors, it would be optimal to reduce demand for labor and to increase it for capital. This change reduces the labor income share, the share of total output allocated to worker compensation—and finally, the income growth of households with low capital. As such, biased technical change has implications both for poverty reduction and income inequality.

In this chapter, the recent evolution of the labor income share in the Dominican Republic is analyzed to test whether biased technical change can help explain why strong economic growth has not translated into improved labor market outcomes. More specifically, the analysis focuses on whether wage stagnation—in the context of favorable economic growth—is explained by a decrease in labor income shares. If, indeed, capital-biased technical change is a determining factor, then sectors that experienced higher output growth also experienced a decrease in the labor income share.

In the context of the classical growth model, technical change is represented by the coefficients interacting with productive factors. Understanding these technical coefficients gives important insights into the transformation of an economy over time. In fact, the labor income share summarizes the production structures and technological conditions of sectors—such that variations reflect changes either in the sectoral composition of output or in the structure of factor utilization (Kravis 1962). While for many years, the constancy of the labor share was a reasonable approximation for the data, at the global level, this indicator has shown a steady decline over the past three decades. For instance, Karabarbounis and Neiman (2013) estimated a 5 percentage point decline in the share of global corporate gross value added paid to labor (from 65 to 59 percent) in a sample of 59 countries, with at least 15 years of data during 1975–2012. This decline is found in the large majority of countries and industries. This trend reflects the lower price of investment goods—driving close to half of the labor share decline, the trend of increasing profits and capital-augmenting growth, and skill composition changes of the labor force.

The results indicate that the labor share in the Dominican Republic fell significantly during the 2003–04 banking crisis, which reflected a large wage correction, but had recovered to precrisis levels by 2010. Thus, an improved measurement of labor share for the Dominican Republic is one of the contributions of this analysis. Specifically, it includes adjustments for wages earned in nonincorporated firms, which are relevant given the country's high self-employment and informality rates, and generates comparable labor share figures across two national accounts data series. Falls in the labor share are notable in the sectors largely driving economic growth, possibly owing to biased technical change that increases productivity while lowering demand for labor. In particular, a negative relationship was found between sectoral changes in labor shares and in growth both before and after the crisis. A decomposition analysis found that, in most years, a decrease in labor share *within* sectors actually drove the decrease in labor shares, rather than a change in the sectoral composition of total output.

This chapter examines these phenomena as follows. First, a framework is provided for understanding the potential channels through which biased technical change can be a factor in explaining the stagnant wages seen in the Dominican Republic. Second, the methodological approach to estimating this economy's labor shares is described and implemented. Third, the sectoral dynamics driving the observed labor share trends are considered.

Relationship between Biased Technical Change and Wages

Inspired by Hicks (1932), the original theory of biased technical change argues that the fluctuation of the relative prices of factors produces incentives to implement cost-saving innovations rather than mere factor substitutions. Beyond the relative prices of factors, new inventions, along with efficiency and technification, also induce technical change through variations in relative factor productivity (for pioneer models, see Kennedy 1964 and Binswanger 1974; for a more recent approach, see Zuleta 2008).

The relationship between biased technical change and the labor share is illustrated by the Cobb-Douglas production function. By assuming that, in addition to the classical inputs of capital (K_t in equation 3.1) and labor (L_t), technology can be expressed by a single factor (A_t), then the output elasticities (the exponents of the productive factors) capture each input's marginal productivity or the distribution of total output between the factors.

In a model with two production inputs, capital and labor, a and $1 - a$ are the output elasticities with respect to each of the factors, such that:

$$Y_t = A_t K_t^a L_t^{1-a} \tag{3.1}$$

Assuming that the markets are competitive and, thus, each factor is paid its marginal product, capital is remunerated a total of $1 - a$ percent of total output and labor receives a, referred to as the *labor income share*.

Total multifactor productivity A_t is a source of technical change that affects the returns to both factors in the same way, without altering the proportions of the returns. The characterization of technology by this unique coefficient and the constancy of the output elasticities have been questioned, and additional modeling solutions have been proposed. A natural extension is to allow a to vary over time, implying that factor productivity asymmetrically increases in favor of one factor. This extension provides an intuitive link between labor income share and technological change.[1] In this context, capital-biased technological change means that innovation results in less of one input being used to produce the same amount of output. This difference in the marginal productivity of input factors affects the optimal choice of factors and the relative prices of inputs. In the above-mentioned model with two productive factors (labor and capital), if one becomes relatively more expensive, firms optimally adjust factors by demanding more of the cheaper factor (substitution effect).[2] Thus, if economic growth is accompanied by biased technical change, growth will be distributed between factors according to their shares in the production function.

Kaldor (1957) found that the share of capital and labor in net income is nearly constant over long periods of time. However, recent research has found evidence of the hypothesis of biased technical change across many countries (Valentinyi and Herrendorf 2008; for the United States, Young 2010 and Elsby, Hobijn, and Şahin 2013; for Colombia, Zuleta, Garcia-Suaza, and Young 2009; for Ireland, Sweeney 2014; for China, Bai and Qian 2010; and for Australia, Parham 2013). Karabarbounis and Neiman (2013) documented the global decline of the income labor share in a set of 59 countries. Between 1975 and 2012, they found a decreasing trend of about 5 percentage points, from an average level of 64 percent in 1975.[3] According to the authors, this change was due to declining relative factor prices favoring capital-augmenting technologies through the substitution effect. Similarly, Estrada and Valdeolivas (2012) found that the average decline among selected OECD economies was about 5 percentage points over the same period. Their estimates suggest that technological factors play a larger role in driving decreasing trends in labor share than globalization or labor market institutional factors.[4]

Measuring Labor Income Shares in the Dominican Republic

Using information from the Dominican Republic's System of National Accounts (SNA), particularly the utilization matrixes, income labor shares are computed for the period 1991–2010. Utilization matrixes provide detailed information on factor utilization, intermediate consumption, exports, investment, and government spending at both the aggregate and the sectoral levels.

Because of a break in the SNA series following a methodological update for 2007 onward, information was used from two different SNAs with references: 1991 (covering 1991–2005) and 2007 (covering 2007–10). A key difference between these two series is how income from unincorporated firms, including most self-employment earnings, is reported. In the SNA-1991 series, this income was included as capital earnings, while in the SNA-2007 series, it was reported as a separate type of income. As shown in the next section, this improvement in the data has implications for how labor share is measured across the two series.

Calculating Adjusted Labor Shares

Following the methodology of Bernanke and Gurkaynak (2002) and Gollin (2002), the labor income share was computed as the proportion of the total output used to compensate workers (shown in equation 3.2). That is, a is the ratio between labor compensation and total output net of taxes on production and imports, which is given by:

$$a_t = \frac{WM_t}{Y_t} \qquad (3.2)$$

where WM is the salary mass and $Y = VA - DT$ is the total value added or aggregate value after direct taxes.

Estimating each component in equation 3.2 requires various assumptions. For example, the SNA reports net taxes on production and imports as one amount, making no distinction over taxes on labor or capital. Therefore, an underlying assumption in this equation is that the labor share is measured as the share of after-tax output.[5]

The break in the SNA series resulted from improvements in measurement (including improved data collection) and methodology undertaken by the Dominican authorities, so that the two series are not strictly comparable. However, because the break in the series occurs in 2006—only two years after the 2003–04 banking crisis—some differences in the two series might also be due to changes in the economy owing to the crisis (figure 3.1). In fact, the years between the SNA-1991 series and the beginning of the SNA-2007 series are high-growth years representing an economic recovery.

As the results in figure 3.2 show, several key sectors of employment show significant changes in the estimated pre- and postcrisis labor shares. Hotels, bars, and restaurants, an important sector in a country with an advanced tourism industry, saw a significant increase in the labor share between the two series—from an average of 0.23 during the precrisis period (1999–2002) to an average of 0.40 in the new series (2007–10). Although this change may reflect an increase in the proportion of compensation allocated to labor in this sector, it may instead be due to increased formalization in the sector or improved measurement of

Figure 3.1 Annual GDP per Capita Growth Rate during Two SNA Series, 2000–14

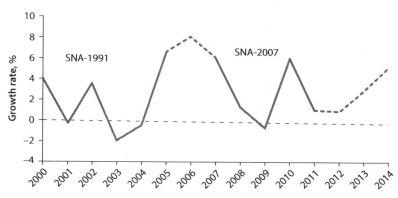

Source: Data from World Development Indicators, World Bank.
Note: SNA = System of National Accounts. Plotting the GDP per capita growth rate by year, the solid line represents years with an SNA series, and the dashed line, those in which the SNA series data are unavailable.

Figure 3.2 Pre- and Postcrisis Labor Income Shares, by Sector, 1999–2002 versus 2007–10

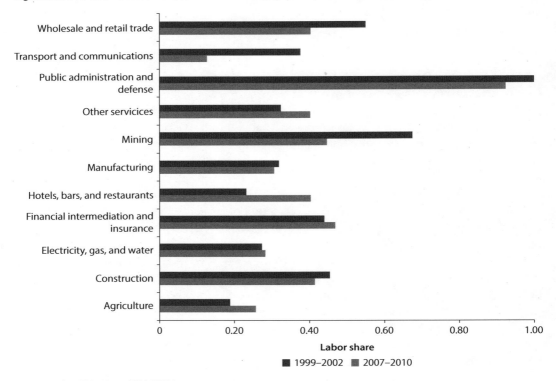

Source: Based on SNA-1991 and SNA-2007 data.
Note: SNA = System of National Accounts.

wages and salary in SNA-2007. On the other hand, the transportation and communications sectors saw a drop in labor share, from 0.38 in the precrisis period to 0.13 in the new series. The transportation sector is highly informal, with significant levels of self-employment. Along with a significant correction downward for the communications sector, resulting from the rebasing for SNA-2007, this change in the labor share level appears to reflect the effect of improved measurement of informal activity in the transportation sector. The financial intermediation and insurance sector, a highly formal sector that was at the center of the 2003–04 crisis, did not see significant changes in its pre- and postcrisis labor share: the sector increased from an average of 0.44 to an average of 0.47. Similarly, labor shares in the manufacturing and utilities sectors (electricity, gas, and water) remained very similar between the two periods.

However, the labor remuneration amounts recorded in the SNAs are limited to wages and salaries from incorporated firms. In the Dominican Republic, the labor market features high informality rates: about 40 percent of workers are self-employed and another 31 percent work for microenterprises of fewer than five workers, greatly increasing the likelihood of informality. While SNA-1991 includes all output from unincorporated firms (including self-employment) as part of the remuneration of capital, the SNA-2007 includes it as a residual amount named *gross mixed income* (GMI). Since self-employment and unincorporated firms are typically less capital-intensive than incorporated firms, the implicit inclusion of GMI in capital remuneration in the original series underestimates the labor share.

To address this issue, the approach by Gollin (2002) is applied to estimate the labor share, under the assumption that GMI is either labor income or a mix of capital and labor income.[6] To do so, two alternative labor income share estimates are computed (equation 3.3 and figure 3.3). First, $a(1)$ assumes that GMI is labor income, which produces an upper bound on the labor income share. The assumption is that the production technology used by self-employed persons and unincorporated firms is predominantly labor-intensive.

More formally:

$$a(1)_t = \frac{WM_t + GMI_t}{Y_t} \qquad a(2)_t = \frac{WM_t}{Y_t - GMI_t} \qquad (3.3)$$

On the other hand, $a(2)$ assumes that GMI is distributed proportionally to preserve the relationship between labor income and capital income with respect to the total (net) product less GMI. This adjustment follows the same logic as the distribution of taxes on production and imports discussed above. This approach implicitly assumes that labor and capital shares are the same for incorporated firms, unincorporated firms, and self-employed persons. Given the importance of self-employment in the Dominican Republic and its propensity to be labor-intensive, most of this analysis uses $a(1)$.

Figure 3.3 Labor Income Shares Based on Two GMI Assumptions, 2007–10

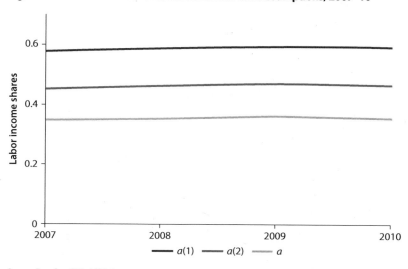

Source: Based on SNA-2007 data.
Note: SNA = System of National Accounts.

Since GMI is not observable in SNA-1991, an adjustment factor was constructed to estimate labor shares for the period 1991–2005, using information from SNA-2007. Previous studies have proposed to impute the GMI as a proportion of the value-added equivalent to the ratio of self-employment to employment. The working assumption behind this approach is that capital and labor are equally productive in the unincorporated sector. However, analysis of SNA-2007 reveals that this results in an overestimation of the GMI share because the self-employed earn less than larger producers (see figure 3.4):

Figure 3.4 Self-Employment Rates and GMI Shares, by Sector, 2007–10

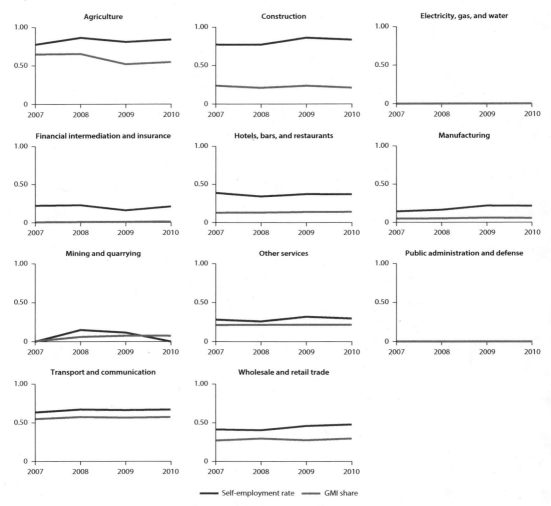

Source: Based on self-employment rates from the ENFT and on GMI share from SNA-2007.
Note: GMI = gross mixed income; ENFT = National Labor Force Survey (Encuesta Nacional de Fuerza de Trabajo); SNA = System of National Accounts.

$$\widehat{GMI}_t = (1-a)Y_t \left[\frac{GMI}{(1-a)Y} \right]_{SNA-2007} \qquad (3.4)$$

Instead, because we have sectoral GMI information from SNA-2007, the GMI share is imputed in each sector in SNA-1991 as the sector's average GMI share to capital income (known as *gross operating surplus*) during 2007–10. In particular, at the sectoral level, it was assumed that the GMI share in SNA-1991 is equivalent to the average GMI share measured in SNA-2007 (equation 3.4). This builds on the observation that self-employment rates have not changed substantially and on assumptions that the following has not changed significantly between the two series: (a) the relationship between self-employment and the GMI share and (b) the measurement of labor share.[7] Indeed, sectoral-level analysis of self-employment rates show they have been stable across time, and for the years with GMI and self-employment data, are highly correlated to the GMI with a correlation of 0.84. This approach also exploits sectoral differences to improve the quality of the adjusted series by imputing at the sector level; for instance, while for the transportation and communications and the agricultural sector, the GMI share is above 59 percent of the value added; in those sectors such as the manufacturing and the hotel, bar, and restaurant (HBR) sectors, this share is 13.2 percent and 5.7 percent, respectively.

Figure 3.5 shows the difference in labor income share between the pre- and postcrisis periods for labor share measured as *a* and for adjusted labor share measured as *a(1)*, the preferred approach. As can be seen from the figure, the adjusted labor share, which takes advantage of the distinction between capital income and GMI in SNA-2007 smooths the differences between the two series at the sectoral level. This finding suggests that the new SNA benefits from improved measurement of the informal sector.

Using the adjusted national accounts data, the calculations show that the labor share in the Dominican Republic remained at approximately 0.57–0.58 throughout the 1990s. This share dipped during the 2003–04 crisis, but as the labor market recovered, as shown by falling unemployment, so has the labor share (figure 3.6). While the SNA series comparability ends in 2005, this year already recorded the beginning of a recovery, with labor share climbing to 0.53. While the 2007–10 series is not strictly comparable, the data suggest that the country's labor share may have reverted to its precrisis level.

While the true level of the labor share in the Dominican Republic can only be approximated, a few important conclusions can be drawn from the trends in figure 3.6. First, the trends do not suggest a significant shift in the labor share, except during the crisis of 2003–04. The labor share fell sharply between 2002 and 2004, from 0.56 to approximately 0.51. The decline coincided with the crisis period, when prices, particularly wages, underwent a severe correction. It is noteworthy that because the same deflator is used for both the numerator

Figure 3.5 Growth in Labor Income Share between the Pre- and Postcrisis Periods, Using Labor Share *a* and Adjusted Labor Share *a(1)*

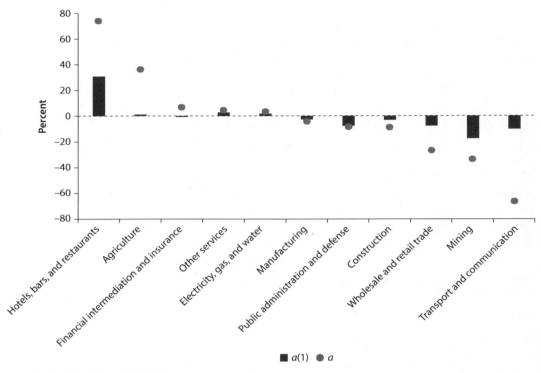

■ *a*(1)   ● *a*

Source: Based on SNA-1991 and SNA-2007 data.
Note: SNA = System of National Accounts.

Figure 3.6 Completed Labor Share Series for the Dominican Republic, 1991–2010

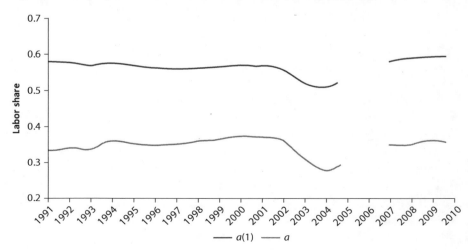

—— *a*(1)   —— *a*

Source: Based on SNA-1991 and SNA-2007 data with gross mixed income adjustments.
Note: SNA = System of National Accounts.

and the denominator, labor income share is not affected by nominal price changes. Instead, the fall of the labor share during the crisis was more likely related to a reduction in the level of employment and the resulting reduction in the total wage bill. In fact, the labor share in the Dominican Republic shows some association with the evolution of the unemployment rate, falling when unemployment increases and recovering as unemployment falls. The end of the first series, SNA-1991, shows the beginning of the recovery in 2005. While SNA-2007 is not strictly comparable to the original series, the result of this analysis suggests a return to the labor share seen before the crisis.

At first glance, the finding that the labor share in the Dominican Republic has recovered following the crisis is surprising because, despite increasing output per worker and increasing labor income share, wages have not recovered. The combination of increasing output per worker and stagnant wages would suggest that the labor income share has fallen. However, closer examination reveals that, while wages are lower, the total number of hours worked has increased by almost as much as real wages have fallen (figure 3.7). Because of the way labor income share is calculated (that is, as the proportion of total output used to compensate total labor), the trends in labor share are not affected by changes in hourly wage levels accompanied by compensating changes in the number of hours worked.

Figure 3.7 Indexes of Labor Share, Total Labor Hours, and Real Hourly Wage, 2000–10

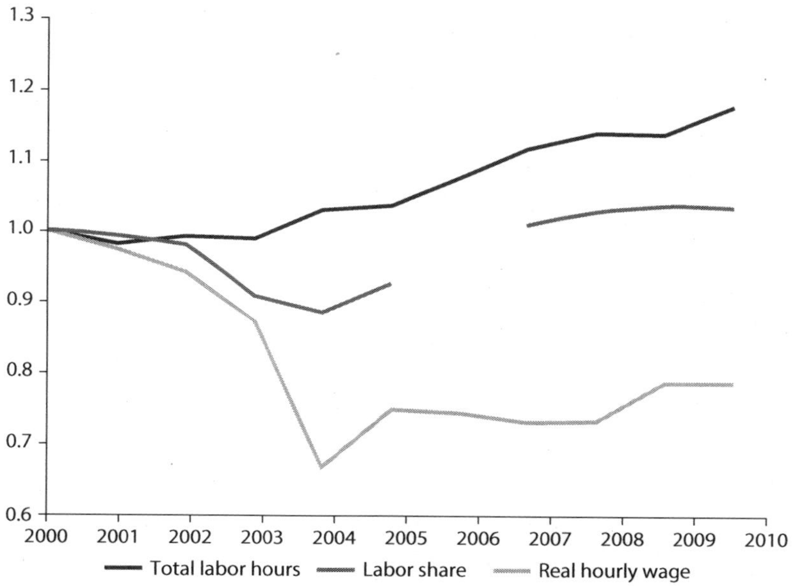

Source: Based on ENFT and labor share estimates from SNA-1991 and SNA-2007 with GMI adjustments.
Note: Trends are indexed to 2000 = 1. Break in labor share line denotes the years with no SNA information.
ENFT = National Labor Force Survey (Encuesta Nacional de Fuerza de Trabajo); SNA = System of National Accounts.

International Comparison of Labor Shares

To place Dominican labor share levels in context, we compare the above estimates with labor shares for some countries in the Latin America and Caribbean region (LAC) and two high-income countries, Germany and the United States (table 3.1). Comparison of labor shares across countries is difficult, owing to limited comparability and coverage of the national accounts. However, standardized national accounts time series show that the labor share in the Dominican Republic is in line with that of other countries in the region if looking at *a(1)*.[8] Because the endpoint of the Dominican series in 2005 may still have been a period of labor share recovery following the 2003–04 crisis, table 3.1 also includes the adjusted series through 2010. Except for Honduras, the labor shares of the LAC region countries included in this analysis are significantly lower than those of Germany and the United States, countries with higher shares of skilled workers and lower rates of informality. This observation implies that between 50 and 60 percent of output in LAC region countries remunerates labor, compared with over 70 percent in Germany and the United States.

Notably, most of the countries considered, including Germany and the United States, saw a reduction in their labor share. As with the above-mentioned studies (see, for instance, Estrada and Valdeolivas 2012; and Karabarbounis and Neiman 2013), the labor share reduction is about 4 to 5 percentage points for many countries. Although the labor share in the

Table 3.1 Labor Share for the Dominican Republic and Selected Countries, by Initial Labor Share

Country	Period		Labor share		Annualized growth rate (%)
	Initial year	Final year	Initial year	Final year	
Dominican Republic	1991	2005	0.580	0.531	−0.64
Precrisis only	1991	2002	0.580	0.562	−0.29
Adjusted series	1991	2010	0.580	0.593	0.11
LAC region countries					
Brazil	2000	2009	0.604	0.609	0.09
Chile	1996	2009	0.557	0.513	−0.63
Colombia	1994	2005	0.695	0.616	−1.09
Guatemala	2001	2012	0.584	0.555	−0.46
Honduras	2000	2012	0.668	0.698	0.37
Mexico	1993	2004	0.601	0.559	−0.66
Panama	1997	2012	0.522	0.476	−0.61
Uruguay	1998	2005	0.639	0.578	−1.42
High-income countries					
Germany	1995	2012	0.72	0.674	−0.39
United States	1990	2012	0.71	0.673	−0.24

Source: Based on National Accounts Statistics (UNSTATS) and on SNA-1991 and SNA-2007 data for the Dominican Republic.
Note: SNA = System of National Accounts.

Dominican Republic fell between 1991 and 2005, a significant part of this reduction may have resulted from the 2003–04 crisis because 2005 was still a recovery year. If one looks only at the precrisis period, the labor share in this country fell by about 0.14 percent per year. If it is assumed, however, that SNA-2007 results in a level comparable to the earlier series, then labor share grew at an annualized rate of 0.11 percent per year between 1991 and 2010, bucking trends in most other countries. Honduras and Brazil also exhibit increases in their labor income shares.

Despite the important differences in the levels of labor income shares, there are interesting common features in term of tendencies. For example, the dynamics of the labor income share are not smooth (figure 3.8). Despite a clear pattern during the medium and long terms, labor income shares are quite volatile and seem to respond to fluctuations in business cycles: the (pooled) correlation between labor shares and GDP growth rates is 33.1 percent. This finding suggests that results in this type of analysis, including those in table 3.1 should be interpreted carefully because they are sensitive to the selection of beginning and ending years.

Figure 3.8 Trends in Labor Income Share for the Dominican Republic and Selected Countries, 2000–10

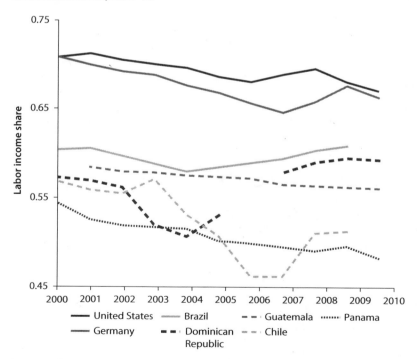

Source: Based on National Accounts Statistics (UNSTATS) and SNA-1991 and SNA-2007 data for the Dominican Republic.
Note: SNA = System of National Accounts.

Labor Income Shares and Biased Technical Change in the Dominican Republic

Building on the measurement exercise presented above, which suggests that the economywide labor share in the Dominican Republic has recovered following the 2003–04 crisis and may have grown between 1990 and 2011, this section tests for evidence of biased technical change. Specifically, it explores the changes in sectoral labor share and sectoral composition of output that underlie the economywide labor share trend presented above. In a situation of capital-biased technical change, favorable macroeconomic performance does not necessarily result in favorable labor market changes because the relative contribution of workers to output falls, causing gains in economic growth to be concentrated in remunerating capital. This generates a cycle in which technical change increases capital income shares, fosters growth, and produces higher incentives to invest in capital-intensive technologies, as explained by Zuleta and Young (2013).

Although evidence of decreased labor share was not found at the economy-wide level in the Dominican Republic, this may be obfuscating changes at the sectoral level. If labor-saving innovations lead to an increase in labor productivity (and, hence, a reduction in labor demand for a fixed level of output), sectors experiencing higher output growth from these innovations may also experience larger falls in the labor income share. For example, investment in telecommunications and information technology can reduce the demand for hotel reservation specialists.[9]

As noted by Abdullaev and Estevao (2013), economic output growth has been concentrated in just a few sectors in the Dominican Republic, and this growth has not necessarily been correlated with employment growth. Specifically, sectors like hotels, bars, and restaurants (HBR); financial intermediation and insurance (FII); electricity; and transportation and communications exhibit the most important economic growth during the period 2001–10 (table 3.2).[10] During 2001–05, the HBR sector's output grew at an annualized rate of 7.0 percent, while transportation and communications grew at 11.4 percent. On the other hand, while 2001–05 was not a high-growth period for FII, in part owing to the banking crisis of 2003–04, this sector grew at an annualized rate of 11.5 percent between 2007 and 2010. Even so, during both periods, FII was the sector with the largest employment increase, growing at an annualized rate of 5.0 percent between 2001 and 2005 and 7.4 percent between 2007 and 2010. Among these dynamic sectors, only HBR experienced a slowdown in its output and employment growth rate during 2007–10. This correlated with employment trends in the sector: HBR had big gains in employment during 2001–05, growing by 3.3 percent per year, but slowed during the second period to just 0.8 percent per year. On the other hand, key sectors such as agriculture and manufacturing grew at slower output rates (respectively, by 1.9 percent and 3.6 percent annualized rate during 2001–05). While manufacturing shed a significant number of jobs during 2007–10, decreasing employment by 7.4 percent per year, its output grew by 2.8 percent per year.

Table 3.2 Sectoral Annualized Output and Employment Growth Rates, 2001–05 versus 2007–10

Percent

Sector	2001–05		2007–10	
	Output	Employment	Output	Employment
Agriculture	1.9	1.3	4.7	4.7
Mining and quarrying	5.5	−4.5	−29.9	5.0
Manufacturing	3.6	2.0	2.8	−7.4
Electricity, gas, and water	−4.9	−2.2	6.2	6.9
Construction	−1.9	2.2	2.0	−1.2
Wholesale and retail trade	0.4	2.0	5.1	3.9
Hotels, bars, and restaurants	7.0	3.3	1.5	0.8
Transport and communications	11.4	0.6	11.3	3.5
Financial intermediation and insurance	1.9	5.0	11.5	7.4
Public administration and defense	3.9	1.2	1.5	6.0
Other services	8.5	0.6	4.2	3.5
Overall	*4.8*	*1.7*	*5.3*	*1.8*

Source: Based on ENFT data for employment rates and on SNA-1991 and SNA-2007 data for output growth.
Note: ENFT = National Labor Force Survey (Encuesta Nacional de Fuerza de Trabajo); SNA = System of National Accounts. Sectors are ordered by Standard Industrial Classification code.

During the first decade of the 2000s, the sectors underlying much of the Dominican Republic's economic growth saw reductions in their labor income share, possibly reflecting technical change that has led to lower demand for labor. During this decade, there was an inverse relationship between changes in the sector's labor income share and the sector's share of value added (that is, the sector's contribution to economic growth). This relationship is seen not only during the 2003–04 crisis, which included a severe wage correction, but also in the second half of the decade (figure 3.9). Between 2001 and 2005, the only sector that saw an increase in both the labor income share and the value-added share was agriculture. Except for agriculture and transportation and communications, all other sectors whose importance in terms of output increased saw a reduction in their labor income share.

This trend of declining labor income share among sectors of growing importance in output is particularly notable in two sectors employing a large share of low-skilled workers: HBR and wholesale/retail trade (commerce). Workers in HBR, for example, saw their labor share fall by an average of 5.1 percent per year during 2001–05. During 2007–10, workers in this same sector saw an increase in the labor share, equivalent to 6 percent per year—however, HBR's contribution to economic growth fell by 3 percent per year. Between 2007 and 2010, the sectors with the largest growth in labor share were those whose share of value added fell. However, three sectors saw both an increase in the labor share and the value-added share—these include commerce and transportation, two sectors employing many low-skilled workers.

Figure 3.9 Annualized Change in Labor Income Share and Value-Added Share, 2000–05 and 2007–10

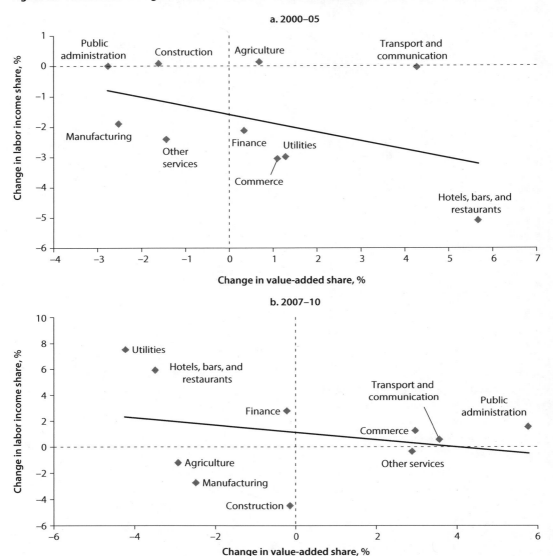

Source: Based on SNA-1991 and SNA-2007 data for output growth.
Note: SNA = System of National Accounts.

A plausible interpretation for the negative relationship between the value-added share and the labor income share is that the sectors that have grown more have seen larger investments in capital-biased technical change, which in turn can result in higher productivity and output growth even as labor costs fall. This insight suggests that recent macroeconomic growth has been potentially driven by biased technical change.[11]

As there is significant heterogeneity across sectors, to systematically assess the evolution of the aggregate labor income share, a decomposition was performed to quantify the importance of (a) change in sectoral labor income shares and (b) the change in the sector's importance on the labor income share of the total economy. To be specific, aggregate income share can be written as the weighted sum of sectoral income shares (equation 3.5). That is:

$$a_t = \sum_i w_i a_{i,t} \tag{3.5}$$

where a_i is the labor income share of the sector i and w_i is its relative size in the economywide labor share. In this scenario, aggregate labor income shares can grow when sectors with higher levels of labor share increase their relative size, even as the sectoral labor income shares remain constant.

The change in the aggregate labor income share is written as shown in equation 3.6):

$$\Delta\alpha_t = \sum_i w_{i,t-1}\Delta\alpha_{i,t} + \sum_i \left(\alpha_{i,t-1} - \alpha_{t-1}\right)\Delta w_{i,t-1} + \sum_i \Delta\alpha_{i,t}\Delta w_{i,t} \tag{3.6}$$

where the first term is the *within* variation, the second term is the *between* variation, and the last component represents the variation of the aggregate labor income share owing to the co-movement of sectoral labor income shares and sectoral size (see Foster, Haltiwanger, and Krizan 2001; Young 2010; and Zuleta, Garcia-Suaza, and Young 2009).

The results indicate that most variation in the aggregate labor share between 1991 and 2005 is due to the *within* component (figure 3.10). That is, the changes in labor share are driven by decreases in the labor share within sectors

Figure 3.10 Decomposition of the Labor Income Share by Sectoral Changes, 1991–2005

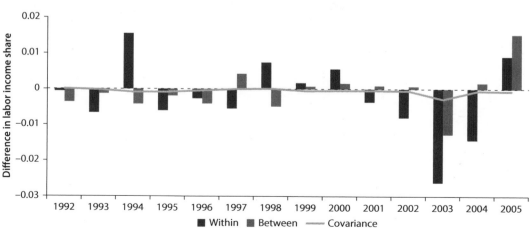

Source: Based on SNA-1991 and SNA-2007 data for output growth.
Note: SNA = System of National Accounts.

rather than by changes in the sectoral composition of output. This is evident mainly in the decreasing pattern that took place beginning in the early 2000s. Even so, the *between* component also explains some of the total variation of the labor share in the Dominican Republic, and this effect has tended to be positive since the late 1990s. This suggests that labor has been moving toward sectors in which the labor share has grown; yet, the pattern of negative values of the within-factor with positive values of the between-factor implies that this positive movement has happened even while the labor shares in these sectors were falling.

Conclusion

The Dominican Republic's remarkable high growth has had only limited success in decreasing poverty. Instead, average wages have remained largely stagnant since the 2003–04 crisis. One possible explanation is that the country's growth has been capital-biased—such that the returns to growth are largely accruing to capital rather than to labor. While the break in SNA series in the Dominican Republic poses a significant challenge to assessing whether a change in the labor share has occurred, the new SNA-2007 series, with its improved measurement of output of the informal sector, also presents an opportunity to better estimate the labor share in the Dominican Republic.

Using information on the output of informal activity as captured by the GMI in the SNA-2007 series, an adjusted labor share series is estimated for the Dominican Republic, stretching from 1991 to 2010. At about 0.59, the Dominican Republic's labor share is in line with the labor share of other LAC countries, though lagging that in the advanced economies of Germany and the United States. Unlike in those countries, in which the labor share has exhibited a downward trend, the Dominican series suggests that the labor share fell significantly during the country's 2003–04 crisis—but that it has recovered. Indeed, the analysis suggests a slight increase in labor share between 1991 and 2010. Despite the growing gap between output and wages following the crisis, at the aggregate, the share of output allocated to labor compensation has not fallen. Instead, labor market indicators suggest that the total number of hours worked has increased—in other words, to compensate for lower wages, workers have increased their labor supply.

The analysis also documents a negative relationship between sectoral changes in labor income share and the change in the value-added share, showing that sectors that increase in importance in output have reduced their labor share. A decomposition analysis reveals that changes in labor share are driven by decreases in labor share *within* sectors more than by changes in the sectoral composition of output. This is consistent with the presence of capital-biased technical change and the adoption of labor-saving innovations that increase per-worker output even as they decrease the demand for labor at a given output level.

While suggestive, this analysis is not conclusive. More research is needed into the topic of technical change in the Dominican economy to better understand whether capital-biased technical change can explain the country's stagnant wages and, by extension, the lack of poverty reduction during most of the past decade. Yet, building from the results of this analysis, a possible explanation is that the complementarity between capital and unskilled labor has led capital-intensive sectors to grow faster, generating relatively more demand for unskilled labor. In turn, this has led to a growing gap between productivity and wages because jobs requiring fewer skills and, hence, paying lower wages would have been created at a faster pace. High capital costs, such as large real estate investments, can be combined with significant low-wage employment, resulting in a capital-intensive sector that also employs large numbers of workers. A relevant example of this type of sector is tourism, which requires significant capital investments and employs large numbers of low-skilled workers. Combined with the destruction of manufacturing jobs, this type of job growth could result in the observed growing gap between productivity and wages.

Notes

1. Alternatively, we can think of a situation in which technology is multidimensional and includes several technology coefficients, one for each productive factor, as follows:

$$Y_t = \left(A_t^K K_t \right)^\alpha \left(A_t^L L_t \right)^{1-\alpha}$$

The behavior of these technology coefficients, A_t^K and A_t^L, may differ over time, for example, if new inventions make capital relatively more productive or change the degree of substitutability between them, producing differences in the ratios between them. For the sake of simplicity, and without losing generality, the classical Cobb-Douglas production function with time-varying output elasticities was kept.

2. This is typically due to differential trends in productivity across factors, but could as well be the result of the relaxation of barriers in the factor markets or changes in the market power (which determine changes in the wedge between the marginal product and the price of a factor).

3. The baseline evidence reported by the authors refers to the income labor share of the corporate sector because this allows them to circumvent some measurement difficulties in order to separate labor and capital income entrepreneurs, sole proprietors, and unincorporated businesses.

4. Similar findings have been reported using cross-sectional data by the International Monetary Fund (IMF 2007), the European Commission (2007), Jacobson and Occhino (2012), and OECD (2012).

5. Gomme and Rupert (2004) note that for some activities, such as self-employment, the distinction between factors' compensation is not clear. They postulate a set of guidelines and considerations needed to get precise estimates of the factors' compensation and output: proprietors' income cannot be trivially divided between labor and capital; the public sector lacks capital (biasing upward the estimate of the labor share); and the housing sector lacks labor (biasing downward the estimate of the labor share). Even though the level of the labor income compensation might be misestimated owing to these and other potential measurement errors, its trend is, in general, robust.

6. Similarly, Guerriero (2012) constructs alternative labor income shares under different treatments of GMI, using data from 89 developed and developing counties. Although the level differs significantly across the different assumptions, the trend of the labor income share is similar.

7. Estimates from the Dominican Republic's ENFT labor force survey indicate small fluctuations in self-employment between 2000 and 2013, with the rate fluctuating from a low of 37 percent to a high of 42 percent during this period; in 2013, the self-employment rate was 39 percent, similar to the 2000 rate of 37 percent.

8. Relying on data for 11 countries from the SNA standardized by the United Nations, labor income shares were estimated according to $a(1)$, that is, assuming that GMI is labor income. Owing to SNA updates across the sample of countries, SNA methodology with the longest time series over the past two decades for each country was selected.

9. Analogous results and explanations have been documented for Colombia over a similar timespan (Zuleta, Garcia-Suaza, and Young 2009).

10. Public sector output is largely measured as public wages (Gomme and Rupert 2004) rather than economic value added (because many of the goods and services are not priced). As such, output is not comparable to the other sectors. It is included in the tables in this section for completeness, but interpretation should be limited.

11. An alternative explanation is that labor is becoming less productive relative to capital.

References

Abdullaev, U. and M. Estevão. 2013. "Growth and Employment in the Dominican Republic: Options for a Job-Rich Growth." International Monetary Fund Working Paper WP/1340, International Monetary Fund, Washington DC.

Bai, C., and Qian, Z. 2010. "The Factor Income Distribution in China: 1978–2007." *China Economic Review* 21 (4): 650–70.

Bernanke, B., and R. Gurkaynak. 2002. "Is Growth Exogenous? Taking Mankiw, Romer, and Weil Seriously." *NBER Macroeconomics Annual 2001* 16: 11–72.

Binswanger, H. 1974. "A Microeconomic Approach to Induced Innovation." *Economic Journal* 84 (326): 940–58.

Elsby, M. W., B. Hobijn, and A. Şahin. 2013. "The Decline of the US Labor Share." *Brookings Papers on Economic Activity* 2: 1–63.

Estrada, A., and E. Valdeolivas. 2012. "The Fall of the Labour Income Share in Advanced Economies." Documentos Ocasionales No. 1209, Banco de España, Madrid.

European Commission. 2007. "The Labor Income Share in the European Union." In *Employment in Europe 2007*. Brussels: Directorate-General for Employment Social Affairs and Equal Opportunities, European Commission.

Foster, L., J. Haltiwanger, and C. J. Krizan. 2001. "Aggregate Productivity Growth: Lessons from Microeconomic Evidence." In *New Developments in Productivity Analysis*, edited by C. Hulten, E. Dean, and M. Harper, 303–63. Chicago: University of Chicago Press.

Gollin, D. 2002. "Getting Income Shares Right." *Journal of Political Economy* 110 (2): 458–74.

Gomme, P., and P. Rupert. 2004. "Measuring Labor's Share of Income." Policy Discussion Paperno. 04-07, Federal Reserve Bank of Cleveland.

Guerriero, M. 2012. "The Labour Share of Income around the World: Evidence from a Panel Dataset." WP No. 32/2012, Development Economics and Public Policy Working Paper Series, Institute of Development Policy and Management, School of Environment and Development, University of Manchester, Manchester. http://hummedia .manchester.ac.uk/institutes/gdi/publications/workingpapers/depp/depp_wp32.pdf.

Hicks, J. 1932. "Marginal Productivity and the Principle of Variation." *Economica* 35: 79–88.

IMF (International Monetary Fund). 2007. *Spillovers and Cycles in the Global Economy*. World Economic Outlook: A Survey by the Staff of the International Monetary Fund. Washington, DC: International Monetary Fund. https://www.imf.org/external/pubs /ft/weo/2007/01/pdf/text.pdf.

Jacobson, M., and F. Occhino. 2012. "Behind the Decline in Labor's Share of Income." Policy Discussion Paper, Federal Reserve Bank of Cleveland.

Kaldor, N. 1957. "A Model of Economic Growth." *Economic Journal* 67 (268): 591–624.

Karabarbounis, L., and Neiman, B. 2013. "The Global Decline of the Labor Share." NBER Working Paper 19136, National Bureau of Economic Research, Cambridge, MA.

Kennedy, C. 1964. "Induced Bias in Innovation and the Theory of Distribution." *Economic Journal* 74: 541–47.

Kravis, I. 1962. *The Structure of Income: Some Quantitative Essays*. Philadelphia: University of Pennsylvania Press.

OECD (Organisation for Economic Co-operation and Development). 2012. "Labour Losing to Capital: What Explains the Declining Labour Share?" In *Employment Outlook 2012*. Paris: OECD Publishing. http://dx.doi.org/10.1787/empl_outlook -2012-en.

Parham, D. 2013. Labour's Share of Growth in Income and Prosperity. Visiting Researcher Paper Series. Canberra: Australian Government Productivity Commission.

Sweeney, P. 2014. "An Inquiry into the Declining Labour Share of National Income and the Consequences for Economies and Societies." *Journal of the Statistical and Social Inquiry Society of Ireland* 42: 109–29.

Valentinyi, A., and B. Herrendorf. 2008. "Measuring Factor Income Shares at the Sectoral Level." *Review of Economic Dynamics* 11: 820–35.

Young, A. 2010. "One of the Things We Know That Ain't So: Is US Labor's Share Relatively Stable?" *Journal of Macroeconomics* 32 (1): 90–102.

Zuleta, H. 2008. "Factor Savings Innovations and Factor Income Shares." *Review of Economic Dynamics* 11 (4): 863–51.

Zuleta, H., A. Garcia-Suaza, and A. Young. 2009. "Factor Shares at the Sector Level, Colombia 1990–2005." Documento de Trabajo 76, Universidad del Rosario, Bogotá.

Zuleta, H., and A. Young. 2013. "Labor Shares in a Model of Induced Innovation." *Structural Change and Economic Dynamics* 24: 112–22.

CHAPTER 4

Wage Effects of Haitian Migration in the Dominican Republic

Liliana D. Sousa, Diana Sanchez, and Javier E. Baez

The Dominican Republic's immigrant population has grown over the past 15 years, representing over 5 percent of the country's population in 2012.[1] About 9 out of 10 immigrants are from neighboring Haiti. At the same time, despite being one of the fastest-growing economies in Latin America, real wages in the Dominican Republic have remained fairly stagnant following the country's recovery from the 2003–04 banking crisis. Wages across all skill groups were about 30 percent lower in real terms in 2013 compared with 2000 (World Bank 2017). As in other immigrant-receiving countries, labor market challenges have resulted in concerns that immigration may be leading to decreased employment opportunities for local workers—and thus contributing to the country's stagnant wages and low rate of poverty reduction.

The authors express their gratitude to collaborators for their useful comments on data analysis and interpretation, namely, Maritza Garcia, Magdalena Lizardo, Antonio Morillo, and Dagmar Romero (Ministerio de Economía, Planificación y Desarrollo, MEPyD). Also to McDonald Benjamin, Oscar Calvo-González, Francisco Carneiro, Gabriela Inchauste, Cecile Niang, Juan Carlos Parra, Mateo Salazar, and Miguel Sanchez (all of the World Bank). This chapter builds on analysis included in "Do Labor Markets Limit the Inclusiveness of Growth in the Dominican Republic?" (World Bank 2017).

Liliana D. Sousa is an economist with the Poverty and Equity Global Practice for the Latin America and the Caribbean Region at the World Bank. She holds a doctorate in economics from Cornell University. Please direct correspondence to lsousa@worldbank.org.

Diana Sanchez-Castro is a consultant in the Development Data Group at the World Bank. She holds a postgraduate degree in statistics from the Universidad Nacional de Colombia. Please direct correspondence to dmarce.sanchezc@gmail.com

Javier E. Baez is a senior economist with the Poverty and Equity Global Practice for the Africa Region at the World Bank. He holds bachelor of arts and master of science degrees in economics from Universidad de los Andes (Bogotá), a master of arts degree in development economics from Harvard University, and a doctorate in economics from Syracuse University. Please direct correspondence to jbaez@worldbank.org.

What effect, if any, does Haitian immigration have on the wages of the native born in the Dominican Republic? This is the key question being explored in this chapter. Based on a classical model of a closed economy, an increase in the labor supply—for instance, owing to immigration—can lead to wage reductions if immigrants are substitutes for the local labor supply. Under the assumption that immigrant and local labor are imperfect substitutes, increased migration can cause a reduction in the cost of immigrant labor. This can result in two opposing effects: (a) as the cost of immigrant labor falls, firms will substitute immigrant labor for native labor, which is referred to as the *substitution effect* and (b) for a given wage level, firms will employ more native workers as output grows, which is called the *scale effect*.

How do the substitution and scale effects play out in the Dominican economy? As shown below, there is evidence that Haitian immigrants do not represent a good substitute for local labor because these workers have significantly lower educational attainment than their Dominican counterparts and face linguistic barriers. Nevertheless, immigration could result in more competition for unskilled jobs, reducing wage growth for the least skilled, while simultaneously increasing returns to capital—to the degree that capital is complemented by unskilled labor.

In this chapter we test the hypothesis that higher Haitian immigration results in lower wages for local workers. The extent to which immigration affects wages in local labor markets is mostly determined by whether immigrants' skills substitute for or complement those of local workers. If their skills are substitutes, these can result in local workers facing increased competition for jobs. On the other hand, if their skills are complements, these can lead to increased demand for local workers as output increases. Haitian workers are highly clustered in the Dominican Republic, not just geographically but also in the labor market, working primarily as unskilled labor in three sectors: agriculture, commerce, and construction. In this context, the heterogeneity of the distribution of Haitian immigrant workers in this country is exploited to test for an empirical relationship between the size of the local Haitian immigrant population and wages of local Dominican-born workers. The empirical exercise suggests no negative relationship between the proportion of the local labor force that is Haitian-born and the wages of local workers. Given the relatively low levels of schooling among Haitian immigrants and the high levels of unemployment among Haitian immigrant women, Dominican-born men with low levels of schooling are the group expected to be most directly affected by Haitian migration. Testing for wage effects across gender and skill groups does not yield a negative effect or correlation between immigration and local wages.

The empirical analysis does not find evidence supporting the hypothesis that Haitian labor in the Dominican Republic has led to stagnating wages for local workers. While data limitations reduce the extent to which this question can be fully explored, the available data suggest relatively few work opportunities for Haitian-born labor in the Dominican Republic. This is also supported by the finding that a significant majority of Haitian immigrant workers are employed in unskilled and informal employment in agriculture, commerce, and construction, suggesting a limited role for immigrant labor in Dominican employment.

The increase in unskilled labor from Haiti cannot on its own explain why wages fell across the board in the Dominican Republic, by similar margins, for highly skilled workers and unskilled workers in both the formal and informal sectors.[2]

The remainder of this chapter is structured as follows. The first section reviews the literature, and the second discusses data challenges in researching immigration and wage effects in the Dominican Republic. The third section describes key characteristics of Haitian migration, and the fourth section presents the empirical model and results.

Literature Review

Most international studies exploring the role of substitution and scale effects of migration have found little or no effect of immigration on native wages (Peri 2014). Card (2009) finds that immigrant and native workers in the United States of similar skill level are imperfect substitutes; instead, additional immigration flows have stronger effects on earlier waves of immigrants than on native workers. Ottaviano and Peri (2011) also find evidence of imperfect substitution between immigrant and native workers in the United States. They estimate that, from 1990 to 2006, immigration had a small effect on the wages of unskilled native workers (those with no high school degree), resulting in a wage increase of between 0.6 percent and 1.7 percent. That is, immigrants were *complements* for low-skilled native labor. On the other hand, immigration had a large negative effect (−6.7 percent) on the wages of previous immigrants. Some studies, however, have found negative wage effects on low-skilled native labor resulting from an increase in the low-skill labor supply. For example, Borjas (2006) estimates that a 10 percent increase in a given skill group's labor supply (from immigration) reduces earnings by close to 4 percent.

However, most studies of the impact of immigrant labor on local labor markets analyzed developed economies; thus, they might not have captured the dynamics of migration in less-developed economies in which institutions and labor markets might differ substantially. Looking at the South-South migration flow between Nicaragua and Costa Rica, Gidding (2009) concludes that, on average, there is no statistically significant relationship between workers' earnings and the share of Nicaraguan immigrants—even after disaggregating them by skill level and gender. The study found no statistically significant relationship between an increased supply of immigrant labor and the earnings of local male workers, including those unskilled workers who are most likely to compete with immigrant labor.

Gidding's study, however, finds a relationship between immigration and female wages. In particular, the study finds a negative effect on wages of low-skilled women and a positive effect on those of women with more schooling. This finding suggests that Nicaraguan immigrants are substitutes for low-skilled Costa Rican women and complements for more-educated women. A potential interpretation of these findings is that both of these effects are driven by domestic workers, the sector of employment for a significant share of Nicaraguan female immigrants. While immigrant domestic workers replace unskilled local workers, the lower costs of domestic workers may allow more women to work outside of the home.

Instrumenting for changes in immigration flows into Malaysia by using population changes in the source countries, Del Carpio et al. (2013) find evidence that international immigration leads to the in-migration of natives and better employment outcomes for native labor. Their analysis suggests that the scale effect—that is, increased demand for local labor as output increases—dominates the substitution effect of immigrant labor in the Malaysian labor market.

Historically, Haitian migration to the Dominican Republic was dominated by rural workers migrating to work in agriculture, particularly sugarcane. However, Duarte and Hasbún (2008) and Silié, Segura, and Dore y Cabral (2002) document a significant change in the Haitian migration stream during the past 20 years. As the Dominican Republic has developed economically and become increasingly urbanized, immigrants have become more likely to migrate from urban areas in Haiti and work in construction. Previous research focused on the Dominican Republic has found some evidence to support the hypothesis that unskilled Haitian migration has negative, but small, effects on the labor market outcomes of Dominican workers and capital owners. Notably, Aristy-Escuder (2008) finds evidence that Haitian immigrant workers earn lower wages than similarly qualified Dominican workers, substituting local low-skilled labor while complementing capital and high-skilled native labor. He estimates a negative but relatively modest native-wage elasticity of −0.37 in the construction sector: that is, a 10 percent increase in the population resulting from immigration reduces average Dominican wages in the construction sector by 3.7 percent.

Data Challenges

A significant challenge to measuring the impact of migration on wages is the scarcity of data on Haitian migration to the Dominican Republic. It is believed that this population is not well measured in official statistics, including the 2002 and 2010 Population and Housing censuses.

The preferred data source on immigrants for this country is the Encuesta Nacional de Inmigrantes de la Republica Dominicana (National Survey of Immigrants from the Dominican Republic, ENI-2012), a national survey collected in 2012 focused exclusively on the country's immigrant population. This survey estimated a total immigrant population of just under 525,000, implying that 5.4 percent of the country's population is foreign-born. Of these, 87 percent are from Haiti (table 4.1). The survey also identified 240,000 individuals (2.5 percent of the total population) with at least one foreign-born parent. However, it is believed that the population of Haitian immigrants and their descendants may have been underestimated, owing to the difficulty of measuring

Table 4.1 Basic Demographics of Haitian Immigrants, by Province Group, 2012

	Total	Group 1	Group 2	Group 3	Group 4	Group 5
Total immigrants						
Population	524,677	250,653	68,976	81,391	65,450	58,206
Percent		47.8	13.1	15.5	12.5	11.1
Haitian immigrants						
Population	458,233	213,915	65,546	70,196	60,353	48,223
Percent		46.7	14.3	15.3	13.2	10.5
Percent of all immigrants	87.3	85.3	95.0	86.2	92.2	82.8
Haitian immigrants only (%)						
Male	65.4	61.9	61.7	69.4	72.9	70.6
Labor force participation rate						
(age 15 and over)	76.5	74.4	82.2	71.6	81.3	79.3
Male	89.4	86.7	95.7	83.5	94.8	94.1
Female	50.9	53.8	58.9	43.3	42.6	41.6
Age distribution						
Under 15	8.5	8.0	13.8	6.4	8.3	6.5
15–24	28.8	28.7	34.1	20.4	32.6	29.6
25–44	52.8	56.6	41.3	54.1	51.2	51.4
45–65	8.0	5.6	9.7	13.6	6.6	9.8
65 and over	1.9	1.1	1.0	5.5	1.2	2.6
Years since migration						
< 1 year	14.7	12.9	22.5	9.8	17.3	15.8
1 year	10.7	13.3	8.3	6.8	10.0	9.0
2 years	9.7	12.0	6.5	7.7	8.9	8.1
3–5 years	18.1	19.4	14.2	20.6	16.2	16.4
6–10 years	15.3	14.1	14.8	16.5	17.5	16.8
11–20 years	13.0	11.5	14.9	14.5	13.0	14.9
21–30 years	3.3	2.0	3.4	7.2	3.6	3.0
More than 30 years	3.2	1.8	2.0	8.2	1.9	5.1
Unknown	12.0	13.0	13.5	8.7	11.5	11.0

Source: Based on ENI-2012 data.

Note: The five province groups are (a) Group 1, *large urban centers,* including the Federal District and the provinces of Santiago and Santo Domingo; (b) Group 2, *provinces near the border,* including Bahoruco, Barahona, Dajabón, Elías Piña, Independencia, Monte Cristi, Pedernales, and San Juan; (c) Group 3, *provinces where sugarcane is grown,* including El Seibo, La Altagracia, La Romana, Puerto Plata, and San Pedro de Macorís; (d) Group 4, *provinces where rice and plantains are produced,* including Azua, Duarte, María Trinidad Sánchez, Monseñor Nouel, Sánchez Ramírez, and Valverde; and (e) Group 5, *provinces with low immigration,* including Espaillat, Hato Mayor, Hermanas Mirabal, La Vega, Monte Plata, Peravia, Samaná, San Cristóbal, Santiago Rodríguez, and San José. ENI = Encuesta Nacional de Inmigrantes de la Republica Dominicana (National Survey of Immigrants from the Dominican Republic).

a largely poor, undocumented population. In fact, in 2012 only 7 percent of Haitian-born immigrants in the Dominican Republic had a Dominican identification card according to ENI-2012. Lack of documentation was also an issue for the Dominican-born of Haitian descent, among whom only 53 percent possessed a Dominican identification card.[3]

Though the ENI-2012 survey's estimate of the immigrant population is higher than that of the 2010 Dominican census, it is not clear how severe the undercount in the census was relative to the survey. The 2010 census counted nearly 312,000 Haitian-born immigrants in the country, while ENI-2012 counted about 460,000 two years later. However, the survey also found that a quarter of these immigrants, over 116,000, had only arrived in the Dominican Republic in the past two years, that is, *after* the census was collected. One possible reason for the high rate of recent immigrants is the presence of high rates of circular migration, for example, for seasonal work during periods of high demand. This does not appear to be the case because, despite the relative ease of border crossing between the two countries, 76 percent of surveyed Haitian immigrants had only migrated to this country once. This implies that a significant share of the Haitian-born population in the Dominican Republic in 2012 were recently arrived immigrants. In other words, the undercount in the census might not be as severe as the initial comparison suggests.

The empirical strategy employed in this chapter relies on ENI-2012, national labor force surveys (Encuesta Nacional de Fuerza de Trabajo, ENFT), and 2002 and 2010 census data. Even if the census undercounts immigrants, *to the extent that this undercount is evenly distributed across the country*, it remains a valuable data source because it is the only source that allows for disaggregated geographical information on immigration in the Dominican Republic. Although nationally representative, ENI-2012 can only provide subnational statistics representative of agglomerations of provinces.[4] As a result, in this study, both data sources are used: ENI-2012 is used to provide a more complete context for the characteristics of the Haitian immigrant population in this country. Meanwhile, as described in greater detail below, a combination of the 2002 and 2010 censuses was used, along with annual labor force surveys, to estimate an empirical model of the effect of Haitian migration on local wages.

Characteristics of Haitian Migration in the Dominican Republic

The impact of migration on native wages depends on the extent to which immigrant and native labor are substitutes or complements. Key characteristics of Haitian migration in the Dominican Republic suggest that the potential for substitution is limited. Notably, the data reveal that (a) labor demand is limited for Haitian-born women in this country; (b) Haitian immigrants are geographically and occupationally clustered; and (c) Haitian immigrants have significantly lower levels of human capital (schooling and Spanish language skills) than local labor. These three factors, on their own, suggest that any direct negative impact on wages from Haitian migration will be limited to certain groups of workers, particularly unskilled men.

ENI-2012 shows that Haitian immigrants are mostly working age (80 percent) and male (65 percent). Over half (53 percent) of Haitian immigrants are between the ages of 25 and 44, whereas another 29 percent are between 15 and 24. The gender bias is most pronounced in those parts of the country that receive

Map 4.1 Haitian Immigrants versus Total Dominican Population, Percent, 2010

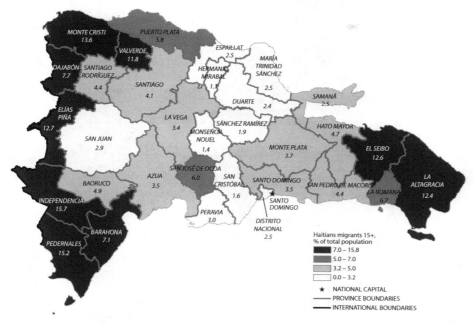

Source: Estimates based on the Dominican Republic 2010 census.
Note: This map shows Haitian immigrants (age 15 and over) as a share of the total population.

fewer immigrants: more than 70 percent of the Haitian-born in the province group known for the production of rice and plantains and the group of provinces with lower immigration are men.[5] Immigrant women from Haiti report levels of labor force participation in line with other women in the Dominican Republic (50.9 percent) but face higher unemployment rates (26.3 percent). This is in stark contrast to the outcomes of their male counterparts—89 percent of Haitian male immigrants are in the labor force, with an unemployment rate of 8.3 percent.

According to ENI-2012, nearly half (47 percent) of Haitian immigrants are concentrated in the country's two large urban centers (the Santo Domingo and Federal District area and the province of Santiago). In contrast, 15 percent live in provinces where sugarcane is grown, and 14 percent in provinces close to the Haitian border. The 2010 census yields a slightly different picture of the geographic distribution of the Haitian-born population, finding that the two largest urban centers are home to only about one-third of Haitian immigrants. It also reports that the Haitian-born represent a higher share of the local population in more sparsely populated parts of the country (map 4.1). Notably, in provinces along the Haitian border and in the eastern part of the Dominican Republic, provinces that are home to significant tourism (La Altagracia) and agriculture (El Seibo) as well as those where sugarcane is grown, the Haitian-born represent more than 7 percent of the population.[6]

Figure 4.1 Distribution of Educational Attainment: Haitian Immigrants versus Overall Dominican Adult Population, 2012

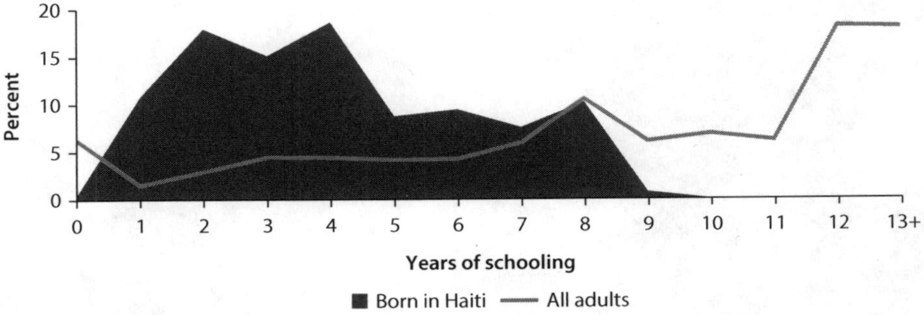

Sources: Estimates based on ENI-2012 data (for Haitian immigrants and Haitian descendants) and 2012 ENFT data (for all adults).
Note: ENFT = Encuesta Nacional de Fuerza de Trabajo (National Labor Force Survey); ENI = Encuesta Nacional de Inmigrantes de la Republica Dominicana (National Survey of Immigrants from the Dominican Republic).

Most important, the Haitian-born are overrepresented among the least-skilled workers: the average years of schooling of a working-age Haitian immigrant were 4.1 in 2012 compared with about 9 years for those born in the Dominican Republic (figure 4.1).[7] In some provinces with high immigration rates—notably El Seibo, Independencia, La Altagracia, Monte Cristi, Pedemales, and Valverde—the 2010 census suggests that Haitian immigrants represent over 20 percent of adults who did not complete primary school. Given the significantly lower educational attainment of Haitian immigrants than most Dominican-born workers, if there is substitution of native labor with immigrant labor, unskilled native labor would be the group that would be most adversely affected by job competition owing to migration. Another human capital factor that could limit the substitutability of local labor with Haitian immigrant labor is the latter's limited Spanish-language skills: only 9.8 percent of Haitian immigrants reported speaking Spanish *very well,* and another 25.3 percent reported speaking Spanish *well,* according to ENI-2012 tabulations.

Haitian-born workers are highly concentrated in two employment sectors—agriculture and construction. Although these sectors employ 72 percent of Haitian-born immigrant laborers, they employ only 7 percent of Dominican-born workers (table 4.2).[8] Conversely, despite accounting for only 7.5 percent of the total Dominican labor force 15 years of age and older, the Haitian-born comprise 21 percent of all agricultural workers and 16 percent of all construction workers. These shares vary significantly across the country—for example, among agricultural workers, the Haitian-born make up half of the labor force in Valverde and about one-third in El Seibo, La Romana, and San Pedro de Macoris. In La Altagracia and Puerto Plata, 40 and 30 percent, respectively, of construction workers were of Haitian birth. Although construction and agriculture are

Table 4.2 Employment Status and Sector of Haitian Immigrants, by Gender and Province Group, 2012

	Men (%)					
	Total	Group 1	Group 2	Group 3	Group 4	Group 5
Employment status						
Unemployed	7	10	4	6	7	5
Out of the labor force	10	13	4	15	5	4
Sector						
Primary sector	33	4	74	21	74	67
Commerce	9	14	6	5	5	4
Construction	26	42	5	31	6	13
Electricity, gas, and water	0	0	0	0	0	0
Financial intermediation and insurance	1	2	1	1	0	0
Hotel, bar, and restaurant	1	1	0	4	0	1
Manufacturing	3	3	3	8	1	1
Mining	0	0	0	0	0	0
Public administration and defense	0	0	0	0	1	0
Transport and storage	2	3	1	3	1	0
Other services	5	8	1	6	1	2
Unknown	1	1	1	0	0	0
	Women (%)					
	Total	Group 1	Group 2	Group 3	Group 4	Group 5
Employment status						
Unemployed	14	15	10	17	10	14
Out of the labor force	49	46	41	55	58	58
Sector						
Primary sector	5	1	20	1	11	5
Commerce	15	16	14	13	15	14
Construction	1	1	0	0	0	1
Electricity, gas, and water	0	0	0	0	0	0
Financial intermediation and insurance	0	0	0	0	0	0
Hotel, bar, and restaurant	3	4	3	5	2	2
Manufacturing	1	1	0	1	1	0
Mining	0	0	0	0	0	0
Public administration and defense	0	0	0	0	0	0
Transport and storage	0	1	0	0	0	0
Other services	11	15	11	7	2	5
Unknown	1	1	1	1	1	1

Source: Based on ENI-2012 data.

Note: The five provincial groups are (a) Group 1, *large urban centers,* including the Federal District, Santiago, and Santo Domingo; (b) Group 2, *provinces near the border,* including Baoruco, Barahona, Dejabón, Elías Piña, Independencia, Monte Cristi, Pedernales, and San Juan; (c) Group 3, *provinces where sugarcane is grown,* including El Seibo, La Altagracia, La Romana, Puerto Plata, and San Pedro de Macorís; (d) Group 4, *provinces where rice and plantains are produced,* including Azua, Duarte, María Trinidad Sánchez, Monseñor Nouel, Sánchez Ramírez, and Valverde; and (e) Group 5, *provinces with low immigration,* including Espaillat, Hato Mayor, Hermanas Mirabal, La Vega, Monte Plata, Peravia, Samaná, San Cristóbal, Santiago Rodríguez, and San José. ENI = Encuesta Nacional de Inmigrantes de la Republica Dominicana (National Survey of Immigrants from the Dominican Republic).

important for low-skilled native labor in the Dominican Republic (together accounting for 29 percent of jobs held by workers who did not finish primary school and 13 percent of jobs held by those who finished primary school or have some secondary schooling), wholesale and retail trade (commerce) is their main sector of employment, accounting for half of the jobs held by these workers. Notably, only 7.2 percent of employed Haitian immigrant women are domestic workers (included in the *other services* entry in table 4.2), a smaller share than expected, given the importance of this sector in female immigrant employment in other countries such as Costa Rica.

The earnings gap between the Haitian-born and the Dominican-born in the construction sector is fully explained by differences in skills, suggesting labor complementarity between the two groups. According to the 2012 Encuesta Nacional de Fuerza de Trabajo (ENFT), Haitian workers earn about 25 percent less than native workers in the construction sector, when adjusting only for region and urban status. This wage gap is fully explained by differences in educational attainment between the two types of workers. This suggests that differences in wages between Dominican- and Haitian-born workers in the construction sector may be related to differences in occupations and tasks, with the higher-skilled Dominicans performing higher-productivity tasks. This is in line with earlier analyses, including World Bank (2012) and an analysis of the construction sector using 2002 data, which find that Haitians earn significantly lower wages and perform very low-skill tasks (Cuello and Santos 2008).

In agriculture, on the other hand, the native–immigrant wage gap of 28 percent (adjusting only for region and urban status) is not fully explained either by worker characteristics (such as education) or by type of employment (wage versus self-employment). Among wage workers, the wage gap is 23 percent, while among the self-employed, it is 20 percent. Because the earnings gap remains for the self-employed, not only the wage employed, this may suggest that Haitian agricultural labor is less productive, perhaps owing to lower access to capital and land.

Despite the concentration of Haitian workers in construction and agriculture, these sectors have not shown different wage trends from other low-skilled sectors. While wages in construction were higher in 2000 than wages in commerce and transportation, following the wage adjustment associated with the crisis of 2003–04, they have been in line with other low-skilled sectors despite the increase in immigrant labor during the postcrisis period (figure 4.2). Of course, the potential wage effects of immigrant labor would not necessarily be limited to the sectors where immigrants are employed. Specifically, one would expect that, as competition for jobs in construction and agriculture intensifies, Dominican-born workers, who may have greater access to other types of employment, would move toward other sectors. This movement would, in effect, increase competition across other sectors, resulting in lower wages across unskilled sectors. Although this is a possibility, the real wages of unskilled workers have followed the same wage trends as those for higher-skilled workers (figure 4.3)—workers who are less

Figure 4.2 Hourly Wage Trends for Unskilled Labor across Sectors, 2000–13

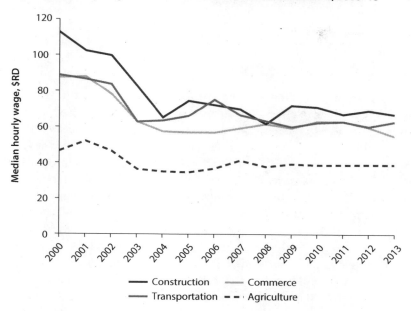

Source: Estimates based on ENFT data.
Note: Wages reported are for workers who did not finish primary school. ENFT = Encuesta Nacional de Fuerza de Trabajo (National Labor Force Survey).

Figure 4.3 Median Hourly Wage Trends by Years of Schooling, 2000, 2004, and 2013

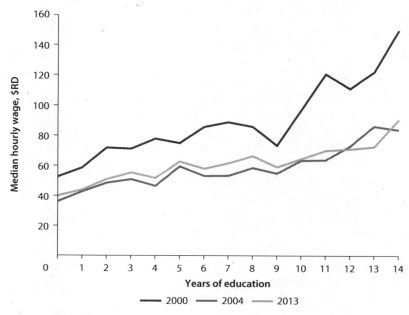

Source: Estimates based on ENFT data.
Note: ENFT = Encuesta Nacional de Fuerza de Trabajo (National Labor Force Survey).

likely to be adversely affected by Haitian immigration. Across the skill distribution, as measured by years of schooling, real wages in 2013 were substantially lower than in 2000 and at the same level as in 2004.

Local Wage Effects of Haitian Workers

The degree to which Haitian immigrants are concentrated in few employment types as well as their relatively low educational attainment suggest limited substitution of immigrant labor for local labor. In this section we test this hypothesis by exploiting the geographical dispersion patterns of Haitian immigrants across the country. To estimate the effects of inflows of migration on the local labor market, previous research in this field has exploited differences in the geographical distribution of immigrants to assess their impact on the employment outcomes, including wages, of the local population.[9] One of the challenges associated with this strategy is the possibility that local economic conditions will affect both the wages of local workers and the flow of immigrant labor, generating a spurious relationship between wages and migration. Beginning with Altonji and Card (1991), an empirical approach often undertaken in the literature has been to use information about an earlier distribution of immigrants as an instrument for future flows of immigrants. The theory behind this instrument is twofold: (a) owing to the importance of social networks, immigrants tend to migrate to areas where co-ethnics have migrated before, hence, the earlier distribution of immigrants is a predictor for future flows, independent of local labor conditions; and (b) local labor markets adjust to labor inflows after some years, hence, earlier inflows of immigrants would not directly affect current labor market conditions.

In theory, even though Haitian unskilled labor is clustered in specific parts of the country, the effect on native wages and employment could be dispersed throughout other regions if immigrant inflows were to cause internal migration of local labor to other parts of the country. For instance, the displacement of local unskilled labor by immigrant labor close to the border could lead to an inflow of native workers to other parts of the country, thus reducing wages across the Dominican Republic. The evidence, however, does not suggest that competition with Haitian labor is causing unskilled Dominican laborers to move to other parts of the country through indirect adjustments of the labor market. Instead, data from the 2002 and 2010 censuses suggest a positive correlation between Haitian immigrant inflows and the share of the native population that is unskilled. In other words, provinces with higher shares of unskilled Dominican workers had a higher proportion of Haitian population. The correlation between unskilled local labor and Haitian immigrant populations rose from 0.30 in 2002 to 0.39 in 2010 as immigration rates increased, suggesting a greater concentration of Haitian immigrants in provinces with less-skilled human capital.

To test the hypothesis that competition from Haitian workers has reduced the wages of Dominican workers, the geographical distribution of the Haitian immigration was exploited in equations 4.1 and 4.2 to estimate the following model specifications:

$$\ln\left(w_i\right) = X_i\beta_1 + \beta_2 ln\left(\frac{H_m}{T_m}\right) + e_i \qquad (4.1)$$

$$\ln\left(w_i\right) = X_i\beta_1 + \beta_2 ln\left(\frac{H_{m,s,g}}{T_{m,s,g}}\right) + e_i \qquad (4.2)$$

where the dependent variable is the log of wages of Dominican-born workers, and X_i is a vector of standard worker-level variables associated with earnings (educational attainment, gender, potential experience and its quadratic, employment sector, employment type, region, and urban status). Exposure to Haitian labor is measured as $ln\left(\frac{H_m}{T_m}\right)$, the natural log of the Haitian immigrant share of the local population (the number of adults who were born in Haiti living in municipality m as a share of all adults in municipality m). The coefficient of interest, β_2, estimates the wage premium (in percentage terms) of local Dominican workers associated with the Haitian immigrant share of the local population.

Specification 4.2 further disaggregates this exposure measure by skill group s and gender g, creating "gender-skill" groups. That is, the wages of a man who did not complete primary school are regressed on the proportion of local similar workers (men with incomplete primary school) who were born in Haiti. This specification addresses the possibility that wages are affected by the presence of similar foreign-born workers, rather than by the overall proportion of immigrants in the local labor force. Owing to the potential endogeneity between local labor market conditions and the location choice of immigrants (for example, an area with higher wages could also attract more migration), all regressions were also run using an instrumental variable approach, following the strategy introduced by Altonji and Card (1991), predicting migration rates in 2010 based on the distribution of immigrants in the Dominican Republic in 2002.

Because it is the only data source that can provide geographically disaggregated information on the Haitian immigrant population in the Dominican Republic, the 2010 population census was used to generate measures of local exposure to Haitian immigration.[10] As shown in figure 4.4, there is significant variation across provinces both for the proportion of the adult population born in Haiti as well as the proportion of unskilled adults born in Haiti.

It is important to note that the census data are believed to undercount the immigrant population. The empirical model employed here is robust in cases of population undercounts, as long as this undercount is orthogonal to the dependent variable and the share of the local population that was born in Haiti. In other words, as long as the undercount is not related to local native wage levels or the size of the local Haitian-born population, the sign of the coefficient β_2 is robust even though its magnitude may be overestimated.

These exposure measures are merged to the 2010 ENFT labor force survey, the Dominican Republic's primary source of labor force data, including

Figure 4.4　Haitian-Born as a Proportion of Unskilled Adult Population, by Municipality, 2010

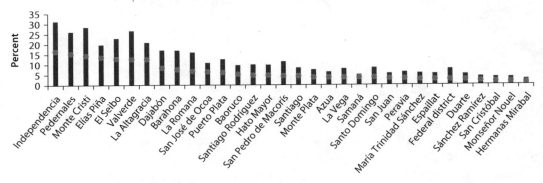

■ Share of Haitian-born local population who did not complete primary school
● Share of Haitian-born local population

Source: Based on the Dominican Republic's 2010 census data.

Figure 4.5　Correlation between the Local Unskilled Population Born in Haiti and the Wages of Dominican-Born Unskilled Workers, 2002 and 2010

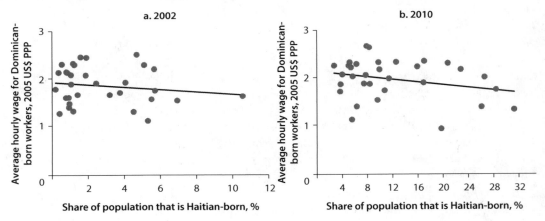

Source: Based on 2002 and 2010 Dominican Censuses, 2002 ENFT, and 2010 ENFT.

nationally representative wage data for Dominican workers. Figure 4.5 shows that there is a negative correlation at the province level between the share of the local population that is Haitian-born and the average hourly wage for Dominican-born workers. In other words, before controlling for individual characteristics, Dominican workers report lower wages in provinces with higher shares of Haitian immigrants. This correlation, however, does not control for differences in human capital and locality effects such as rural and urban differences.

Equations 4.1 and 4.2 are run on the wages of local nonimmigrant workers—that is, the sample from the ENFT is limited to individuals born in the Dominican

Table 4.3 Estimated Relationship between the Haitian-Born Share of the Local Labor Market and the Wages of Dominican-Born Workers

Exposure measure: log of share of local working age population that is Haitian-born

	Ordinary least squares			Instrumental variable		
	All	Incomplete primary	Primary complete	All	Incomplete primary	Primary complete
Haitian share (municipality)	0.0234	0.0231	0.0150	0.0188	0.0487*	−0.00140
	(0.0157)	(0.0212)	(0.0346)	(0.0204)	(0.0272)	(0.0453)
Male	0.173***	0.113***	0.278***	0.173***	0.113***	0.278***
	(0.0202)	(0.0366)	(0.0425)	(0.0202)	(0.0364)	(0.0422)
Experience	0.0256***	0.0230***	0.0219***	0.0257***	0.0231***	0.0219***
	(0.00155)	(0.00266)	(0.00394)	(0.00155)	(0.00266)	(0.00391)
Wage worker	−0.809***	−0.981***	−0.569***	−0.809***	−0.984***	−0.570***
	(0.0454)	(0.0951)	(0.0997)	(0.0453)	(0.0947)	(0.0990)
Self-employed	−0.751***	−0.902***	−0.456***	−0.751***	−0.903***	−0.457***
	(0.0454)	(0.0918)	(0.0987)	(0.0453)	(0.0914)	(0.0980)
Urban	−0.115***	−0.149***	−0.230***	−0.115***	−0.150***	−0.231***
	(0.0191)	(0.0269)	(0.0373)	(0.0191)	(0.0268)	(0.0371)
Education controls	X			X		
Region controls	X	X	X	X	X	X
Sector controls	X	X	X	X	X	X
Constant	0.669***	0.794***	0.500***	0.673***	0.760***	0.525***
	(0.0663)	(0.124)	(0.139)	(0.0685)	(0.125)	(0.145)
First stage F-test	n.a.	n.a.	n.a.	727.41	355.95	206.69
First stage T-test	n.a.	n.a.	n.a.	102.01	70.09	49.34
Observations	7,367	3,257	1,820	7,363	3,256	1,818
R-squared	0.285	0.182	0.159	0.285	0.182	0.159

Source: Estimates based on 2010 ENFT and the Dominican 2002 and 2010 censuses.
Note: ENFT = Encuesta Nacional de Fuerza de Trabajo (National Labor Force Survey); *n.a.* means = not applicable; X = a set of controls was included in the model. Share of local population of Haitian birth is reported in logs; estimated at the municipal level, using 2010 census tabulations; and instrumented, using 2002 census tabulations. Dependent variable is log of hourly wage of Dominican-born workers. Standard errors in parentheses.
***$p < 0.01$, **$p < 0.05$, *$p < 0.1$.

Republic who reported positive wages. Each specification is run for three sub-samples: (a) all workers, (b) workers who did not complete primary school, and (c) workers who completed primary school but did not complete secondary school. The results for specification 4.1 are reported in table 4.3, and those for specification 4.2 are given in table 4.4.

The first set of results, corresponding to specification 4.1, does not find statistically significant relationships between the earnings of locals and the share of the local population that was born in Haiti. This is true for all workers, as well as for the two groups of unskilled workers (those with incomplete primary school and those who completed primary and did not complete secondary school).

Table 4.4 Estimated Relationship between the Haitian-Born Share of the Local Labor Market and the Wages of Dominican-Born Workers

Exposure measure: log of share of local gender-skill group that is Haitian-born

	Ordinary least squares			Instrumental variable		
	All	Incomplete primary	Primary complete	All	Incomplete primary	Primary complete
Haitian share (municipality)	0.0469***	0.0155	0.00442	0.0586**	0.0752**	−0.0286
	(0.0133)	(0.0231)	(0.0335)	(0.0230)	(0.0315)	(0.0575)
Male	0.145***	0.105***	0.276***	0.141***	0.0783**	0.292***
	(0.0218)	(0.0382)	(0.0458)	(0.0244)	(0.0392)	(0.0518)
Experience	0.0256***	0.0230***	0.0219***	0.0252***	0.0233***	0.0210***
	(0.00156)	(0.00266)	(0.00394)	(0.00161)	(0.00266)	(0.00400)
Wage worker	−0.806***	−0.980***	−0.570***	−0.828***	−0.983***	−0.571***
	(0.0454)	(0.0951)	(0.0998)	(0.0469)	(0.0946)	(0.0999)
Self-employed	−0.745***	−0.901***	−0.457***	−0.758***	−0.899***	−0.456***
	(0.0455)	(0.0918)	(0.0988)	(0.0469)	(0.0913)	(0.0989)
Urban	−0.118***	−0.150***	−0.231***	−0.124***	−0.157***	−0.229***
	(0.0192)	(0.0269)	(0.0373)	(0.0200)	(0.0268)	(0.0378)
Education controls	X			X		
Region controls	X	X	X	X	X	X
Sector controls	X	X	X	X	X	X
Constant	0.598***	0.794***	0.517***	0.585***	0.680***	0.564***
	(0.0693)	(0.128)	(0.135)	(0.0814)	(0.134)	(0.144)
First stage F-test	n.a.	n.a.	n.a.	1285.94	349.99	132.96
First stage T-test	n.a.	n.a.	n.a.	67.64	62.61	31.82
Observations	7,341	3,257	1,820	6,831	3,246	1,756
R-squared	0.286	0.182	0.159	0.287	0.183	0.155

Source: Estimates based on 2010 ENFT and the Dominican 2002 and 2010 censuses.

Note: ENFT = Encuesta Nacional de Fuerza de Trabajo (National Labor Force Survey); *n.a.* means = not applicable; X = a set of controls was included in the model. Share of local population who is of Haitian birth is reported in logs and is estimated at the municipal level, using 2010 census tabulations and is instrumented using 2002 census tabulations. Dependent variable is log hourly wage of Dominican-born workers. Standard errors in parentheses.

***$p < 0.01$, **$p < 0.05$, *$p < 0.1$.

The instrumental variable model estimates a weakly significant and economically small positive relationship for the lowest-skilled group, suggesting that an increase of 10 percentage points in the share of the local population that is Haitian-born would yield a wage premium of about half a percent for local workers with an incomplete primary education.

The results of specification 4.2 find a positive yet economically small correlation between the share of workers in a given gender-skill group who were born in Haiti and wages for Dominican-born members of that group. The base specification model, which does not address the endogeneity of immigrant inflows, finds a small positive effect on wages of having a greater share of Haitian immigrants in one's gender-skill group, though this effect is not statistically significant for either of the low-skill groups. After addressing the endogeneity of immigrant inflows, the instrumental variable regressions find a similar effect on overall workers and a larger, statistically significant effect on the lowest-skilled Dominican workers. For Dominican workers who did not finish primary school, the instrumental variable model suggests that an increase of 10 percentage points in the Haitian share of the local population that did not finish primary school results in a wage increase of 0.7 percent. As shown in figure 4.4, this share can reach 30 percent in some provinces, suggesting that in some localities with a high concentration of Haitian workers, local Dominicans who did not complete primary school could be seeing a wage premium of almost 1.3 percent. A small negative coefficient is found for local workers who completed primary school but not secondary school, though this is not statistically significant from 0.

Conclusion

Although the number of Haitian immigrants to the Dominican Republic has increased substantially over the past decade and a half, scant evidence supports the hypothesis that Haitian labor reduces wages for local labor. Instead, the evidence suggests that labor demand for Haitian workers in the Dominican Republic is largely limited to low-wage informal work, particularly in agriculture, commerce, and construction. Applying methods used widely in the immigration literature to the case of the Dominican Republic, a set of wage regressions does not find a negative correlation between the wages of nationals and the share of the local labor force that is Haitian-born. The analysis finds no evidence that even unskilled Dominican men—those who are the most likely to compete directly with Haitian labor—are adversely affected by wages. If anything, the regression analysis suggests an economically small, yet positive, effect on wages for the least-skilled. This may suggest a small scale effect for the least-skilled Dominican workers, wherein the presence of low-skilled Haitian labor increases firm output and, hence, the wages of unskilled local labor.

A significant obstacle encountered in researching the wage effects of immigrants in the Dominican Republic is the limited data available on this topic. While there are legitimate questions on how well this topic can be explored with the available data, to the extent that the geographical distribution of the immigrant population is well measured in the census data, the empirical approach employed in this analysis does not support the hypothesis that competition with Haitian labor can explain why wages in this country have remained stagnant during a time of increased macroeconomic growth. The socioeconomic detail available from ENI-2012, the country's immigrant survey, suggests that Haitian workers remain largely employed in low-productivity and highly informal sectors, particularly in agriculture, construction, and commerce. This is likely due to the less-skilled human capital base of Haitian immigrants— in particular, as measured by educational attainment and Spanish-language skills, compared with native Dominican workers. This limits their ability to compete for better-quality jobs and higher wages. An increase in unskilled labor from Haiti cannot, on its own, explain why wages have remained stagnant across all skill levels for Dominican workers. This analysis further suggests that this increase in immigrant labor also does not explain why wages have remained stagnant for unskilled workers.

Notes

1. Owing to data limitations in the 2010 census, only individuals born outside of the Dominican Republic are considered immigrants for the purposes of this report.

2. According to World Bank (2017), "Compared to their level in 2000, wages for workers with one or more years of education were on average 34 percent lower during the time of domestic crisis. The rapid post-crisis growth period did not do much to return wages to their baseline. As of 2013, real wages remained 31 percent below the level observed in 2000."

3. In 2014, the Domican Republic began implementing its National Plan of Regularization, including the passage of Law 169–14, for the purpose of registering individuals without documentation. An estimated 55,000 Dominicans of Haitian descent registered through 2015.

4. Specifically, ENI's national coverage is split between five groups of provinces: (a) the large urban centers include the Federal District and the provinces of Santiago and Santo Domingo; (b) the provinces near the border include Baoruco, Barahona, Dejabón, Elías Piña, Independencia, Monte Cristi, Pedernales, and San Juan; (c) the provinces where sugarcane is grown include El Seibo, La Altagracia, La Romana, Puerto Plata, and San Pedro de Macorís; (d) the provinces where rice and plantains are produced include Azua, Duarte, María Trinidad Sánchez, Sánchez Ramírez, Valverde, and Monseñor Nouel; and (e) the provinces with low immigration include Espaillat, La Vega, Peravia, Hermanas Mirabal, Samaná, San Cristóbal, Santiago Rodríguez, Monte Plata, Hato Mayor, and San José.

5. See note 4 above for a list of provinces by group.

6. Between 2002 and 2010, the regions that saw the highest growth in local Haitian population were those along the border with Haiti.

7. Educational attainment is from ENI-2012 for the Haitian-born population and from the 2010 census for the Dominican-born population.

8. These estimates are based on the 2010 census. ENI-2012 finds that 62 percent of jobs of Haitian-born labor in the Dominican Republic are in these two sectors.

9. An example of this methodology is given by Bertrand, Luttmer, and Mullainathan (2000).

10. As mentioned above, in interpreting these results, it is important to note that the census data are believed to undercount the immigrant population. If the undercount was not evenly distributed throughout the country, it may reduce the statistical value of this analysis.

References

Altonji, J. G., and D. Card. 1991. "The Effects of Immigration on the Labor Market Outcomes of Less-Skilled Natives." *Immigration, Trade and Labor*, edited by J. M. Abowd and R. B. Freedman. Chicago: University of Chicago Press.

Aristy-Escuder, J. 2008. "Impacto de la inmigración haitiana sobre el mercado laboral y las finanzas públicas de la República Dominicana." Pontificia Universidad Católica Madre y Maestra Working Paper Series, Santiago de los Caballeros, Dominican Republic.

Bertrand, M., E. Luttmer, and S. Mullainathan. 2000. "Network Effects and Welfare Cultures." *Quarterly Journal of Economics* 115 (3): 1019–55.

Borjas, G. 2006. "Native Internal Migration and the Labor Market Impact of Immigration." *Journal of Human Resources* 41 (2): 221–58.

Card, D. 2009. "Immigration and Inequality." *American Economic Review: Papers & Proceedings* 99 (2): 1–21.

Cuello, M., and F. Santos. 2008. "Costos y beneficios de la mano de obra Haitiana en el sector construcción." Report prepared for Servicio Jesuita a Refugiados/as y Migrantes, Santo Domingo.

Del Carpio, X., C. Ozden, M. Testaverde, and M. Wagner. 2013. "Local Labor Supply Responses to Immigration." *Scandinavian Journal of Economics* 117 (2): 493–521.

Duarte T. I., and J. Hasbún. 2008. *La mano de obra Haitiana en la construcción: Caracteristicas, valoraciones y prácticas*. Report prepared for the Fondo Para el Fomento de la Investigacion Economica y Social (FIES), Santo Domingo.

Gidding, T. H. 2009. "South-South Migration: The Impact of Nicaraguan Immigrants on Earnings, Inequality and Poverty in Costa Rica." *World Development* 37 (1): 116–26.

Ottaviano, G. I., and G. Peri. 2011. "Rethinking the Effect of Immigration on Wages." *Journal of the European Economic Association* 10 (1): 152–97.

Peri, G. 2014. "Do Immigrant Workers Depress the Wages of Native Workers?" IZA World of Labor 2014: 42. doi:10.15185/izawol.42.

Silié, R., C. C. Segura, and C. Dore y Cabral. 2002. *La nueva inmigración haitiana*. Santo Domingo: FLASCO.

World Bank. 2012. *Haiti, Dominican Republic: More Than the Sum of Its Parts*. Washington, DC: World Bank.

———. 2017. "Do Labor Markets Limit the Inclusiveness of Growth in the Dominican Republic?" Washington, DC: World Bank.

CHAPTER 5

Labor Market Implications of Immigration and Emigration in the Dominican Republic

Zovanga L. Kone and Caglar Ozden

Although the epicenter of the catastrophic January 2010 Haitian earthquake was 25 miles west of Port-au-Prince, the aftershocks were immediately felt in the Dominican Republic, on the other side of Quisqueya Island. As with all natural disasters of this scale, the devastation following the 2010 earthquake was immediate: it triggered a blow to the Haitian economy, which was already weak from a low economic growth rate, persistent poverty, and income inequality. Furthermore, such disasters overwhelm neighboring countries through sudden inflows of often-desperate populations fleeing disasters. Over the next years, thousands of Haitians crossed the border in a mass migration to the Dominican Republic, becoming one of the most cited examples of "environmental" migration.

The economic costs and negative effects of the inflow of migrants immediately became a central social and economic issue in the Dominican Republic's politics after the earthquake. The government initiated legal proceedings to deport hundreds of thousands of migrants and their descendants, including many of whom had been born in the Dominican Republic or had lived there for decades. Because it is unlikely to be resolved any time soon, this ongoing issue is

The authors express their gratitude to Francisco Carneiro for his guidance, comments, and patience at each stage of the preparation of this analysis. We are also grateful to Frederic Docquier and Chris Parsons, our collaborators in closely related projects over the years, without implicating them for the shortcomings and errors here. Finally, we are grateful to Cecile T. Niang, Oscar Calvo-González, and especially McDonald P. Benjamin for useful comments and suggestions.

Zovanga L. Kone is a research fellow at the Centre on Migration, Policy, and Society of the University of Oxford. He holds a master of science in econometrics and mathematical economics from the London School of Economics and a doctorate in economics from the University of Nottingham, United Kingdom.

Caglar Ozden is a lead economist in the World Bank's Development Research Group. He holds a doctorate in economics from Stanford University. Please direct correspondence to cozden@worldbank.org.

a source of continuing diplomatic and political tensions between the governments of the Dominican Republic, Haiti, and many Western countries, as well as the United Nations and numerous human rights organizations that aim to help and protect Haitian migrants.

Haitian migration to the Dominican Republic has long historical roots that precede the 2010 earthquake. However, the number of Haitian migrants in the Dominican Republic is unclear. While estimates vary widely and existing data are fraught with numerous problems (a critical point, discussed in the data section), the 1991 Dominican census identified about 250,000 Haitians in the Dominican Republic, and this was generally considered a low estimate. Migration was already on the rise, as Haiti continued to struggle with poverty during the past two decades, with some surveys putting the number of Haitians in this country right before the earthquake at about 1 million.

The critical, yet unanswered, question in this debate is: What is the labor market impact of Haitian immigration into the Dominican Republic?

Standard economic theory would predict a large negative wage impact as the labor supply rapidly increases, especially among low-skilled workers who are directly competing with the incoming immigrants. However, the effects on different groups of native workers, such as the high-skilled or the low-skilled, depend on the underlying extent of substitutability or complementary, or both, between these different skill groups as well as between natives and immigrants in the labor market.

Furthermore, two additional labor market features of countries need to be considered. First, although it is an important destination for Haitian immigrants, the Dominican Republic is also a large migrant-sending country, mainly to the United States. Owing to selection effects, the skill composition and other features of the Dominican emigrants differ from those of the nonmigrants and, hence, have differential labor market impacts across workers of different skill groups. Second, like many developing economies, the labor market in the Dominican Republic is characterized by significant informality, especially among low-skilled workers. The overall impact of the arrival of immigrants will thus depend on their sectoral distribution or their formality status, or both.

This chapter aims to identify the impact of *both* immigration and emigration on natives in the Dominican labor market through an aggregate production function model that captures the presence of multiple sectors of employment in the economy. The labor market outcomes examined are the employment and wage levels of natives. The analytical model used is an extension of the standard models that have become popular in the literature and have been commonly used to explore similar issues, especially in the context of countries that are members of the Organisation for Economic Co-operation and Development (OECD).[1] Similar models were used to study macroeconomic growth, productivity, and skill premiums.

The main innovation of the analytical model used in this chapter is to add another level of nest—formal versus informal production sectors—to a standard nested production model. The basic framework enables one to derive labor demand by two skill groups—the low-skilled and the high-skilled. A simple labor supply decision is then added, one that generates an aggregate supply curve for each skill group. Within each skill group, natives and immigrants are imperfect substitutes. With this model, the wage and employment effects of immigration and emigration on nonmigrant native workers can be estimated across different skill levels and different sectors of employment.

Once the analytical model is constructed and the channels through which immigration and emigration affects different labor groups are identified, various scenarios can be considered by using different estimates of the model's fundamental parameters. In particular, the study uses different values of the elasticity of (a) relative demand between high- and low-skilled workers, (b) relative demand between migrant and native workers, (c) human capital externalities, (d) aggregate labor supply, and (e) substitution between the informal and the formal sector in producing final output. In addition, the number of new immigrants and the share of informal employment among them are used as additional variables in these scenarios. The goal is to see which assumptions are critical and how sensitive the results are to different immigration levels while severe data constraints are circumvented.

The findings show that low-skilled native workers in the informal sector are the most negatively affected by immigration because they are in closer competition with the new incoming immigrants. High-skilled workers are not much affected by immigration. This is mainly because immigrants are unskilled and concentrated in the informal sector. Low-skilled workers in the formal sector, however, gain from immigration. Put differently, the results suggest native workers switching from the informal to the formal sectors, owing to immigration-generated pressures in the informal sector. The results for emigration indicate that its effects can be as important as those of immigration.

Emigrants are positively selected, and would generally be more skilled than the native labor force. Thus, the relatively higher-skilled intensity of emigration hurts low-skilled nonmigrants because they are complements in production. On the other hand, nonmigrant high-skilled workers benefit owing to less competition in the labor market. Its impact on low-skilled workers in the formal and informal sectors depend on the extent of the predeparture sectoral distribution among those who emigrated, as one might expect.

Background

This section provides background on the Dominican labor market and a discussion of the data, outlining its shortcomings. In subsequent sections, the analytical stylized model is presented, followed by a discussion of the results.

The Dominican Labor Market between 2000 and 2010

The Dominican Republic experienced a noticeable increase in its gross domestic product (GDP) per capita over the past decade, rising from a (purchasing power parity) value of about RD$6,400 in the year 2000 to over RD$11,000 in 2010.

There is, however, a certain level of discord between the GDP numbers and wage levels. Real average wages declined between 2000 and 2010, according to International Monetary Fund (IMF) research (Abdullaev and Estevão 2013). Wages dipped to 60 percent of their 2000 value in 2004, before stabilizing at about 80 percent between 2009 and 2010. On the other hand, labor productivity experienced a noticeable increase. There was also a moderate increase in employment rates during 2000–10 (Abdullaev and Estevão 2013).

The informal sector seems to have experienced a faster rate of growth in terms of employment. The share of informal sector workers among the employed in nonagricultural jobs steadily increased, from 34.4 percent in 2000 to 42.6 percent in 2010, according to the International Labour Organization (ILO) (Parisotto 2013). Recent labor force data from a number of surveys suggest that the share of informal sector workers might actually be higher, passing the 50 percent level. In the formal sector, the trend in the sectoral distribution of employment remained quite stable between 2000 and 2010, albeit with 4 percentage point increase of employment in the service sector and a slight decrease in the manufacturing sector.

The *unemployment rate*, defined broadly to include discouraged workers, fluctuated between 14 percent and 20 percent during 2000 and 2010 (Abdullaev and Estevão 2013). The lack of job prospects, in addition to uncertain political climates, was cited as a main reason for emigration among those who left the country (Rodriguez 2011). In fact, the emigration rate was estimated at 16 percent. This process might have also been driven by the easy access into the United States from which many Dominican migrants benefit, owing to both proximity and extensive diaspora linkages.

Dominican Migrants in the United States

Migrants from the Dominican Republic represent one of the largest diasporas in the United States. The laxity of visa requirements in earlier decades and geographic proximity made the country a popular destination. In 2012, close to 960,000 Dominican-born persons were living in the United States, accounting for about 2 percent of the foreign-born population in the country (Nwosu and Batalova 2014). About 9 percent of these individuals entered the country from 2010 onward. Moreover, 50 percent are naturalized citizens, suggesting a significant number of long-term stayers, and about 22 percent of those over age 18 who are married have an American-born spouse. This large diaspora with relatively deep roots in the United States can be expected to result in more immigrants to enter the United States through family reunification programs and other informal support networks, as suggested by the literature on the role of networks (for example, on the role of networks, see Beine, Docquier, and Özden 2011 and Munshi 2003).

Roughly 800,000 immigrants from the Dominican Republic were of working age, according to the 2012 American Community Survey, a survey conducted by the U.S. Census Bureau (table 5.1). Their mean duration of stay in the United States was 18 years. Nevertheless, those staying for fewer than 10 years in the

Table 5.1 Employment and Education Levels of Dominican Immigrants in the United States (Ages 18–65), 2000–12

Year	Employment rate (%)	College-educated (%)	Number
2000	52.80	9.10	572,360
2001	62.88	9.79	546,217
2002	63.92	11.45	554,827
2003	66.09	11.50	579,806
2004	64.70	12.03	575,222
2005	66.45	12.15	609,530
2006	68.85	13.45	648,343
2007	68.22	14.12	631,689
2008	69.69	14.12	672,822
2009	65.71	13.30	675,866
2010	64.77	12.90	754,372
2011	65.78	14.27	754,373
2012	66.06	14.13	802,191

Source: Based on 2012 American Community Survey (ACS) data.

United States accounted for a quarter of individuals of working age. The employment rate for this group of immigrants stood at 66 percent, higher than the corresponding rate in the Dominican Republic. However, their employment appears to be concentrated in low to mid-level-skill occupations; more generally, personal services occupations and elementary occupations (that is, occupations that consist of simple and routine tasks that mainly require the use of hand-held tools, often some physical effort, and no formal qualifications) accounted for about one-third of employment for this diaspora population. The top-five occupations (at the three-digit OCC1990 level) of employment were cashiers, drivers, janitors, nursing aids, and housekeepers and stewards, and accounted for 24 percent of employment.

The high share of employment in low-skilled to semiskilled occupations could be linked to the immigrants' educational attainments. Although those completing secondary school accounted for about 50 percent of this group of immigrants, as of 2012, slightly more than 14 percent completed a degree. The latter share is quite low compared to the 30 percent level among all foreign-born of the same age group in the United States. These findings corroborate the fact that emigrants from the Dominican Republic are predominantly nontertiary educated, an empirical observation that is used in the simulation.

Haitian Migrants in the Dominican Republic

While many people migrate from the Dominican Republic, mostly to the United States, the Dominican Republic itself hosts many immigrants from other countries. As highlighted previously, the majority of these immigrants are from Haiti. Migration from Haiti to the Dominican Republic has deep historical roots, being a typical example of South-South migration. When close neighbors, such as Haitians, cannot easily access the labor market of a high-income country like the United States, migrating to a relatively more stable, prosperous neighboring country like the Dominican Republic becomes an attractive alternative.

The main difficulty in analyzing the patterns and impact of Haitian migration to the Dominican Republic is the lack of reliable data. There are various reasons for the absence of high-quality data on immigrants. Some relate to the difficulties of collecting consistent, high-quality data, especially on labor market variables, in developing countries. Data collection becomes especially challenging when a large portion of the labor market is informal. Other problems arise from the special situations related to Haitian immigrants. The vast majority of these immigrants are undocumented and have entered the Dominican Republic through informal channels. As such, they have the incentives to avoid surveys and answer them truthfully, owing to fear of arrest and deportation.

The historical and geographic ties between Haiti and the Dominican Republic explain the extent of migration. Haitian soldiers invaded the Dominican Republic in 1822, known then as Santo Domingo, and annexed the country to Haiti until it regained independence in 1844. The two countries first signed a migration agreement in 1918, which provided for the recruitment of 20,000 Haitian workers each year. Although periods of restrictive migration measures followed, the renewal of recruitment agreements in 1970 boosted Haitian emigration during the 1980s and 1990s. Thus, Haiti became a source of cheap labor for the Dominican Republic. Immigrants from Haiti were (and still are) principally employed in the informal sectors and in the agriculture sector, for example sugarcane plantations.

Official reports suggest that 245,000 Haitians immigrants were in the Dominican Republic according to the 1991 Dominican census. Moreover, the Embassy of Haiti in Santo Domingo estimated that nearly 1.1 million Haitians lived in the Dominican Republic in 2009 (which potentially also included Dominican-born individuals with Haitian parents), a figure that is much higher than the 313,040 estimate from the 2010 census. The lack of a consensus about the number of Haitian-born people in the Dominican Republic is further shown in the United Nations' estimate of about 260,000 people in 2013. Despite minor differences in the years pertaining to these estimates, the differences in numbers from the various sources are considerable.

The number of Haitians in the Dominican Republic soared following the 2010 earthquake because many sought refuge. The exact count, as of 2015, remains unclear. The estimates from the media suggest that the figure is about 460,000.[2,3] Somewhat close to this number is the estimate from a national survey, the Primera Encuesta Nacional de Inmigrantes en la Republica Dominicana (ENI, or the First National Survey of Immigrants from the Dominican Republic). It suggests that out of the 524,632 foreign-born individuals in the Dominican Republic in 2012, those born in Haiti accounted for 458,233.

The currently available standard labor force surveys from the Dominican Republic underestimate the count of immigrants in the country because they do

Table 5.2 Comparison of Native versus Foreign-Born Population, by Data Source

Population group	DIOC 2010	LFS 2010	ENFT 2012
Native-born	9,042,360	9,541,742	9,191,608
Foreign-born			
Non-Haitian	395,480	281,278	524,632
Haitians	308,010	—	458,233
Total	9,437,840	9,823,020	9,716,240

Source: Based on DIOC census data and on ENFT and LFS survey data.
Note: — = not available; DIOC = Database on Immigrants in OECD and Non-OECD Countries; ENFT = National Labor Force Survey; LFS = Labour Force Survey.

not clearly distinguish the respondent's place of birth from the respondent's place of last residence. For example, while the Database on Immigrants in OECD and Non-OECD Countries (DIOC), which draws on census data, puts the count of all immigrants in the Dominican Republic at 395,480 in 2010, labor force survey estimates suggest that 281,278 immigrants were in the country that same year (table 5.2). The former is more likely to be a better estimate because it is based on census data, while the labor survey is based on a sample. Moreover, comparing labor force survey estimates to those reported officially by the statistical bureau of the country would imply that there was a decline in the total population and the native population, and as such, the survey may not be undercounting only Haitian immigrants.

According to the Primera Encuesta Nacional de Inmigrantes en la Republica Dominicana, conducted in 2012, immigrants are predominantly younger than the natives. The share of immigrants between 15 to 64 is over 86 percent, compared with less than 65 percent for natives of this age group. The main origin countries, other than Haiti, are Cuba, the United States and the self-governing Commonwealth of Puerto Rico, and Venezuela. Haitians remain the predominant immigrant group in the Dominican Republic, accounting for about 90 percent of all immigrants according to most data sources. Their employment rate, however, is much lower in comparison with that of the natives, standing at less than 40 percent.

The Data

This section examines the implications of immigration and emigration for the wage and employment levels of natives, as discussed previously. In our simple aggregate model of an economy, workers are differentiated by their place of birth (that is, native or foreign-born) and education levels, used as a measure of skill. Unlike the model of Docquier, Ozden, and Peri (2014), the model presented in this chapter is extended to consider an economy with a formal sector and an informal sector that accounts for close to 50 percent of employment in the Dominican Republic. As such, data are required for education levels and nativity status as well as for the formality status of individuals.

The interest of this analysis lies in examining the effects of immigration and emigration flows on labor market outcomes of natives of the Dominican Republic. A reference year must be chosen and these flows obtained at a particular point in time. As such, the period 2000–10 was chosen, with 2000 as the starting reference point. Information on the number of immigrants and natives in the country in the reference year is crucial because this is used to examine how (a) the inflow of immigrants (by skill level) and (b) the outflow of natives (again, by skill level) over the next 10 years will affect labor market outcomes of interest.

Two sets of data are available for this analysis: (a) Dominican labor force surveys (LFS) from the World Bank and (b) immigration and emigration data from DIOC, which are collated from national census data of destination countries (the Dominican Republic in this case). Table 5.3 reports the numbers of the working-age population (that is, ages15–64) from these two sets of data. While both sources suggest that this was slightly over 5 million in 2000, the labor force survey places the number of immigrants at less than 72,000; but in comparison, DIOC places this figure at a little over 400,000. For the year 2010, DIOC places the numbers of immigrants at about 325,000, and the labor force survey, at about 243,000. As outlined in the background section, DIOC data better align with the official statistics from the Dominican Republic, which place the number of foreign-born individuals of working age in 2012 at a little less than 459,000. Both data sources (LFS and DIOC) are arguably unreliable for identifying the number of immigrants in 2000 and 2010 as well changes during this 10-year period. DIOC is, however, likely to be more reliable for the year 2000, but possibly underestimates immigrants in 2010. The LFS, on the other hand, seems unreliable for both years.

Our model, outlined in the next section, contains two skill groups: the high-skilled and the low-skilled. The first group comprises those with a tertiary education and the second comprises all those with no tertiary education qualifications. DIOC contains information on educational attainment, which is used to obtain the skill composition of the working-age population by nativity status. This is reported in table 5.4. Individuals with a tertiary education accounted for 9 percent of the population in 2000; the corresponding shares were respectively about 9 percent and 10 percent among natives and immigrants.

Table 5.3 Immigration Status of Working-Age Population (Ages 15–64), 2000 and 2010

Population group	2000		2010	
	DIOC	LFS	DIOC	LFS
Native	4,774,069	4,937,217	5,718,950	5,998,063
Immigrant	403,916	71,938	324,910	242,601
Total	5,177,985	5,009,155	6,043,860	6,240,664

Sources: DIOC 2000 and 2010; LFS 2000 and 2010.
Note: An *immigrant* is classified by last place of residence in the LFS but by country of birth in DIOC.
DIOC = Database on Immigrants in OECD and Non-OECD Countries; LFS = Labour Force Survey.

Table 5.4 Immigration Status of Working-Age Population (Ages 15–64), by Skill Group, 2000 and 2010

Population group	2000			2010		
	Nontertiary	Tertiary	Unknown	Nontertiary	Tertiary	Unknown
Native	4,356,369	385,192	32,508	5,202,570	516,380	—
Immigrant	361,780	37,448	4,688	305,670	19,240	—
Total	4,718,149	422,640	37,196	5,508,240	535,620	—

Source: DIOC 2000 and 2010.
Note: — = not available; DIOC = Database on Immigrants in OECD and Non-OECD Countries.

Table 5.5 Sectoral Distribution of Employment, by Skill Group and Formality Status, 2000 and 2010

Skill group	2000				2010			
	Formal		Informal		Formal		Informal	
	Number	Share (%)	Number	Share (%)	Number	Share (%)	Number	Share (%)
Tertiary	294,930	94.56	16,977	5.44	453,666	95.01	23,841	4.99
Nontertiary	1,121,750	44.01	1,427,214	55.99	1,243,314	39.68	1,889,925	60.32
Total	1,416,680	49.52	1,444,191	50.48	1,696,980	47.00	1,913,766	53.00

Source: LFS 2000 and 2010.
Note: LFS = Labour Force Survey. "Tertiary" and "nontertiary" refer to level of education.

Table 5.5 shows the employment shares of the formal and informal sectors, for both 2000 and 2010, using labor force survey data. The informal sector accounts for at least half of all jobs in both years. These shares drop by 2–5 percentage points when one omits the agriculture sector. This figure also suggests that most of the increase in the number of people employed occurred in the informal sector (that is, 62 percent). To a large extent, this justifies the need to consider the effects of immigration and emigration on wages and employment in the formal and informal sectors separately.

Average wages computed using labor force surveys between 2000 and 2012 paint a similar result to that reported by the IMF, as illustrated in figure 5.1. It is also observed that the decline in wages appears to have been more pronounced among the tertiary educated between 2000 and 2004 when one examines the trend in adjusted wages by purchasing power parity. In comparison, the dip in wages among those who did not complete tertiary education was much smaller. Wage levels remained relatively stable from 2004 onward for both skill groups. Comparison across sectors shows that wages in the formal sector were consistently higher than wages in the informal sector, which further supports the need to consider that workers across sectors may have different productivity levels.

An additional dimension of the data explored is the educational attainment distribution of Dominican-born people residing outside the country. Net emigration flows by skill group were obtained using the DIOC 2000 and DIOC 2010 surveys. The number of Dominican-born people residing outside the country

Figure 5.1 Monthly Earnings by Sector, in Dominican Dollars and Adjusted by Purchasing Power Parity, 2000–12

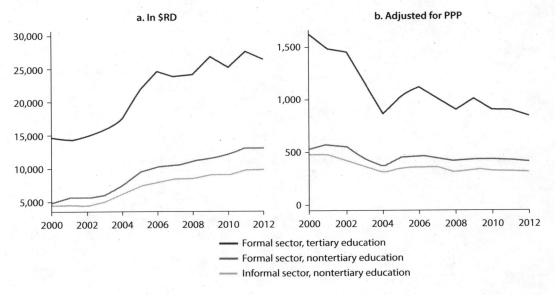

a. In $RD

b. Adjusted for PPP

— Formal sector, tertiary education
▬ Formal sector, nontertiary education
— Informal sector, nontertiary education

Table 5.6 Dominican-Born Working-Age Population Residing Abroad, 2000 and 2010

Skill group	2000	2010	Change
Tertiary education	90,915	169,004	78,089
Nontertiary education	630,118	786,809	156,691
Total	721,033	955,813	234,780

Source: DIOC 2000 and 2010.
Note: DIOC = Database on Immigrants in OECD and Non-OECD Countries.

increased by 234,780 between 2000 and 2010. Moreover, out of 955,813 emigrants in 2010, 786,809 had a nontertiary education. On the other hand, the number of the tertiary educated increased by almost 86 percent, whereas the corresponding increase among the nontertiary educated was about 25 percent (table 5.6).

Analytical Model

Aggregate Production Function

The analytical model used in this study is an extension of the model developed by Docquier, Ozden, and Peri (2014) (referred to as the *DOP model*, hereafter). This is a variant of the standard nested production models used in many different strands of the economics literature. The main variation here, as mentioned previously, is the inclusion of another production layer to capture an economy with a dual sector of employment. Output (that is, *y*) is assumed to be homogeneous and perfectly tradable. It is produced with a constant-return-to-scale production function, f, using two factors: physical capital (k) and a composite labor input (q):

$$y = Af(k, q) \tag{5.1}$$

where A is the total factor productivity (TFP) parameter. The production of a unit of good requires labor from two sectors: the formal sector and the informal sector, as seen in figure 5.2. One can also view q in effective units, and equation 5.1 can be rewritten as equation 5.2:

$$y = Aq \tag{5.2}$$

such that

$$q = \left[\theta_s q_f^{\frac{\delta_s - 1}{\delta_s}} + (1 - \theta_s) q_i^{\frac{\delta_s - 1}{\delta_s}} \right]^{\frac{\delta_s}{\delta_s - 1}} \tag{5.3}$$

where q_f denotes formal sector labor and q_i denotes informal sector labor. Here, θ_s and $1 - \theta_s$ are the respective relative sectoral productivity parameters. Finally, δ_s is the elasticity of substitution of labor between the two sectors, one of the key parameters of the model and the simulations.

The labor market is divided into two skill groups: high-skilled and low-skilled.

It is assumed that the labor aggregate consists of high- and low-skill workers in each sector (see equation 5.4), although the informal sector will later be assumed to only employ low-skilled workers, as shown in figure 5.2:

$$q_s = \left[\theta_e q_{s,h}^{\frac{\delta_e - 1}{\delta_e}} + (1 - \theta_e) q_{s,l}^{\frac{\delta_e - 1}{\delta_e}} \right]^{\frac{\delta_e}{\delta_e - 1}} \tag{5.4}$$

where $s = f, i$.

Figure 5.2 Composite Labor of Nest Structure

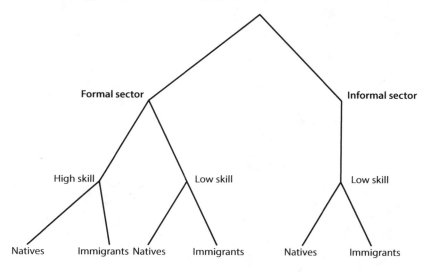

In equation 5.4, $q_{s,h}$ stands for high-skill labor and $q_{s,l}$ is low-skill labor. Here, θ_e and $1-\theta_e$ are the respective relative productivity levels of each skill level, and δ_e is the elasticity of substitution between skill groups, the second important elasticity parameter.

The next and final nest is for worker nationality or migration status. Each education or skill group comprises foreign-born workers and native-born workers, such that:

$$q_{s,e} = \left[\theta_m q_{s,e,n}^{\frac{\delta_m-1}{\delta_m}} + \left(1-\theta_m\right) q_{s,e,m}^{\frac{\delta_m-1}{\delta_m}} \right]^{\frac{\delta_m}{\delta_m-1}}$$

(5.5)

where $e = h, l$

Here, $q_{s,e,n}$ represents native workers and $q_{s,e,m}$ represents their corresponding foreign-born workers; θ_m and $1-\theta_m$ are the respective relative productivity levels of the natives and immigrants; and δ_m is the elasticity of substitution between natives and immigrants, the third critical elasticity parameter. The nest structure is as presented in figure 5.2.

Externality of Education

In light of the importance of human capital for TFP and the externalities of schooling (see Docquier, Ozden, and Peri 2014; and Lucas 1988), the TFP of a country is expressed as

$$A = A_0 * e^{\lambda f h}$$

(5.6)

where A_o represents the independent component of TFP to human capital externality, f_h denotes the share of high-skilled individuals in the workforce, and λ denotes the semi-elasticity of TFP to f_h.

Labor Demand

The Dominican Republic is assumed to be a single labor market. Marginal productivity of each type of native worker $\{s, e, n\}$ can be obtained by substituting equations 5.3 through 5.5 into 5.2 and by differentiating q with respect to $q_{s, e, n}$. Proceeding as such gives the demand for labor of type $\{s, e, n\}$ as shown in equations 5.7–5.9:

$$W_{f,h,n} = A * \theta_s * \theta_e * \theta_m \left[\frac{q}{q_f} \right]^{\frac{1}{\delta_s}} \left[\frac{q_f}{q_{f,h}} \right]^{\frac{1}{\delta_e}} \left[\frac{q_{f,h}}{q_{f,h,n}} \right]^{\frac{1}{\delta_m}}$$

(5.7)

$$W_{f,l,n} = A * \theta_s \left(1-\theta_e\right) * \theta_m \left[\frac{q}{q_f} \right]^{\frac{1}{\delta_s}} \left[\frac{q_f}{q_{f,l}} \right]^{\frac{1}{\delta_e}} \left[\frac{q_{f,l}}{q_{f,l,n}} \right]^{\frac{1}{\delta_m}}$$

(5.8)

$$W_{i,l,n} = A\left(1-\theta_s\right)\left(1-\theta_e\right)*\theta_m\left[\frac{q}{q_i}\right]^{\frac{1}{\delta_s}}\left[\frac{q_i}{q_{i,l}}\right]^{\frac{1}{\delta_e}}\left[\frac{q_{i,l}}{q_{i,l,n}}\right]^{\frac{1}{\delta_m}} \qquad (5.9)$$

Next, one needs to take the total differentials of equations 5.7 through 5.9 with respect to variations (Δ) of the employment of each type of worker to obtain the percentage change in marginal productivity for native workers, which arises from a change in employment of immigrants of a given type (that is, $\hat{q}_{s,e,m}$), natives (that is, $\hat{q}_{s,e,n}$), or both. This percentage change is defined as $\hat{x} = \Delta x/x$. This leads to equations 5.10 and 5.11:

$$\frac{\partial \ln w_{s,e,n}}{\partial w_{s,e,n}} \Delta w_{s,e,n} = \frac{1}{\delta_s}\left[\frac{\partial q}{\partial q_{f,h,m}}\frac{\Delta q_{f,h,m}}{q} + \frac{\partial q}{\partial q_{f,l,m}}\frac{\Delta q_{f,l,m}}{q} + \frac{\partial q}{\partial q_{i,l,m}}\frac{\Delta q_{i,l,m}}{q}\right]$$

$$+\frac{1}{\delta_s}\left[\frac{\partial q}{\partial q_{f,h,n}}\frac{\Delta q_{f,h,n}}{q} + \frac{\partial q}{\partial q_{f,l,n}}\frac{\Delta q_{f,l,n}}{q} + \frac{\partial q}{\partial q_{i,l,n}}\frac{\Delta q_{i,l,n}}{q}\right]$$

$$+\left(\frac{1}{\delta_e}-\frac{1}{\delta_s}\right)\left[\frac{\partial q_s}{\partial q_{s,h,m}}\frac{\Delta q_{s,h,m}}{q_s} + \frac{\partial q_s}{\partial q_{s,l,m}}\frac{\Delta q_{s,l,m}}{q_s}\right]$$

$$+\left(\frac{1}{\delta_e}-\frac{1}{\delta_s}\right)\left[\frac{\partial q_s}{\partial q_{s,h,n}}\frac{\Delta q_{s,h,n}}{q_s} + \frac{\partial q_s}{\partial q_{s,l,n}}\frac{\Delta q_{s,l,n}}{q_s}\right]$$

$$+\left(\frac{1}{\delta_m}-\frac{1}{\delta_e}\right)\left[\frac{\partial q_{s,e}}{\partial q_{s,e,m}}\frac{\Delta q_{s,e,m}}{q_{s,e}}\right]$$

$$+\left(\frac{1}{\delta_m}-\frac{1}{\delta_e}\right)\left[\frac{\partial q_{s,e}}{\partial q_{s,e,n}}\frac{\Delta q_{s,e,n}}{q_{s,e}}\right]$$

$$-\frac{1}{\delta_m}*\frac{\Delta q_{s,e,n}}{q_{s,e,n}} + \lambda\Delta f_h \quad \text{for } s = f \text{ and } e = (h,l) \qquad (5.10)$$

$$\frac{\partial \ln w_{i,l,n}}{\partial w_{i,l,n}} \Delta w_{i,l,n} = \frac{1}{\delta_s}\left[\frac{\partial q}{\partial q_{f,h,m}}\frac{\Delta q_{f,h,m}}{q} + \frac{\partial q}{\partial q_{f,l,m}}\frac{\Delta q_{f,l,m}}{q} + \frac{\partial q}{\partial q_{i,l,m}}\frac{\Delta q_{i,l,m}}{q}\right]$$

$$+\frac{1}{\delta_s}\left[\frac{\partial q}{\partial q_{f,h,n}}\frac{\Delta q_{f,h,n}}{q} + \frac{\partial q}{\partial q_{f,l,n}}\frac{\Delta q_{f,l,n}}{q} + \frac{\partial q}{\partial q_{i,l,n}}\frac{\Delta q_{i,l,n}}{q}\right]$$

$$+\left(\frac{1}{\delta_e}-\frac{1}{\delta_s}\right)\left[\frac{\partial q_i}{\partial q_{i,l,m}}\frac{\Delta q_{i,l,m}}{q_i}\right]+\left(\frac{1}{\delta_l}-\frac{1}{\delta_i}\right)\left[\frac{\partial q_i}{\partial q_{i,l,n}}\frac{\Delta q_{i,l,n}}{q_i}\right]$$

$$+\left(\frac{1}{\delta_m}-\frac{1}{\delta_l}\right)\left[\frac{\partial q_{i,l}}{\partial q_{i,l,m}}\frac{\Delta q}{q_{i,l}}\right]+\left(\frac{1}{\delta_m}-\frac{1}{\delta_l}\right)\left[\frac{\partial q_{i,l}}{\partial q_{i,l,n}}\frac{\Delta q_{i,l,n}}{q_{i,l}}\right]$$

$$-\frac{1}{\delta_m}\frac{\Delta q_{i,l,n}}{q_{i,l,n}} + \lambda\Delta f_h \qquad (5.11)$$

At equilibrium, each type of labor is paid its marginal productivity, and given that labor is the only factor of production, the share of the total wage bill, shr_k, for any k group of workers can be expressed as $shr_k = \dfrac{w_k * q_k}{y}$ such that:

$$shr_{s,e,j} = \frac{w_{s,e,j} * q_{s,e,j}}{y} = w_{s,e,j} * \frac{q_{s,e,j}}{y} = \frac{\partial q}{\partial q_{s,e,j}} * \frac{q_{s,e,j}}{q} \tag{5.12}$$

where $j = n, m$

$$shr_{s,e} = \frac{w_{s,e} * q_{s,e}}{y} = w_{s,e} * \frac{q_{s,e}}{y} = \frac{\partial q}{\partial q_{s,e}} * \frac{q_{s,e}}{q} \tag{5.13}$$

$$shr_s = \frac{w_s * q_s}{y} = w_s * \frac{q_s}{y} = \frac{\partial q}{\partial q_s} * \frac{q_s}{q} \tag{5.14}$$

Equation 5.12 implies that

$$shr_{s,e,j} * \frac{\Delta q_{s,e,j}}{q_{s,e,j}} = \frac{\partial q}{\partial q_{s,e,j}} \frac{\Delta q_{s,e,j}}{q} \tag{5.15}$$

Equations 5.12 and 5.14 imply that

$$\frac{shr_{s,e,j}}{shr_s} * \frac{\Delta q_{s,e,j}}{q_{s,e,j}} = \frac{\partial q_s}{\partial q_{s,e,j}} * \frac{\Delta q_{s,e,j}}{q_s} \tag{5.16}$$

Equations 5.12 and 5.13 imply that

$$\frac{shr_{s,e,j}}{shr_{s,e}} \frac{\Delta q_{s,e,j}}{q_{s,e,j}} = \frac{\partial q_{s,e}}{\partial q_{s,e,j}} * \frac{\Delta q_{s,e,j}}{q_{s,e}} \tag{5.17}$$

Equation 5.15 equates to the first set of terms in equations 5.10 and 5.11, equation 5.16 equates to the second set, and equation 5.17 equates to the third set. Substituting these equivalences into equations 5.10 and 5.11, the result shown in equation 5.18 is obtained:

$$
\begin{aligned}
\hat{w}_{f,h,n} = \frac{1}{\delta_s} & \Big[\left(shr_{f,h,m}\hat{q}_{f,h,m} + shr_{f,l,m}\hat{q}_{f,l,m} + shr_{i,l,m}\hat{q}_{i,l,m} \right) \\
& + \left(shr_{f,h,n}\hat{q}_{f,h,n} + shr_{f,l,n}\hat{q}_{f,l,n} + shr_{i,l,n}\hat{q}_{i,l,n} \right) \Big] \\
& + \left(\frac{1}{\delta_e} - \frac{1}{\delta_s} \right) \Big[\left(\frac{shr_{f,h,m}}{shr_f}\hat{q}_{f,h,m} + \frac{shr_{f,l,m}}{shr_f}\hat{q}_{f,l,m} \right) \\
& + \left(\frac{shr_{f,h,n}}{shr_f}\hat{q}_{f,h,n} + \frac{shr_{f,l,n}}{shr_f}\hat{q}_{f,l,n} \right) \Big] \\
& + \left(\frac{1}{\delta_m} - \frac{1}{\delta_e} \right) \left[\frac{shr_{f,h,m}}{shr_{f,h}}\hat{q}_{f,h,m} + \frac{shr_{f,h,n}}{shr_{f,h}}\hat{q}_{f,h,n} \right] \\
& - \frac{1}{\delta_m}\hat{q}_{f,h,n} + \lambda \Delta f_h
\end{aligned}
\tag{5.18}
$$

$$\hat{w}_{f,l,n} = \frac{1}{\delta_s} \Big[\big(shr_{f,h,m}\hat{q}_{f,h,m} + shr_{f,l,m}\hat{q}_{f,l,m} + shr_{i,l,m}\hat{q}_{i,l,m} \big)$$

$$+ \big(shr_{f,h,n}\hat{q}_{f,h,n} + shr_{f,l,n}\hat{q}_{f,l,n} + shr_{i,l,n}\hat{q}_{i,l,n} \big) \Big]$$

$$+ \left(\frac{1}{\delta_e} - \frac{1}{\delta_s} \right) \left[\left(\frac{shr_{f,h,m}}{shr_f}\hat{q}_{f,h,m} + \frac{shr_{f,l,m}}{shr_f}\hat{q}_{f,l,m} \right) \right.$$

$$\left. + \left(\frac{shr_{f,h,n}}{shr_f}\hat{q}_{f,h,n} + \frac{shr_{f,l,n}}{shr_f}\hat{q}_{f,l,n} \right) \right]$$

$$+ \left(\frac{1}{\delta_m} - \frac{1}{\delta_e} \right) \left[\frac{shr_{f,l,m}}{shr_{f,l}}\hat{q}_{f,l,m} + \frac{shr_{f,l,n}}{shr_{f,l}}\hat{q}_{f,l,n} \right]$$

$$- \frac{1}{\delta_m}\hat{q}_{f,l,n} + \lambda\Delta f_h \qquad (5.19)$$

$$\hat{w}_{i,l,n} = \frac{1}{\delta_s} \Big[\big(shr_{f,h,m}\hat{q}_{f,h,m} + shr_{f,l,m}\hat{q}_{f,l,m} + shr_{i,l,m}\hat{q}_{i,l,m} \big)$$

$$+ \big(shr_{f,h,n}\hat{q}_{f,h,n} + shr_{f,l,n}\hat{q}_{f,l,n} + shr_{i,l,n}\hat{q}_{i,l,n} \big) \Big]$$

$$+ \left(\frac{1}{\delta_e} - \frac{1}{\delta_s} \right) \left[\frac{shr_{i,l,m}}{shr_i}\hat{q}_{i,l,m} + \frac{shr_{i,l,n}}{shr_i}\hat{q}_{i,l,n} \right]$$

$$+ \left(\frac{1}{\delta_m} - \frac{1}{\delta_e} \right) \left[\frac{shr_{i,l,m}}{shr_{i,l}}\hat{q}_{i,l,m} + \frac{shr_{i,l,n}}{shr_{i,l}}\hat{q}_{i,l,n} \right]$$

$$- \frac{1}{\delta_m}\hat{q}_{i,l,n} \qquad (5.20)$$

A further assumption of the model, which is observed from contrasting equation 5.19 and equation 5.20, is that, the externality of high-skilled workers affects the formal labor group only. A close inspection of the last three equations (equations 5.18–5.20) tells us that changes in the wages for any given type of worker occur through the sum of changes in employment of all types of workers. This can be seen from the common expression on the first two lines of all three equations. The next set of expressions, which comprise only sector-specific terms, capture the effects through changes in employment in the worker's own sector. $\frac{1}{\delta_m}\hat{q}_{s,e,n}$ represents changes arising from change in employment of the worker's own type, and $\lambda\Delta f_h$ denotes the effect that can be attributed to the change in the share of the high-skilled in the workforce, through TFP. Thus, all other things being equal, changes in the number of a given type of worker could affect the relative wages and employment levels of all other types of workers.

Labor Supply

The work/leisure choice allocation of a unit of time for a given native of type $\{s, e, n\}$ is such that they work $l_{s,e,n}$ units of time and allocate the remaining $1 - l_{s,e,n}$ unit to leisure. This allocation maximizes an instant utility function, which depends positively on their consumption, $c_{s,e,n}$, but negatively on the amount of labor supplied, $l_{s,e,n}$:

$$U_{s,e,n} = \theta_c c_{s,e,n}^{\varsigma} - \theta_l l_{s,e,n}^{\eta} \tag{5.21}$$

For simplicity, the parameters θ_c, θ_l, ς, and η are assumed to be identical across all types of individuals. Furthermore, in line with the DOP model, it is assumed that individuals consume all their labor income, such that $c_{s,e,n} = l_{s,e,n} w_{s,e,n}$.[4] Substituting this constraint into equation 5.21, labor supply is obtained by maximizing equation 5.21 with respect to $l_{s,e,n}$, which gives the following:

$$l_{s,e,n} = \phi w_{s,e,n}^{\gamma} \tag{5.22}$$

with $\phi = \left[\dfrac{\theta_c \varsigma}{\theta_\eta} \right]^{\frac{1}{\eta - \varsigma}}$, a constant, and $\gamma = \dfrac{\varsigma}{\eta - \varsigma}$. The latter captures the elasticity of labor supply, θ_η, $\eta - \varsigma$, which is assumed to be nonzero positive.

Aggregate labor supply for a given type of worker $\{s, e, n\}$ is obtained by multiplying equation 5.22 with the total workforce of the same type, $Q_{s,e,n}$. This results in the following:

$$q_{s,e,n} = \phi Q_{s,e,n} w_{s,e,n}^{\gamma} \tag{5.23}$$

We follow the DOP model in making the simplifying assumption that all working-age immigrants supply a constant amount of labor, say τ, such that total employment among immigrants of type $\{s, e, m\}$ is given by:

$$q_{s,e,m} = \tau Q_{s,e,m} \tag{5.24}$$

The assumption that all working-age immigrants supply a constant amount of labor has the following implications: γ, the elasticity of labor supply, is assumed to be zero among immigrants; and a given percentage change in the immigrant workforce population equates to the same percentage change in their employment.

Equilibrium Effects of Immigration and Emigration

This section presents solutions for the equilibrium changes in the wage and employment of a given type of native worker. Changes in the pool of immigrants of working age (that is, $\Delta Q_{s,e,m}$) and in the pool of working-age natives (that is, $\Delta Q_{s,e,n}$) arising from migration are, as in the DOP model, what are considered as net immigration flow and net emigration flow. These are taken as given. Here, the interest lies in examining their implications for the wages and employment levels of natives left in the home country. Equilibrium is set at the point where wage and employment levels of each type of native worker, through demand and supply, adjust to net immigration flow and net emigration flow.

As noted previously, a given percentage change in $Q_{s,e,m}$ corresponds to the same percentage change in $q_{s,e,m}$. The wage equation arising from the demand side—that is, equations 5.18 through 5.20—is thus:

$$\hat{w}_{s,e,n} = \frac{1}{\delta_s}\left[shr_{f,h,m}\hat{Q}_{f,h,m} + shr_{f,l,m}\hat{Q}_{f,l,m} + shr_{i,l,m}\hat{Q}_{i,l,m} \right]$$

$$+ \frac{1}{\delta_s}\left[shr_{f,h,n}\hat{q}_{f,h,n} + shr_{f,l,n}\hat{q}_{f,l,n} + shr_{i,l,n}\hat{q}_{i,l,n} \right]$$

$$+ \left(\frac{1}{\delta_e} - \frac{1}{\delta_s}\right)\left[\frac{shr_{s,h,m}}{shr_s}\hat{Q}_{s,h,m} + \frac{shr_{s,l,m}}{shr_s}\hat{Q}_{s,l,m} \right]$$

$$+ \left(\frac{1}{\delta_e} - \frac{1}{\delta_s}\right)\left[\frac{shr_{s,h,n}}{shr_s}\hat{q}_{s,h,n} + \frac{shr_{s,l,n}}{shr_s}\hat{q}_{s,l,n} \right]$$

$$+ \left(\frac{1}{\delta_m} - \frac{1}{\delta_e}\right)\left[\frac{shr_{s,e,m}}{shr_{s,e}}\hat{Q}_{s,e,m} \right] + \left(\frac{1}{\delta_m} - \frac{1}{\delta_e}\right)$$

$$\left[\frac{shr_{s,e,n}}{shr_{s,e}}\hat{q}_{s,e,n} \right] - \frac{1}{\delta_m}\hat{q}_{s,e,n} + \lambda\Delta f_h \qquad (5.25)$$

with $shr_{s,h,m} = shr_{s,h,n} = 0$ when $s = i$

The wage equation arising from the supply side—that is, 5.24—implies that:

$$\hat{w}_{s,e,n} = \frac{1}{\gamma}\left[\hat{q}_{s,e,n} - \hat{Q}_{s,e,n} \right] \qquad (5.26)$$

Recall the share of employment of high-skilled workers being negligible in the informal sector; it is assumed to be zero because it simplifies the task of solving for equilibrium solutions—hence, six unknowns have to be solved. The implications of a net immigration flow, $\hat{Q}_{s,e,m}$, and a net emigration flow, $\hat{Q}_{s,e,n}$ for wages and employment of a given type of worker are obtained by simultaneously solving equations 5.25 and 5.26. The next step solves equations 5.25 and 5.26 for three quantities of interest, which are as follows: $\hat{q}^*_{f,h,n}, \hat{q}^*_{f,l,n}$, and $\hat{q}^*_{i,l,n}$.

The equilibrium quantities

$$
\begin{aligned}
\hat{q}^*_{f,h,n} = \delta_e \delta_s shr_f \Big[&-\delta_e shr_f \left(\alpha_{f,l,n} \alpha_{i,l,n} \delta_s^2 - shr_{f,l} shr_{i,l} \right) \left(\gamma m \hat{p} l^m_{f,h,n} + \hat{Q}_{f,h,n} \right) \\
&- shr_{f,l} \left(\alpha_{i,l,n} shr_f \delta_e \delta_s - \alpha_{i,l,n} q \delta_s + \alpha_{i,l,n} \delta_s^2 + shr_{i,l} shr_f \delta_e \right) \\
&\left(\gamma m \hat{p} l^m_{f,l,n} + \hat{Q}_{f,l,n} \right) - shr_{i,l} \left(\alpha_{f,l,n} shr_f \delta_e \delta_s + shr_{f,l} shr_f \delta_e \right. \\
&\left. - shr_{f,l} \delta_e + shr_{f,l} \delta_s \right) \left(\gamma m \hat{p} l^m_{i,l,n} + \hat{Q}_{i,l,n} \right) \Big] \Omega - 1
\end{aligned}
$$

(5.27)

$$
\begin{aligned}
\hat{q}^*_{f,l,n} = \delta_e \delta_s shr_f \Big[&\delta_e shr_f \left(-\alpha_{f,h,n} \alpha_{i,l,n} \delta_s^2 + shr_{f,h} shr_{i,l} \right) \left(\gamma m \hat{p} l^m_{f,l,n} + \hat{Q}_{f,l,n} \right) \\
&- shr_{f,h} \left(\alpha_{i,l,n} shr_f \delta_e \delta_s - \alpha_{i,l,n} \delta_e \delta_s + \alpha_{i,l,n} \delta_s^2 + shr_{i,l} shr_f \delta_e \right) \left(\gamma m \hat{p} l^m_{f,h,n} + \hat{Q}_{f,h,n} \right) \\
&- shr_{i,l} \left(\alpha_{f,h,n} shr_f \delta_e \delta_s + shr_{f,h} shr_f \delta_e - shr_{f,h} \delta_e + shr_{f,h} \delta_s \right) \\
&\left(\gamma m \hat{p} l^m_{i,l,n} + \hat{Q}_{i,l,n} \right) \Big] \Omega - 1
\end{aligned}
$$

(5.28)

$$
\begin{aligned}
\hat{q}^*_{i,l,n} = \Big(&shr_{f,l} \left(\left(shr_f - 1 \right) \delta_e + \delta_s \right)^2 shr_{f,h} - \alpha_{f,h,n} \alpha_{f,l,n} shr_f^2 \delta_e^2 \delta_s^2 \Big) \\
&\delta_s \left(km \hat{p} l^m_{i,l,n} + \hat{Q}_{i,l,n} \right) \Omega - 1 - \delta_e \delta_s shr_f \Big[shr_{f,h} \left(\alpha_{f,l,n} shr_f \delta_e \delta_s \right. \\
&+ shr_{f,l} shr_f \delta_e - shr_{f,l} \delta_e + shr_{f,l} \right) \delta_s \left(km \hat{p} l^m_{f,h,n} + \hat{Q}_{f,h,n} \right) \\
&+ shr_{f,l} \left(\alpha_{f,h,n} shr_f \delta_e \delta_s + shr_{f,h} shr_f \delta_e - shr_{f,h} \delta_e + shr_{f,h} \delta_s \right) \\
&\left(km \hat{p} l^m_{f,l,n} + \hat{Q}_{f,l,n} \right) \Big] \Omega - 1
\end{aligned}
$$

(5.29)

and:

$$
\hat{w}^*_{s,e,n} = \frac{1}{\gamma} \left[\hat{q}^*_{s,e,n} - \hat{Q}_{s,e,n} \right]
$$

(5.30)

The effect of immigration and emigration on the employment level, $\hat{q}_{s,e,n}$, is negative if $\hat{w}^*_{s,e,n} < \dfrac{-1}{\gamma} \hat{Q}^*_{s,e,n}$, and is positive if $\hat{w}^*_{s,e,n} > \dfrac{-1}{\gamma} \hat{Q}^*_{s,e,n}$.

It is apparent also from equations 5.27 and 5.29 that changes in employment in one sector affect demand for workers in another sector; and that in the formal sector, changes in employment in one skill group affect demand for workers of the second skill group. In the above equations, for the change in employment,

$$\Omega = \left(\left(2\gamma shr_f \delta_e \left(shr_f \delta_e - \delta_e + \delta_s \right) shr_{i,l} + \gamma \alpha_{i,l,n} \delta_s \left(shr_f \delta_e - \delta_e + \delta_s \right)^2 \right) \right.$$
$$shr_{f,l} + \gamma \alpha_{f,l,n} shr_{i,l} shr_f^2 \delta_e^2 \delta_s \right) shr_{f,h} + \gamma \alpha l shr_f^2 \delta_e^2 \delta_s \qquad (5.31)$$
$$\left(shr_{f,l} shr_{i,l} - \alpha_{f,l,n} \alpha_{i,l,n} \delta_s^2 \right)$$

$$\hat{mpl}_{f,e,n}^m = \frac{1}{\delta_s} \left[shr_{f,h,m} \hat{Q}_{f,h,m} + shr_{f,l,m} \hat{Q}_{f,l,m} + shr_{i,l,m} \hat{Q}_{i,l,m} \right]$$
$$+ \left(\frac{1}{\delta} - \frac{1}{\delta} \right) \left[\frac{shr_{f,h,m}}{shr_f} \hat{Q}_{f,h,m} + \frac{shr_{f,l,m}}{shr_f} \hat{Q}_{f,l,m} \right] \qquad (5.32)$$
$$+ \left(\frac{1}{\delta_m} - \frac{1}{\delta_e} \right) \left[\frac{shr_{f,e,m}}{shr_{f,e}} \hat{Q}_{f,e,m} \right] + \lambda \Delta f_h$$

$$\hat{mpl}_{i,l,n}^m = \frac{1}{\delta_s} \left[shr_{f,h,m} \hat{Q}_{f,h,m} + shr_{f,l,m} \hat{Q}_{f,l,m} + shr_{i,l,m} \hat{Q}_{i,l,m} \right]$$
$$+ \left(\frac{1}{\delta_e} - \frac{1}{\delta_s} \right) \left[\frac{shr_{i,l,m}}{shr_i} \hat{Q}_{i,l,m} \right] + \left(\frac{1}{\delta_m} - \frac{1}{\delta_e} \right) \left[\frac{shr_{i,l,m}}{shr_{i,l}} \hat{Q}_{i,l,m} \right] + \lambda \Delta f_h \qquad (5.33)$$

$\hat{mpl}_k^m$ can be viewed as the change in the marginal productivity of labor for a given type of worker that results from net immigration and the externality, through TPF, of skilled labor:

$$\alpha_{f,h,n} = \frac{1}{\gamma} - \frac{shr_{f,h,n}}{\delta_s} - \left(\frac{1}{\delta_e} - \frac{1}{\delta_s} \right) \frac{shr_{f,h,n}}{shr_f} - \left(\frac{1}{\delta_m} - \frac{1}{\delta_e} \right) \frac{shr_{f,h,n}}{shr_{f,h}} + \frac{1}{\delta_m} \qquad (5.34)$$

$$\alpha_{f,l,n} = \frac{1}{\gamma} - \frac{shr_{f,l,n}}{\delta_s} - \left(\frac{1}{\delta_e} - \frac{1}{\delta_s} \right) \frac{shr_{f,l,n}}{shr_f} - \left(\frac{1}{\delta_m} - \frac{1}{\delta_e} \right) \frac{shr_{f,l,n}}{shr_{f,l}} + \frac{1}{\delta_m} \qquad (5.35)$$

$$\alpha_{i,l,n} = \frac{1}{\gamma} - \frac{shr_{i,l,n}}{\delta_s} - \left(\frac{1}{\delta_e} - \frac{1}{\delta_s} \right) \frac{shr_{i,l,n}}{shr_i} - \left(\frac{1}{\delta_m} - \frac{1}{\delta_e} \right) \frac{shr_{i,h,n}}{shr_{i,l}} + \frac{1}{\delta_m} \qquad (5.36)$$

which are weighted contributions by a type of worker to the total labor wage bill, adjusted by their elasticity of labor supply and their elasticity of substitution with immigrants of the same type.

Simulated Labor Market Effects

The model does not impose any form of restrictions on the wage structure of individuals of a given type except for those arising from the economic theory that underlines it. The key issue is how changes in the composition of the labor force affect the relative wages and employment levels of different groups of natives (by skill level or formality status). Data are required on wage levels in the initial period for each type of native worker. A parsimonious, mincerian regression suggests that low-skilled workers in the formal sector earn more than their counterparts in the informal sector (as shown in table 5A.1). High-skilled workers earn the most. These regressions confirm the average levels presented in figure 5.1: low-skilled workers in the informal sector earn 7–12 percent less than their counterparts in the formal sector, depending on the specification considered. Also, the evidence affirms that earnings levels differ across workers with different levels of education (as can be seen in table 5A.1). Based on this evidence, wages in the informal sector are used as the unit of measure, normalizing the average wage in the informal sector to 1. This is then used to compute wage bill shares for each group of workers of a given type.

In addition to net flows of immigration into the country and emigration to other countries, the simulation requires values for the following key parameters of the model: (a) the elasticity of labor supply, γ; (b) the elasticity of substitution between skill groups, δ_e; (c) the elasticity of substitution between formal and informal sectors, δ_s; (d) the elasticity of substitution between natives and immigrants, δ_m; and (e) the externality of the high-skilled, λ.

Specific estimates of these parameters for the Dominican Republic do not exist (to the best of the authors' knowledge), so estimates from other Latin American countries are used. Manacorda, Sánchez-Páramo, and Schady (2010) suggest that δ_e ranges from about 2.5 to slightly over 5 in their study of Latin American countries. Behar (2009), on the other hand, puts this range between 1.3 and 3.2. Focusing on Mexico, Schramm (2014) suggests a value between 1.5 and 1.7. In addition, the same study estimates δ_s to be approximately 1.7. In their study of OECD countries, Docquier, Ozden, and Peri (2014) use different values of δ_m (6, 20, and infinity) and equate γ to 0.2, 0.1, and 0 for different scenarios. They use values of λ between 0 and 0.75. Their paper applies a different range of these parameters in the simulations.

The simulation also requires estimates of the numbers of people in the labor force in the country in each period. Although the estimate of net emigration flow between 2000 and 2010 concurs with what one may expect, confusion exists regarding which estimate to use for net immigration flow (as detailed in the analytical model section). Although DIOC provides better estimates for numbers of immigrants in comparison to the LFS, especially for 2000, the former data set suggests a negative net immigration flow. This is highly unlikely in light of the recent earthquake in Haiti and the subsequent political and social debate over the large inflow of Haitian immigrants into the Dominican Republic. The Primera Encuesta Nacional de Inmigrantes en la República Dominicana

Table 5.7 Emigrants of Working Age from the Dominican Republic, by Skill Group, 2000 and 2010

	2000		2010	
	Nontertiary	Tertiary	Nontertiary	Tertiary
Emigrants	370,912	68,701	578,608	144,111

Source: DIOC 2000 and 2010.

Note: DIOC = Database on Immigrants in OECD and Non-OECD Countries. "Tertiary" and "nontertiary" refer to level of education.

(National Survey of Immigrants from the Dominican Republic, or ENI-2012), a 2012 survey conducted by the country's statistical office, puts the number of immigrants at 524,632, of which 458,233 were Haitian-born. It further suggests that immigrants living fewer than 10 years in the country accounted for a little over 60 percent of this population; the corresponding value for the non-Haitian-born is 43 percent. Adjusting for the economic activity rate, this yields an approximate count of 227,246 for the net immigration flow.

In light of this discrepancy, a different analytical approach is needed to illustrate the impact of immigration on wages and employment levels with a range of potential net immigration flows, rather than a single number. One can interpret this approach as a "modified sensitivity analysis" and see how labor market outcomes are affected by different levels of immigration.

Another important, yet missing, type of data is on the formal and informal sectoral distribution of low-skilled immigrants. It is assumed that those in the country in 2000 had the same formality distribution as the natives, that is, 50 percent in the formal sector and 50 percent in the informal sector. However, it is also assumed that new immigrants are more likely to be concentrated in the informal sector because they are, by definition, new in the host country and thereby less familiar with the labor market structure or may need time to acquire host-country-specific skills (Chiswick 1978), if not a combination of both. ENI-2012 puts the informality rate at about 75 percent among new Haitian immigrants, who account for about 90 percent of all new immigrants (that is, those with fewer than 10 years in the country). Additionally, more recent Haitian immigrants are shown to be more concentrated in sectors with higher shares of informality, so 75 percent is likely to be an underestimate.

Net emigration among those of working age is reported in table 5.7. Here, it is not possible to distinguish the low-skilled that came from the informal sector versus those that came from the formal sector. As such, it is reasonable to assume that they would predominantly have come from the formal sector. Nevertheless, the analysis proceeds by using different scenarios in which the share of emigrants coming from the formal sector is allowed to vary.

Results

The results from the simulations of the implications of immigration for the wages and employment probabilities of natives are illustrated in figures 5.3 and 5.4. Similarly, figures 5.5 and 5.6 present the implications of

Figure 5.3 Wage Effects of Immigration for Low-Skilled Informal and High- and Low-Skilled Formal Workers

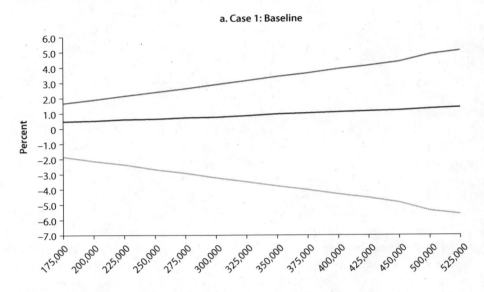

a. Case 1: Baseline

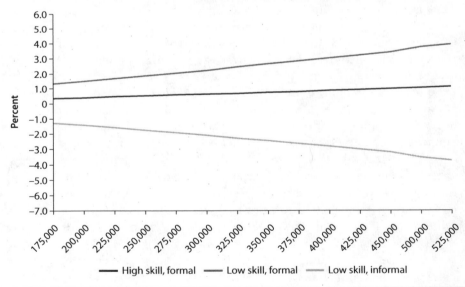

b. Case 2: Reduced share of informality among immigrants

—— High skill, formal   —— Low skill, formal   —— Low skill, informal

figure continues next page

Figure 5.3 Wage Effects of Immigration for Low-Skilled Informal and High- and Low-Skilled Formal Workers *(continued)*

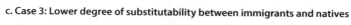

c. Case 3: Lower degree of substitutability between immigrants and natives

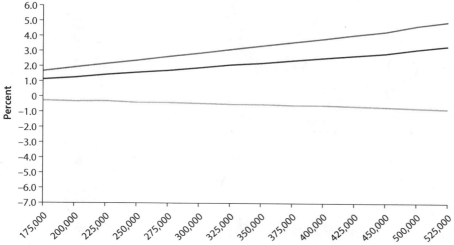

d. Case 4: Lower degree of substitutability between sectors

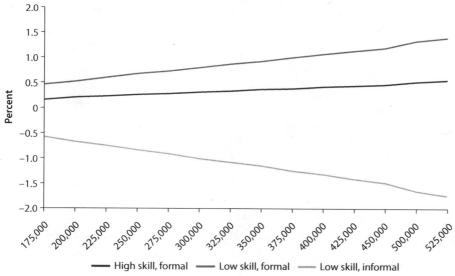

High skill, formal ——— Low skill, formal ——— Low skill, informal

Figure 5.4 Employment Effects of Immigration for Low-Skilled Informal and High- and Low-Skilled Formal Workers

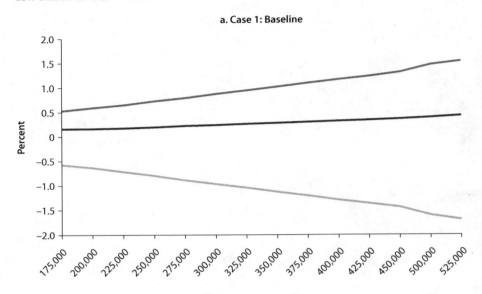

a. Case 1: Baseline

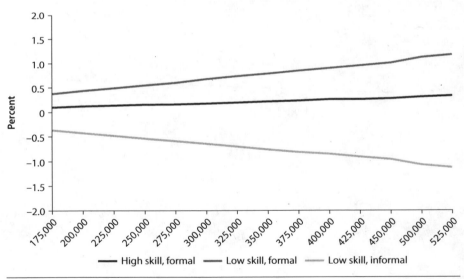

b. Case 2: Reduced share of informality among immigrants

—— High skill, formal   —— Low skill, formal   —— Low skill, informal

figure continues next page

Figure 5.4 Employment Effects of Immigration for Low-Skilled Informal and High- and Low-Skilled Formal Workers *(continued)*

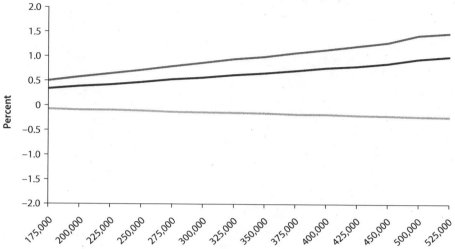

c. Case 3: Lower degree of substitutability between immigrants and natives

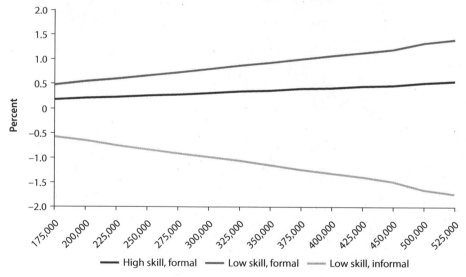

d. Case 4: Lower degree of substitutability between sectors

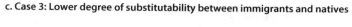

—— High skill, formal   —— Low skill, formal   ‑‑‑‑‑ Low skill, informal

Figure 5.5 Wage Effects of Emigration for Low-Skilled Informal and High- and Low-Skilled Formal Workers

a. Case 1: Baseline

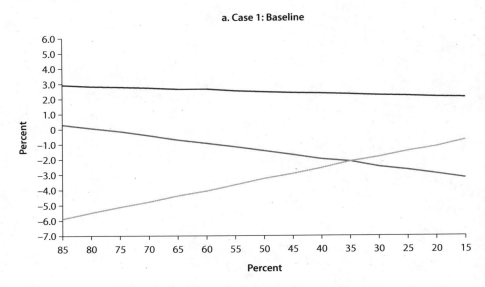

b. Case 2: Reduced share of informality among immigrants

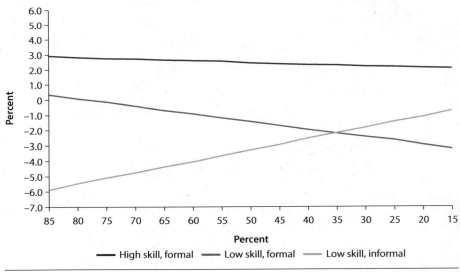

————— High skill, formal   ————— Low skill, formal   ········· Low skill, informal

figure continues next page

Figure 5.5 Wage Effects of Emigration for Low-Skilled Informal and High- and Low-Skilled Formal Workers *(continued)*

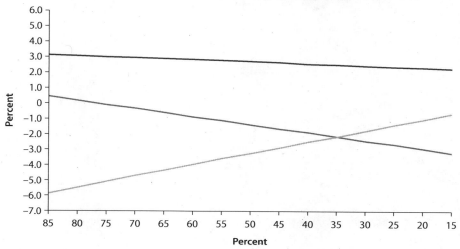

c. Case 3: Lower degree of substitutability between immigrants and natives

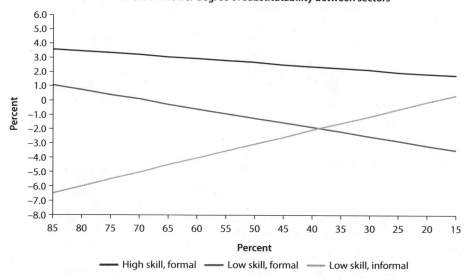

d. Case 4: Lower degree of substitutability between sectors

——— High skill, formal ———— Low skill, formal ········· Low skill, informal

Figure 5.6 Employment Effects of Emigration for Low-Skilled Informal and High- and Low-Skilled Formal Workers

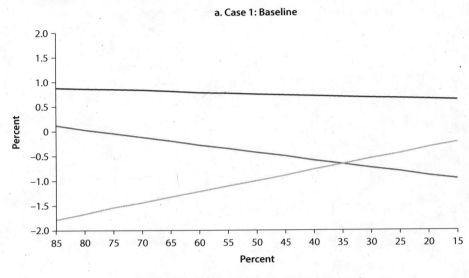

a. Case 1: Baseline

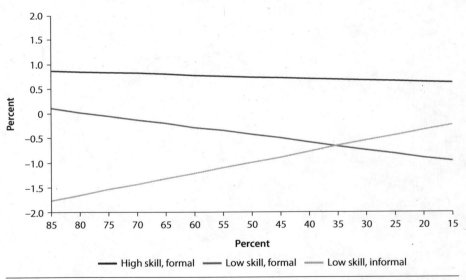

b. Case 2: Reduced share of informality among immigrants

— High skill, formal   — Low skill, formal   ⋯ Low skill, informal

figure continues next page

Figure 5.6 Employment Effects of Emigration for Low-Skilled Informal and High- and Low-Skilled Formal Workers *(continued)*

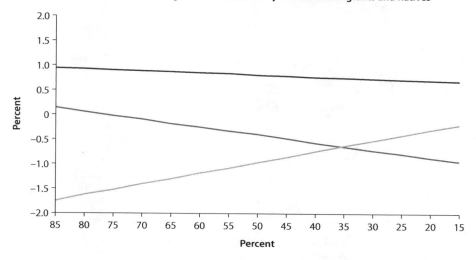

c. Case 3: Lower degree of substitutability between immigrants and natives

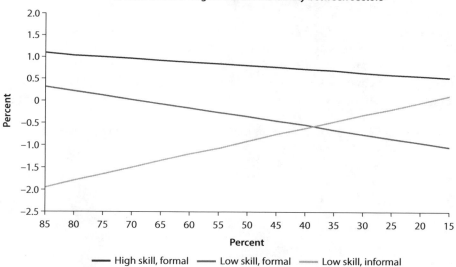

d. Case 4: Lower degree of substitutability between sectors

High skill, formal ——— Low skill, formal ——— Low skill, informal

emigration for both wages and employment probabilities. Each chart in the figures contains three graphs: the blue lines present the effects on the labor market outcomes of the high-skilled; the orange lines, of the low-skilled in the formal sector; and the green lines, of the low-skilled in the informal sector.

Each figure comprises four panels, each of which corresponds to different combinations of values for the key parameters of the model. These scenarios are presented in table 5.8. In all of the simulations, the elasticity of substitution between skill groups is set to 3 (that is $\delta_e = 3$), which is in the middle of the range suggested by Manacorda, Sánchez-Páramo, and Schady (2010) but at the upper range of the one reported by Behar (2009). Other scenarios with different values of δ_e show that there is a relatively small impact on the overall results, especially when compared to other parameters. The next parameter to be determined is the externality of the high-skilled, γ, which is set to 0.45 in all cases. The labor supply elasticity, λ, was also set to a constant value in all scenarios. This is a higher elasticity in comparison to the ones used in the DOP model, reflecting relatively flexible labor markets in a developing country. Finally, the share of the high-skilled among the new immigrants is assumed to be the same as that among preexisting immigrants. This stands at 12 percent.

The next set of parameters differs in each scenario that was considered. First, the elasticity of substitution between the formal and informal sectors, δ_s, is set at 1.7 in the first three scenarios. This is the upper value of the only range of estimates available (that is, for the case of Mexico, from Schramm 2014). In the last scenario, the value is set equal to 1.2. Second, the analysis uses a value of elasticity of substitution between immigrants and natives, δ_m, equal to 20, the value used for an intermediary scenario of substitution between immigrants and natives in the DOP model. Only in the third case, the value was lowered to 6 to capture less substitutability. Finally, 75 percent is set as the share of the new low-skilled immigrants going into the informal sector in all scenarios, except in the

Table 5.8 Parameters and Sectoral Split of New Immigrants

	Case 1	Case 2	Case 3	Case 4
Elasticity of substitution between sectors	1.7	1.7	1.7	1.2
Elasticity of substitution between skill groups	3	3	3	3
Elasticity of substitution between immigrants and natives	20	20	6	20
Externality of high-skilled (affects formal sector only)	0.45	0.45	0.45	0.45
Labor supply elasticity for all three groups (above)	0.3	0.3	0.3	0.3
Share of high-skilled for new immigrants	0.12	0.12	0.12	0.12
Share of low-skilled new immigrants going into informal sectors	0.85	0.75	0.75	0.75

Note: Case 1 = baseline; Case 2 = reduced share of informality among immigrants; Case 3 = lower degree of substitutability between immigrants and natives; and Case 4 = lower degree of substitutability between sectors.

baseline scenario (that is Case 1), where it is set at 85 percent. Table 5.8 lists these different values just outlined.

The impact of immigration on the wages of natives varies depending on their skill group and sector of employment (see the panels in figure 5.3). For low-skilled natives in the informal sector, wages decline by up to 7 percent, depending on the parameter values and the net flow of immigrants considered. The effect is most severe in Case 1 because it has the largest share of low-skilled immigrants now entering the informal sector. The results indicate that each additional 100,000 immigrants lower informal wages by about 1 percent in this case. The scenario with the least impact for wages in the informal sector is Case 3, where immigrants and natives are least substitutable. There are virtually no effects arising from the inflow of new immigrants here.

The main winners from immigration are low-skilled workers in the formal sector. Even though this might be surprising at first sight, the analytical framework adopted would suggest that this is because the vast majority of new immigrants work in the informal sector, they do not directly compete with low-skilled native workers in the formal sector. Instead, the expansion of the informal sector and lower wages increase the relative demand and wages for formal low-skilled workers. As a result, the largest wage gain for low-skilled formal workers is observed in Case 1, where each additional 100,000 immigrant workers lead to a 1 percent wage gain. The lowest wage gain, in contrast, happens in Case 4, where the formal and informal sectors have a low elasticity of substitution. The impact on the wages of the high-skilled from immigration is almost negligible, always between 1 and 2 percent. Increased levels of immigration flow have a slight positive effect in each scenario, with the strongest effect being observed in Case 3, where natives and immigrants are not good substitutes.

Another way to discuss the results is to fix a level of immigration, which is set at 500,000, a number frequently cited in the media. In this case, about 60,000 of these immigrants will be high-skilled, and about 330,000 (the remaining 75 percent) will work in the informal sector. This level of immigration flow results in a wage decline among workers in the informal sector of at least about 1 percent (Cases 3 and 4)—recall that this occurs when sectors or immigrants have lower degrees of substitutability. The decline will be much higher if the elasticity of substitution between immigrants and natives were to increase. For the same levels of immigration flow, the highest net gains are observed among low-skilled workers in the formal sector—this is about 4 percent in all cases, except in Case 4, where the elasticity of substitution between sectors is low. Finally, the effects on high-skilled workers are all between 1 and 2 percent.

Employment responds much less to immigration, as seen in panels a–d of figure 5.4. The effects are negligible for the high-skilled here as well, between 0.2 and 0.5 percent in all scenarios regardless of the immigration level.

Low-skilled informal workers are again the hardest hit, experiencing declines in employment levels of up to 2 percent. The most severe effects are in Cases 1 and 4, when a higher share of immigrants are informal workers or the sectors are least substitutable. For formal low-skilled workers, gains in employment are between 0.5 and 1.5 percent. This can be interpreted as informal native workers moving to the formal sector. The positive effects are quite similar in all cases, with the exception of Case 2.

On the other side of the coin is the effect of emigration on the labor market outcomes of those who stay behind. Docquier, Ozden, and Peri (2014) argue that, in many European countries, emigration has a bigger impact on the stayers than immigration. This strongly counters the public image and political debate, in which immigrants are seen as taking away jobs from natives. The wage effects of emigration are presented in figure 5.5. The x-axis in these figures presents the share of low-skilled emigrants who are drawn from the informal sector. The analysis presents scenarios in which it is assumed that this share varies between 15 and 85 percent.

The first clear observation is that the results are quite similar in all cases. This is mainly because (a) the assumptions in each case differ mainly for immigrants and (b) the overall effects are quite similar. The impact on high-skilled non-immigrants is always positive. Emigrants are positively selected; the share of the high-skilled is higher among emigrants than the underlying native labor force. Thus, the relative supply of the high-skilled declines with emigration and their wages increase. Wages increase by 3 percent if low-skilled emigrants are mostly drawn from the informal sector and decline by 2 percent if they are mostly drawn from the formal sector.

The wage impact on low-skilled formal workers is almost always negative because they are complementary to high-skilled workers in production, and the departure of the latter hurts the labor market prospects of the former. The wage effect ranges from slightly above 0 to −3 percent as the (assumed) share of the informal workers among emigrants declines to 15 percent and the (assumed) share of formal workers among emigrants increases to 85 percent. In other words, as more (fewer) emigrant workers are drawn from the informal (formal) sector (moving to the left on the axis), then the remaining formal low-skilled naturally gain. The effect on low-skilled workers in the informal sector is the opposite. Their wages also decline from emigration by between zero and −6 percent, depending on the extent of informality among the emigrants. If it were assumed that low-skilled emigrants were equally employed in the formal and informal sectors (that is, at 50 percent on the x-axis), then formal and informal low-skilled workers would experience a wage decline of 1.5 and 3.5 percent, respectively.

The employment effects of emigration are presented in figure 5.6, showing similar patterns as the wage effects. The high-skilled gain, and the overall effect is within a rather narrow range of 0.5 and 1 percent. The low-skilled experience potentially large negative effects. For those in the formal sector, the range is between 0 and −1 percent; it is between −0.25 and −1.75 percent for informal workers. If a 50–50 split is assumed, as above, employment levels for formal and informal low-skilled workers would decline by 0.5 and 1 percent, respectively.

Conclusion

The Dominican Republic is one of the few countries that is *both* an immigration and an emigration country. While a large number of immigrants from the Caribbean region, mostly from Haiti, live in the Dominican Republic, a similarly large number of people emigrate from the country, mostly to the United States. Both corridors, especially those from Haiti, received much attention in the policy debate, which led to controversial policy decisions such as mass deportations.

One of the critical issues is the labor market impact of migration patterns, especially those of Haitian immigrants, which intensified after the massive 2010 earthquake. Many efforts, unfortunately, hit significant roadblocks owing to the lack of data, as clearly exemplified by the wide range of estimates put out by different sources. To circumvent these constraints, this study uses a different approach. It uses a stylized model of a nested production that captures the extent of substitution between natives and immigrants, between high- and low-skilled workers, and between the formal and informal sectors in producing output. Then, the effects of both immigration and emigration flows are simulated for a wide range of substitution parameters as well as for immigration levels. The goal is to see which assumptions are critical and how sensitive the results are to different levels of immigration.

The wages of native workers across the formal and informal sectors are sensitive to the international mobility of labor. Our findings indicate that the group that is most negatively affected by immigration are low-skilled native workers in the informal sector because they are in most direct competition with immigrants. The impact on high-skilled natives is minimal, and low-skilled workers in the formal sector gain the most. In fact, the results can be interpreted as showing native workers switching to the formal sector owing to immigration. The results on emigration indicate that it is as important as immigration. The high-skill composition of emigration (a) hurts low-skilled nonmigrants because they are complements and (b) benefits high-skilled nonmigrants who remained in the country. The effects on low-skilled workers in the formal sector and the informal sector depend on the extent of formality among emigrants, as expected.

The results of this analysis seek to lead to more exploration and highlight the role of the assumptions on the underlying structure of the labor market. Formality, skill levels and spillovers, and substitution elasticities are all critical parameters that influence the effects of immigration and emigration on labor market outcomes. It should be emphasized that reliable, detailed data are needed to provide more answers.

Annex 5A

Table 5A.1 Mincerian Regression of Sectoral Log Earnings of Low-Skilled Workers

	(1)	(2)	(3)	(4)
	M1	M2	M3	M4
	b/se	b/se	b/se	b/se
Formal	0.218***	0.143***	0.136***	0.087***
	(0.020)	(0.020)	(0.020)	(0.024)
Tertiary educated	0.579***	0.460***	0.408***	0.329***
	(0.073)	(0.068)	(0.068)	(0.066)
Formal × tertiary educated	0.273***	0.345***	0.351***	0.403***
	(0.078)	(0.073)	(0.072)	(0.071)
Male	0.404***	0.428***	0.452***	0.368***
	(0.019)	(0.019)	(0.019)	(0.020)
Age	0.012***	0.012***	0.147***	0.136***
	(0.001)	(0.001)	(0.019)	(0.018)
Age square			0.003***	0.002***
			(0.001)	(0.000)
Constant	5.069***	5.266***	3.356***	3.213***
	(0.034)	(0.035)	(0.209)	(0.205)
Age cube	No	No	Yes	Yes
Region of residence dummies	No	Yes	Yes	Yes
Industry dummies	No	No	No	Yes
Adjusted R-square	0.235	0.287	0.316	0.369
Observations	7,732	7,732	7,732	7,732

Source: Labor Force Survey.
Note: Controls include age cube and region of residence.
$*p < 0.05, **p < 0.01, ***p < 0.001.$

Notes

1. Recent examples are Borjas (2003); D'Amuri, Ottaviano, and Peri (2010); Ottaviano and Peri (2012); Manacorda, Sánchez-Páramo, and Schady (2010); and Docquier, Ozden, and Peri (2014).

2. See Raul A. Reyes, "Dominican Americans: Views Against, and For, D.R.'s Immigration Policy," *NBC News*, June 25, 2015. http://www.nbcnews.com/news/latino/among-dominican-americans-different-views-d-r-immigration-policy-n381686.

3. See "Junot Díaz and Edwidge Danticat Condemn Deportations of Haitians," *The Guardian*, June 25, 2015. http://www.theguardian.com/us-news/2015/jun/25/junot-diaz-edwidge-danticat-condemn-dominican-republic-haitian-migrants.

4. Allowing consumption to be a constant share of labor income does not alter the implications.

References

Abdullaev, U., and M. Estevão. 2013. "Growth and Employment in the Dominican Republic: Options for a Job-Rich Growth." IMF Working Paper 13/40, International Monetary Fund, Washington, DC.

Arslan, C., J.-C. Dumont, Z. Kone, Y. Moullan, C. Parsons, C. Ozden, and T. Xenogiani. 2014. "A New Profile of Migrants in the Aftermath of the Recent Economic Crisis." OECD Social, Employment and Migration Working Paper 160, Organisation for Economic Co-operation and Development, Paris.

Behar, A. 2009. "Directed Technical Change, the Elasticity of Substitution and Wage Inequality in Developing Countries." Department of Economics Discussion Paper Series (Ref: 467), Oxford, University of Oxford.

Beine, M., F. Docquier, and Ç. Özden. 2011. "Diasporas." *Journal of Development Economics* 95 (1): 30–41.

Borjas, G. J. 2003. "The Labor Demand Curve Is Downward Sloping: Reexamining the Impact of Immigration on the Labor Market." *Quarterly Journal of Economics* 118 (4): 133–574.

D'Amuri, F., G. I. P. Ottaviano, and G. Peri. 2010. "The Labor Market Impact of Immigration in Western Germany in the 1990s." *European Economic Review* 54 (4): 550–70.

Docquier, F., Ç. Ozden, and G. Peri. 2014. "The Labour Market Effects of Immigration and Emigration in OECD Countries." *Economic Journal* 124 (579): 1106–45.

Lucas, R. E. 1988. "On the Mechanics of Economic Development." *Journal of Monetary Economics* 22 (1): 3–42.

Manacorda, M., A. Manning, and J. Wadsworth. 2012. "The Impact of Immigration on the Structure of Wages: Theory and Evidence from Britain." *Journal of the European Economic Association* 10 (1): 120–51.

Manacorda, M., C. Sánchez-Páramo, and N. Schady. 2010. "Changes in Returns to Education in Latin America: The Role of Demand and Supply of Skills." *Industrial Labour Relations Review* 63 (2): 307–26.

Munshi, K. 2003. "Networks in the Modern Economy: Mexican Migrants in the U.S. Labor Market." *Quarterly Journal of Economics* 118 (2): 549–99.

Nwosu, C., and J. Batalova. 2014. "Immigrants from the Dominican Republic in the United States." Spotlight, July 18. http://www.migrationpolicy.org/article/foreign-born-dominican-republic-united-states.

ONE (Oficina Nacional de Estadística). 2013. *Primera Encuesta Nacional de Inmigrantes en la Republica Dominicana: ENI-2012*. Santo Domingo: Oficina Nacional de Estadística. http://media.onu.org.do/ONU_DO_web/596/sala_prensa_publicaciones/docs/0565341001372885891.pdf.

Ottaviano, G. I. P., and G. Peri. 2012. "Rethinking the Effect of Immigration on Wages." *Journal of the European Economic Association* 10 (1): 152–97.

Parisotto, A. 2013. "Growth, Employment and Social Cohesion in the Dominican Republic." ILO background paper presented at the ILO-IMF Tripartite Consultation on Job-Rich and Inclusive Growth in the Dominican Republic, held in Santo Domingo, January 30. https://www.imf.org/external/country/DOM/rr/2013/013113.pdf.

Rodriguez, R. D. 2011. *Proyecto Piloto: Migracion de retorno a la Republica Dominicana*. Madrid: Fundación Internacional y para Iberoamérica de Administración y Políticas Públicas (FIIAPP); Geneva: International Organization for Migration (IOM). http://www.migracion-ue-alc.eu/documents/proyecto_piloto_dominicana/Informe_proyectopiloto_RD.pdf.

Schramm, H. R. 2014. "The Equilibrium Effects of Income Taxation on Formal and Informal Labor Markets." NEUDC 2014 Working Paper. Presented at the Northeast Universities Development Consortium Conference, Boston University, Boston, November.

United Nations, DESA–Population Division and UNICEF. 2014. "Migration Profiles Common Set of Indicators: Dominican Republic." https://esa.un.org/miggmgprofiles /indicators/files/DominicanRepublic.pdf.

Environmental Benefits Statement

The World Bank Group is committed to reducing its environmental footprint. In support of this commitment, we leverage electronic publishing options and print-on-demand technology, which is located in regional hubs worldwide. Together, these initiatives enable print runs to be lowered and shipping distances decreased, resulting in reduced paper consumption, chemical use, greenhouse gas emissions, and waste.

We follow the recommended standards for paper use set by the Green Press Initiative. The majority of our books are printed on Forest Stewardship Council (FSC)–certified paper, with nearly all containing 50–100 percent recycled content. The recycled fiber in our book paper is either unbleached or bleached using totally chlorine-free (TCF), processed chlorine-free (PCF), or enhanced elemental chlorine-free (EECF) processes.

More information about the Bank's environmental philosophy can be found at http://www.worldbank.org/corporateresponsibility.